Anti-Democratic Attitudes in American Schools

Roy E. Horton, Jr.

Richard D. Franklin

Arthur D. Kirsch

Robert F. Corder

Robert E. Mainer

Dorothy Gates Rodgers

Elmer L. Struening

Larry Dennis Cannon

W. H. Vermillion, Jr.

W. H. Leftwich

ANTI-DEMOCRATIC ATTITUDES IN AMERICAN SCHOOLS

Edited by

H. H. Remmers

Northwestern University Press/1963

CONTENTS

PART I
Attitude Studies of High School Youth

PART II
Attitude Studies in Higher Education

FIGURES

TABLES

PART I

ATTITUDE STUDIES OF HIGH SCHOOL YOUTH

I ORIGINS AND OVERVIEW

H. H. Remmers

INTRODUCTION

To point up the importance of democratic-authoritarian attitudes one needs only to refer to the current domestic and world tensions. Domestically we see the bipolar concept that is the theme of this book in operation in the conflict concerning desegregation—economically, politically and particularly educationally. Less violent but clearly visible conflicts exist in other areas of our society—labor versus management, creed versus creed, and dogma versus dogma in many group relationships.

Nor are these domestic conflicts any longer self-contained. It is now almost a cliché to assert their effects upon the rest of the world and its perception of our democracy. But cliché or not, the statement needs emphasizing to the point where the average citizen understands it and is fully aware of its import not only as it affects our nation but ultimately himself and his way of life. Supreme Court Justice William O. Douglas has expressed it eloquently: "We cannot glorify Little Rock, anti-Semitism, supremacy of the police, downgrading of education at home, and at the same time be strong abroad. We are the same people in Guinea as we are in Boston. We cannot be leaders of people abroad unless we honor at home the democratic ideal in race relations, in labor relations, in community development."

Mere emphasis, however, will not, it is safe to say, by itself accomplish the implementation of democratic values and the freedoms they imply. The schizophrenia from which we suffer has made possible the verbal espousal of the high ethical principles of the Judean-Christian heritage of the West while at the same time its other behavior has often emphatically denied these principles in practice.

3

Physical science and technology have in a very brief span of time, as history counts time, produced revolutionary changes, particularly in the relative annihilation of space and time. Within the memory of many living today the distance from Chicago to St. Louis was greater than the distance from New York to Tokyo is now when measured in terms of time required to go from one to the other.

The world has become very small. We have unlocked sources of energy that now makes it possible on the one hand to increase world living standards beyond the hopes of yesteryear or, on the other, to incinerate most of the human race within a single day. Bertrand Russell has phrased the consequences for humanity as grim alternatives:

Man has hitherto survived because he was too ignorant to realize his wishes. Now that he can realize them, he must either change them or perish.

But to bring about such changes in man's wishes is not a simple matter. Man's nature and the institutions, the culture that he has developed and their accompanying values strongly resist change. Whether he has developed or can develop the necessary flexibility to adapt himself to the consequences of his own discoveries and innovations in the physical sciences and technology remains to be seen. The "race between chaos and education" that H. G. Wells called civilization is more critical than ever before. Survival or annihilation are now real and near alternatives of choice.

To know the size and dimensions of the educational task requires that we discover, in operational terms, where we are, so that we may know how to proceed toward our educational goals. The behavioral sciences have only begun the task of implementing Pope's observation that "The proper study of mankind is man."

That the ten studies by my former students and myself reported in this book are a contribution to the study of mankind is the conviction that has led me to edit and put them together, rather than leaving them to collect dust on library shelves. The task of directing these researches of capable, curious, inquiring young people and to share their joys of accomplishment and

4

discovery has been a source of much pleasure and satisfaction.

Deletion of a good deal of technical tabular material from some of the original reports was dictated both by consideration of costs and the desire to mute somewhat the clanking of the machinery. An important element of strength of these studies is their decent respect for the principles of sampling and being able to generalize for defined populations, principles "more often honored in the breach than in the observance" in otherwise well-designed and executed studies in social psychology, where college sophomores are too often the basis of generalizations for mankind. The following two sections present the background, the origins and an overview of the studies.

THE PURDUE OPINION PANEL STUDIES

The first seven studies are of nationally representative samples of high school youth via the *Purdue Opinion Panel* polls. These polls, originally conceived of for the single state of Indiana, gradually were increased to include since 1945 all of the continental United States. Its original conceptualization I have described elsewhere (Remmers, 1941). Quoting a slightly adapted part of that paper will make clear its purposes and rationale.

THE PROBLEM

The present generation of youth of high school age will be responsible for carrying on the business of life tomorrow. It is, therefore, of great practical importance to obtain if possible a continuous inventory of their views on matters of common concern—government, education, economic enterprise, and cultural aspirations and values. Such a continuous inventory of the public opinion of tomorrow would obviously serve a number of highly important purposes.

1. It would serve as a guide for evaluating the process of education in many of its important aspects so that ends and means of education in its broadest sense could be more effectively geared to each other.

2. It could serve as a catalytic agent and revitalizing force particularly in the social studies.

3. To the extent that dependable trends were obtained, extrapolations of such trends would constitute the basis for effective planning for the future, not only in education, but also in government and social arrangements generally.

5

4. It would serve as a vantage point from which to explore the origins, the factors that change, make and unmake attitudes, interests, wants, and needs of youth.

5. It could serve as at least a starting point for more effective community integration—community here being thought of not merely as the face-to-face social relationships of a relatively small geographic area, but as the state, region, nation and ultimately the world community.

6. In the present [1941] defense program it may serve as an important part of the psychological front.

7. It would make possible positive contributions to social psychology with respect to content, research methodology, and theory.

Granted that such a continuous inventory of things that matter is desirable, is it feasible in terms of cost in time, energy, and money? And are the costs warranted by the social and educational returns to be anticipated? An affirmative answer to both these questions can be given with considerable confidence.

The public opinion polls such as those of the American Institute of Public Opinion and Fortune magazine have demonstrated the feasibility of validly polling the adult population with reference to important issues on the basis of relatively small samplings of the total population. The area of consumer research is rapidly demonstrating the same thing. There is a fast-growing recognition of the fact that these things "pay."

PROPOSED PROCEDURE

For the first time in history all but a relatively negligible fraction of our population of high school youth *are* in high school. From information already available it should be rather readily possible to choose a weighted sampling of high schools . . . in such a way as to have the sampling representative of all high school youth. The census and the State Departments of Public Instruction are sources of data for choosing such a representative sample.

Nor need such a sample be very large. The sampling error of even a few hundred is very small—of the order of 0.5 to 2.0 per cent.

Now these high school youths, being in school for eight and one-half to ten months of the year, are much more conveniently available than are adults for purposes of polling. With the co-operation of a relatively small number of high schools it is thus possible to obtain the required responses quickly and easily. These responses can be quickly forwarded to Purdue University, where they can be immediately analyzed and interpreted.

The polls have operated substantially as outlined here,[1] except for improvements in the mechanics of processing the data—such,

6

for example, as the use of IBM mark-sensed cards and the use of other IBM equipment for making and printing out individual school reports and the computation and printing of thousands of percentages. At this writing a program has been written for the Remington Rand Univac, recently acquired by the Purdue Statistical Laboratory. This computer, once the cards have been scanned for imperfect marking and the representative sample drawn, will process each poll completely in a matter of a few hours.

The validity of such polls is often called into question. Variations on the question, "Don't these kids often give you would-be funny answers?" are perhaps the most frequent. Such questions deserve answers. One criterion of validity often used by pollsters of adults—Gallup, Roper, Crosley, and many others—are pre-election polls predictive of election results. With this criterion the *Purdue Opinion Panel* polls compare favorably with polls of adults in predicting the national popular adult vote from answers to the question, "If you could vote in this election for whom would you vote?" In the two Eisenhower-Nixon and in the 1960 Kennedy-Johnson campaigns, the latter a very close contest, the *Purdue Opinion Panel* predictions were correct in predicting the popular vote within less than one-half per cent error, a result on the whole somewhat more accurate than those of the pollsters of adults.

When in pre-testing one poll [2] we asked the students to indicate what their grades were, their answers correlated approximately .9 with their recorded grades.

Many other evidences of validity can be cited. For example, on a question on school integration 86% of students in the East approved as against 26% in the South; the upper socio-economic group much more than the lower group was concerned with problems of going to college; the lower group, on the other hand, is much more frequently concerned about the fact that their "teeth need fixing"; and much more of the like. There is every evidence that the youngsters respond seriously and to the best of their ability, and none to the contrary.

No doubt the accuracy of our pre-election predictions and of other objective criteria is a function of the fact that we use a stratified random sample of 2,000–3,000 cases. The stratification variables are sex, grade, region, and rural or urban residence. An example in non-technical language of the explanation of the polling procedure given in every poll report follows.

The sample composition for Poll No. 61 is given by way of example in Tables 1 and 2.

A WORD ABOUT TECHNIQUE

The reader may wish to clarify his thinking about the distinction in terminology which is made in this report between "poll" and "panel." The term "poll" is used to refer to the questions asked students. The term "panel" refers to the annual body or sample of students whose schools have subscribed to the polls.

Polls of *The Purdue Opinion Panel* are given by the high schools to approximately 8,000–17,000 students in high schools all over the nation. Students record their answers anonymously on a special ballot card. When the cards are returned to Purdue University, these marks are converted into punched holes, making it possible for all the data to be tabulated on International Business Machine equipment. Each school is sent a report of its own results in addition to this national report.

The first part of each poll asks a number of questions establishing the individual's sex, school grade, and home environment. A pupil's response to the "house-home" scale gives an estimate of socio-economic status. Students are also asked to give the level of education their mothers reached, since we found this to be related to many attitudes.

About 12,000 high school pupils from all sections of the United States replied to this poll. A sample of 2,000 pupils was drawn so that analysis of results could be made on a group as nearly representative of the nation's high school pupils as our data would permit. The sample was stratified according to grade, sex, residence, geographical region, not Catholic or Non-Catholic religious preference; but strictly randomized from our total return with respect to all other characteristics. The composition of this sample is shown in the following tables.

TABLE 1
COMPOSITION IN PERCENTAGES OF THE HIGH SCHOOL SAMPLE
ON WHICH ANALYSIS IS BASED
Total Number in Sample
2,000

	Census	Poll		Poll
Boys	48.8	49.0	Mothers Education	
Girls	51.2	51.0	Grade School	42.2
			High School	44.9
10th Grade	39.7	39.4	College	12.9
11th Grade	32.8	32.7		
12th Grade	27.5	27.9	Income	
			Low	10.9
East	23.4	23.4	Medium	58.9
Midwest	30.1	31.5	High	29.6
South	32.0	30.6		
West	14.5	14.5	Protestant	64.0
			Catholic	24.1
Rural	35.9	42.1	Jewish	.8
Urban	64.1	57.9	Other	11.1

TABLE 2
PERCENTAGE IN EACH STRATIFICATION CELL OF THE SAMPLE

	Total		East		Midwest		South		West	
	Census	Poll	Census	Poll	Census	Poll	Census	Poll	Census	Poll
Rural Boy										
Grade 10	6.3	6.7	.9	.9	2.0	2.2	2.8	2.8	.6	.8
Grade 11	5.2	5.2	.8	.8	1.7	1.9	2.2	2.0	.5	.5
Grade 12	4.4	4.4	.6	.6	1.5	1.5	1.8	1.8	.4	.4
Rural Girl										
Grade 10	6.8	7.0	1.0	1.4	2.0	2.4	3.1	2.4	.6	.7
Grade 11	5.7	6.1	.8	.8	1.9	2.2	2.4	2.5	.6	.6
Grade 12	4.5	4.5	.6	.6	1.4	1.4	2.0	2.0	.4	.4
Urban Boy										
Grade 10	13.0	12.8	3.6	3.6	3.8	3.8	3.4	3.4	2.3	2.1
Grade 11	10.8	10.7	3.0	3.0	3.2	3.2	2.7	2.6	1.9	1.9
Grade 12	9.0	9.4	2.6	2.6	2.8	2.8	2.2	2.6	1.5	1.5
Urban Girl										
Grade 10	13.6	13.1	3.7	3.3	3.8	3.9	3.8	3.7	2.2	2.1
Grade 11	11.2	10.7	3.1	3.1	3.2	3.5	3.0	2.2	1.8	1.8
Grade 12	9.5	9.5	2.6	2.6	2.8	2.8	2.5	2.5	1.5	1.5
Total	100.0	100.0	23.4	23.4	30.1	31.5	32.0	30.6	14.5	14.5

Statistics from the Biennial Survey of Education (1953–54) and the U. S. Census, 1950.

Following stratification comparison of the sample with other known characteristics such as distribution by religion, parental education and political party preference generally shows these to be within the allowable sampling error.

In addition to the criterion checks already mentioned we asked about a television set in the home. The proportion of homes with television sets was within two per cent of the proportion in the population.

My emphasis upon the details of sampling are perhaps a bit wearisome. But they are crucially important for establishing the scientific validity of the sample and the generalizations to the population. Now to the studies themselves.

The careful procedures in the construction of the questionnaires are described by Dr. Horton in the first of these studies to follow. This is the pattern for all of the questionnaires administered in the polls generally. Various appendices—the Manual of Instruction for Poll Administrators, The Final Questionnaire, The Report to the Schools, the Bill of Rights—for consideration of space are omitted from this book. They are of course available to the interested scholar in the original dissertation on file in the Purdue University Library.

Dr. Horton's findings will give pause to anyone seriously concerned about the Constitution, the Bill of Rights, and their interiorization by the young citizen in the educational process. In Poll Report No. 30, administered in 1951, we first discovered the willingness of many youngsters to forego the rights guaranteed by the Bill of Rights. A repetition of many of the same items after an eight and ten year interval shows relatively little change as shown in Chapters 3 and 7.

Chapter 3 is an item-by-item comparison of changes over time in items (poll 30) that were repeated at different intervals from two to four times over a ten-year span. These data have not been further analyzed except by means of percentage comparisons. Since most of the percentages are based on from 2,000 to 3,000 cases, the sampling errors will be very small and hence small differences will be *statistically* significant without being necessarily *practically* significant.

What must concern a putative democratic society is the very

10

slight change for the better in most of the items and the retrogression for several of them. The not so very latent hostilities apparent in the results will be strongly resistant to change and thus imply a long term educational problem.

Dr. Kirsch's study of social distance in voting behavior clearly establishes that attitudes toward candidates for public office is a single psychological "dimension" in the context of the candidate's religion or "race," an interesting finding in light of the fact that in 1960 we elected a Catholic as President, the office most socially distant.

It is noteworthy also that the social distance scales rather closely approximate the actual voting situation; the individual "votes" his preference anonymously. It is also interesting to note that the study corroborates Dr. Horton's study with respect to degrees of liberalism in regions of the country.

Chapter 5 reports results of a repetition of Dr. Kirsch's scaling experiment in the 1954 Presidential election. Our 1960 experiment was all the more interesting in that for more than 30 years no Catholic had been a presidential candidate. Now there was one. That Kennedy's candidacy might put a strain on the single dimension discovered by Dr. Kirsch seemed to us a not unlikely occurrence. The facts turned out otherwise. That it did not appears to be further evidence for the strength of this social-psychological dimension.

That minorities are under serious hazard, even in a community very close to a great university is evidenced by the following news item, which appeared in the local paper while this was being written:

SWASTIKA PAINTED
ON SYNAGOGUE

Vandals splashed red paint on the walls and front door of the Sons of Abraham synagogue Friday night while services were in progress.

They painted a swastika 30 inches high on the door, and the word "Jew" in seven-inch letters was painted beneath it, police said.

The factorial analysis by Dr. Corder yielded two meaningful factors. The summated factor scores can be useful additions to the armamentarium not only of the social research scientist but for

11

the practicing educator as well. As will appear in Chapter 7, it enabled Dr. Mainer to capitalize on Dr. Corder's finding that only two factors were needed to explain his correlation matrix. Dr. Corder's further finding that social discrimination is related to geographical region comes as no surprise and in a sense again validates the kind of instruments developed in this and the other studies in this book.

Dr. Mainer's study of attitude change is in one sense the most important of the four here considered. The other three established and measured the status quo of certain important social-psychological attitudes, with some speculations as to the educational procedures relevant to changing attitudes undesirable and deleterious in our society. In Dr. Mainer's study we undertook, on a national scale, an experiment designed to measure the effectiveness of educational programs on intergroup relations.

Because of the importance of this kind of experimentation I have included nearly all of the full technical details of his original report. Thus those who may be in a position to undertake similar experiments will have a useful reference at hand.

Methodologically our elimination of the "undecided" alternative response to item stems and substituting the four alternatives "agree"; "undecided, probably agree"; "undecided, probably disagree"; and "disagree" removed the easy escape from taking a position. It also facilitated processing the data. Colored IBM cards with pre-punched code numbers enabling longitudinal follow-up without sacrificing anonymity was another very useful innovation.

Such an experiment, using the entire nation as its laboratory, clearly leaves something to be desired in the way of controls. On the other hand, it is in no danger of overgeneralizing from too narrow a population base.

Substantively Dr. Mainer's findings are interesting and important. Dr. Corder's findings, having obviated the use of the E (ethnocentrism) Scale, enabled narrowing the area of search to discriminatory and authoritarian attitudes, their changes, and their correlates.

The attitudes under study are largely irrational, hence particularly resistant to change. That a five-month exposure to varied

12

intergroup education programs nevertheless produced reliably measurable changes of discriminatory attitudes in desired directions is encouraging. No doubt further research in discovering the more effective aspects of intergroup education and application of such findings plus what I have advocated elsewhere (Remmers, 1953) will be most effective:

The solution of the problem, I suggested is "——a long-range problem of education aided wherever possible by legislative support. While one cannot force fairer attitudes upon people, nevertheless there is probably no surer way of making generations of prejudiced people than to let children grow up in a physical environment of segregation and a psychological climate geared to such segregation. Hence, if enough people support anti-discrimination regulations or laws to make them enforceable, a prejudiced generation can be constrained to change its outward behavior. To the extent that this occurs, children will have more of a chance to grow up knowing and liking those who differ from them in race, creed, or national origin."

THE COLLEGE AND UNIVERSITY STUDIES

These studies were an indirect outgrowth of the Midwestern Conference on Discriminations in Higher Education. This organization, under the auspices of the American Council on Education and financed by the Anti-Defamation League of the B'nai B'rith, functioned beginning about 1948 in bringing together representatives from the colleges and universities of some nine Midwestern states for periodical conferences to study problems and to initiate action programs concerning discriminatory practices.

The Indiana delegation, of which I have had the honor of serving as chairman for several years, decided that a logical first step would be a study of attitudes of college students toward social issues related to discriminatory practices and commissioned me to draw up a prospectus of such a study. At a meeting on January 1953 in Indianapolis the committee [3] agreed upon the details of the proposed measuring devices. These were most of the items of Poll 33 of the *Purdue Opinion Panel* (See Dr. Horton's study, Chapter II) plus certain items aimed at issues peculiarly

13

relevant to higher education, such as discriminatory clauses in fraternity and sorority constitutions and the like. It was also agreed to include both students and faculties in the program. Of the 32 institutions in the state, 25 participated.

Details of instructions for drawing the samples were assigned to me and my staff.[4] By dint of careful written instructions to the institutions on procedure and finally by obtaining from registrars their enrollment figures for each of the four undergraduate years we obtained an excellent stratified random sample of the undergraduate population. We were less successful in obtaining, except in a few instances, representative faculty data. One of these exceptions was the sample from the institution whose data were the basis of Dr. Struening's study.

Because her study has a good theoretical framework and an excellent review and critique of the more important literature in that context, Dorothy Gates Rodgers study has been put first in this series of attitude studies in higher education. While, as she cautiously observes, her results are strictly generalizable only to the undergraduate population of institutions that participated in the study, it is reasonably safe to assume that they would apply generally at least to college populations in the Middle West.

I have, I hope, perceptively muted the clanking of the technical machinery. Appendices A (the measuring devices) and B (the instructions for sampling) are included for the same reason. Readers not already conversant with factor analysis will have to take it on faith. It is too complex to be briefly described.

The three factors that Mrs. Rodgers discovered and their reliabilities as measured by their factorial multiple regression weights provide convenient tools for further research.

Dr. Struening's study is unique in that it explores, for the first time to the best of my knowledge, a large and representative sample of a large university faculty with respect to the dimensions of democratic-anti-democratic attitudes. The reader will note the similarity of the factor structure he discovered to that reported by Dorothy Gates Rodgers (Chapter VIII) for an undergraduate population across institutions in the preceding study and Corder (Chapter VI) for further insight of a similar kind for stability

14

across institutions of the factors discovered by Struening (Chapter IX).

Certainly one of Dr. Struening's most interesting and important findings are the rather linear gradients on five scales for the mean scores by fields of vocational specialization. For example, the F' authoritarian scale ranges from a high mean of 49.0 for Administration to a low of 13.2 for Psychology and Sociology. Interesting also is the observed positive relationship between mean scores on the same scale and frequency of church attendance, a finding reported a number of times by other investigators with similar scales. The reader will find many other interesting and important generalizations.

A large university faculty is of course recruited from no limited geographical region. It represents in its membership probably nearly every state in the country and many foreign countries. All the more interesting, therefore, are the observed significant relationships of the various mean scale scores with the various other personal data items.

At this writing (1962) Dr. Struening is making further analyses of the data, so far as full-time employment in a veterans' hospital as a clinical research psychologist will permit. It is to be hoped that he will soon be able to make these results available in the journal literature.

Because we had faculty data from reasonably adequate samples of five institutions besides the large university studied by Dr. Struening, we decided to study in these five institutions the stability of three of the factors he discovered. Dr. Cannon's study is the result.

The results of Dr. Cannon's study, while they reveal similarities of his three factors A, B, and C with Dr. Struening's factors I,' II,' and III,' (authoritarian religious submission, cynical and suspicious view of the human environment, and aggressive authoritarian nationalism, respectively) they do not allow the conclusion that this set of three factors is entirely invariant across the six institutions studied. That a cynical and suspicious view of human nature is a factor stable across these institutions is perhaps not too surprising. "You can't change human nature" is a

15

refrain that for many persons settles all arguments about the reasons for "man's inhumanity to man."

In any case, Dr. Corder's results must be viewed with caution because of the rather accidental and possibly biased faculty samples available for study in these five institutions.[5] To the extent that true variations across institutions exist, they clearly represent cultural, i.e., learned differences in the relevant attitudes. Much informal observation as well as not a little controlled experimentation attest to the proposition that so far as these attitudes are a part of "human nature" it *can* be changed.

Concerning the entire series of studies, it must not be forgotten that the kinds of attitudes at issue are *learned,* notwithstanding the fact that one of every four or five high school students believes, as found in a number of our polls, that racial prejudice is "inborn," a belief, incidentally, much more widely held by teenagers in the South than the rest of the nation. The democratic-value oriented learning theorist as well as the educator will find this not too disheartening, for what has been learned can be unlearned. More importantly, better learning situations can be programmed, given the kind of bench marks provided by these studies and the legal implementation going on apace. Chief Justice Warren has said that the Bill of Rights, if referred to a referendum, could probably not be passed today. The educational task is to negate his proposition.

NOTES

1. This is doubtless the only public opinion polling operation in which the pollees—or rather their schools—pay directly for being polled! For the individual school report and the report on the national sample—usually three but sometimes four per year—each participating school pays a nominal fee of ten cents per pupil for the year. This, of course pays only a relatively small fraction of the costs of operation. Income from sale of the results helps to finance it. The *Chicago Tribune* beginning in 1957 purchased first publication rights. Occasional sale of magazine articles and royalties from one book further help to underwrite costs.

2. Poll Report No. 41, Youth's knowledge of learning principles and study practices, March, 1955.

3. As per the minutes of this meeting, present were Mrs. A. B. Counselbaum, representing the Midwestern Conference on Higher Education; Pro-

fessor Paul Bowman, Manchester College; Dean Richard Burkhart, Ball State Teachers College; Dean J. E. Grinnell, Indiana State Teachers College; Dr. John Mahoney, Indiana University Medical School; Dr. H. H. Remmers, Purdue University; Dean Robert H. Shaffer, Indiana University; and Dean Albert Wehling, Valparaiso University.

Unable to attend were Professor Smelser of Notre Dame University, Father Maline of West Baden College, and President Beckes of Vincennes University.

4. Those of my assistants who participated in this task were P. C. Baker, Dorothy Gates Rodgers and E. L. Struening, the latter acting as Project Director under my general supervision.

5. One biasing factor found by other social scientists is the greater resistance of the authoritarian person to respond to such scales because of his intolerance of ambiguity and his need for maximally structured situations and social environment. (H. H. R.)

II AMERICAN FREEDOM AND THE VALUES OF YOUTH [1]

Roy E. Horton, Jr.

INTRODUCTION

PURPOSE OF THE STUDY

Freedom, one of the most important concepts in our modern world, has been defined in many ways, in many times, and it is difficult to find a clear-cut meaning on which all men will agree. But whether freedom is discussed in a political sense, an ideological sense, a psychological sense, or in other ways, it is recognized as one of the greatest aspects of our cultural heritage. In this country, one meaning of freedom has been traditionally defined in the Bill of Rights, the first ten amendments to the Constitution (Becker, 1947).

The purpose of the present research is to study attitudes toward freedom as defined by the Bill of Rights. The study is concerned with the ideology of the nation's high school youth, with the values of freedom and fascism. This research is an attempt at a more systematic inquiry in the important area of ideology, using research techniques of social science. The measurement of opinion, belief, and attitude provides an empirical approach to some of the problems in this area.

In view of the *Zeitgeist* or current climate of opinion, there is little necessity for justifying the value of such research. The periodicals and journals are filled with comment and speculation concerning freedom. Civil liberties, economic freedom, the problem of potential fascism, the suppression of ideas, censorship, Americanism and patriotism, and similar topics are all subjects of widespread discussion and debate. These topics are the focus of the present research.

18

A Word About Values

At this point, let us consider the role of values in a scientific investigation. Myrdal (1944) has described some important implications of values in the social sciences, with regard to the ways in which values and biases influence scientific research. He points out that most social scientists erroneously believe that by "keeping to the facts," "being objective," and using refined statistical treatment of their data, all traces of bias and valuation may be eliminated. Myrdal's point is that values permeate research in social science, regardless of the scientists' attempts at concealing or avoiding them. Even the apparently simple concepts used in research presume elaborate theories; each hypothesis contains speculation and is judged "significant" by the scientists' valuations. Choice of procedure, decisions as to kinds of analyses, and conclusions are all influenced by the value premises of the investigator. Myrdal urges the social scientist to bring his valuations into the open, rather than to proceed with hidden biases:

Biases in research are much deeper seated than in the formulation of avowedly practical conclusions. They are not valuations *attached* to research but rather they *permeate* research. They are the unfortunate results of concealed valuations that insinuate themselves into research in all stages, from its planning to its final presentation.

The valuations will, when driven underground, hinder observation and inference from becoming truly objective. This can be avoided only by making the valuations explicit. There is no other device for excluding biases in the social sciences than to face the valuations and to introduce them as explicitly stated, specific, and sufficiently concretized value premises.

The formulation of specific valuations to be utilized as instrumental norms in a scientific investigation is likely to emphasize the tremendous moral responsibility placed upon social scientists. A number of points already made, however, should be borne in mind. First, the same responsibility is actually carried by every student, whether he chooses to make his value premises explicit or not. Second, if he makes his value premises explicit, his responsibility is, in fact, smaller, as he then fixes the readers' attention on the matter and thus aids them to criticize his value premises and conclusions. Third, the research part

19

of the work is mainly dependent on the value premises as to viewpoints and direction. Fourth, his method means that he has taken precautions to avoid hidden valuations, that is, biases.

Certain value premises underlying the present research have been touched upon, implicitly, in the introductory statements of this section. The topics of the present research, dealing with some of the most highly value-loaded aspects of the current American scene, are such that Myrdal's comments are particularly relevant. Other investigators of the ideology of freedom and fascism, notably Frenkel-Brunswick (1954) have recognized that the problem of values permeates such research. It is impossible to deal with the ideology of freedom and its related attitudes without being influenced by certain value premises.

Value Premises in this Study. For the present research, dealing with the concept of freedom and related topics, one could find no more adequate and appropriate set of value premises than the "American Creed," as Myrdal calls it. In other words, the norm or criterion guiding the formulation of hypotheses and procedures is the pattern of American ideals, the American democratic faith. Specifically, the value premises underlying this research are those formally stated in documents such as the Constitution, especially the Bill of Rights, and the Supreme Court's interpretation of those statements. The values are less formally stated in the writings of Thomas Jefferson, Thomas Paine, and other spokesmen for the American democracy.

The importance of stating these value premises will become clear as the study proceeds. Certain judgments, scoring techniques, procedures, and interpretations stem directly from these premises and find justification in them.

It is worthwhile to note that these values of democracy are more than arbitrary dogma. There is little doubt for the social scientist that the democratic society and democratic values promise the greater individual fulfillment and happiness; in our society there is both clinical and experimental evidence to support the conclusion that the democratic life is more constructive, less frustrating, and less generative of conflict and maladjustment than the authoritarian way (Eager and Smith, 1951; Fromm, 1941; Lewin *et al.*, 1939; Sanford, 1950).

METHODOLOGY

While a variety of methods of studying attitudes are available this study uses the methods of survey research.

Methods in this Study. None of the earlier studies in the area of authoritarian attitudes of the ideology of freedom were conducted on a representative, wide-scale sample which would provide an adequate basis for generalizing about the population studied. The present study is designed to give a nationwide picture of the acceptance or rejection of democratic values, as opposed to authoritarian values, for the population studied. The problems of obtaining a representative nationwide sample are such that few investigators find such a study feasible. In the present research, the population studied is limited to the nation's high school pupils, since the operation of the *Purdue Opinion Panel* enables an adequate sample of that population. Aside from the considerations in obtaining a sample, there are a number of reasons for studying the ideology of the nation's high school youth. They are the "citizens of tomorrow," and from this group will come the leaders of the next generation. Educators and others are interested in the quality of the products of today's educational system; some of the data from this study may provide information useful to those who diagnose our educational needs and plan our educational procedures.

At this point in the discussion of methods, the limitations of research techniques should be pointed out. In obtaining data through the facilities of a nationwide polling organization, restrictions are imposed by the nature of the procedure. The means of obtaining data are limited to group administered questionnaires, answered within the time of the ordinary classroom period. The questions must be more highly structured than in an individual interview, for example, so that the methods of this study do not allow the intensive study which is characteristic of the clinical method. Though the investigator gains in adequacy of sampling, he loses in the amount and kind of information acquired. The group survey approach is apparently doomed to dealing with what are assumed to be the more superficial aspects of personality, rather than the deeper lying variables

21

obtained in the clinic. This limitation of the present study should be recognized at the beginning; it is only through the interaction and cooperative research by different techniques that we shall gain a thorough and widespread knowledge of personality, ideology, and attitudes.

The Sample of Schools. At the beginning of each school year a number of schools are invited to participate in the *Purdue Opinion Panel.* Schools invited to participate are randomly selected from the national directory of secondary schools, with the number of selected schools stratified by geographic region and size of city in proportion to the desired number of schools for a representative sample, and in proportion to the response rate in previous years. No more than one-third of the schools participating in any year are renewals from the previous year; the continual turnover in schools prevents "panelitis," or non-representativeness of the sample due to continuous polling of the same groups, who would become sensitized to the polling issues. The *Panel* during a school year usually contains between sixty and one hundred schools, with the number of participating pupils between 8,000 and 15,000. The schools pay for participation, currently at the rate of ten cents per pupil, but before 1952 at the rate of six cents per pupil. This charge covers only a relatively small part of the total expenses of poll operations.

For the present study, the sample of schools was larger and more adequate than earlier *Purdue Opinion Panel* samples. The sample in the school year 1951–52, which was used in the present study, consisted of 103 schools, with 18,052 pupils participating in the polls. The schools were widely distributed geographically, with 34 states represented.

The Sampling of Pupils. In selecting a sample for detailed analysis, only a part of the total returns was used. The poll report of the national sample, prepared for use in the participating schools, was based upon analysis of a stratified random sample of 3,000 pupils. Despite efforts to obtain a representative sample of schools, the response to the mailed invitations to participate cannot be predicted with high accuracy. With regard to geographic region, for example, the schools in the East and Midwest are generally more strongly represented in the sample than are the schools in the South and West. The smaller rural schools more frequently respond than do the larger urban schools; and the upper grades are sometimes over-represented. For these reasons, the sample used in analysis of nationwide returns is stratified with respect to certain variables; i.e., the proportions of the sample in each geographic region, each grade, sex of respondent, and rural-urban communities are controlled so that the sample composition parallels the characteristics of the population. These characteristics of the population (secondary school pupils) are determined from statistics of the U. S. Census (1953) and the *Biennial Survey of Education* (1952). Within each cell of the sample, the pupils are randomly selected; the result is known as a "stratified random sample." Following stratification on these variables, other known characteristics of the sample are compared with the population: distribution by religion, parental education, and political party preference are generally found to be within the allowable random sampling error. These variables are strictly randomized, since control by stratification is unnecessary.

The representativeness of this stratified random sample is very high, as determined by the available evidence. Tests of the validity of generalizations based upon the sample are possible on occasions.

The Sample Used in this Study. For the analyses in this study, and for the main focus of research, the sample is limited to twelfth graders only. There are several reasons for limiting the analyses in this way.

By making the high school senior the focus of the research, we gain knowledge and insight concerning the final product of our high schools. The meaning and the interpretation of the results are clarified, to the extent that the reader knows the findings are based upon the more mature twelfth grader.

An additional factor of importance concerns the reliability of the data. The analysis of final returns and experience in pretesting the questionnaire, have shown that the reliability of response is higher among the twelfth graders. Specifically, the errors in marking are fewer among the older pupils; the proportion of non-usable cards due to incomplete response is smaller.

23

The specific composition of the sample of twelfth graders has been controlled by stratification on the relevant variables, to insure a sample which is highly representative of the nationwide population of twelfth graders. The description of the sample will be included in the analyses.

CONSTRUCTION OF THE QUESTIONNAIRE

General Rationale. The broad purpose of the research having been defined as the study of the ideology—especially with regard to the values of freedom—of the nation's youth, as determined from a nationwide sample of high school seniors, the task remains to specify the operations by which this ideology will be appraised.

The term "ideology" generally refers to an organization or pattern of beliefs, opinions, and attitudes (Adorno *et al;* Krech and Crutchfield, 1948). An attitude, per se, is a relatively enduring predisposition with respect to some aspect of an individual's world, and involves the organization of emotional, motivational, perceptual, and cognitive processes (Krech and Crutchfield; Remmers, 1954). The concept of attitude, as currently used, is such that an attitude is an underlying characteristic of an individual, and, of course, cannot be measured directly. Rather, a person's attitude is inferred from the appraisal of certain samples of behavior. Among the commonly appraised samples of behavior are opinions and beliefs, the verbal and cognitive expressions of attitude and ideology. With the use of the paper-and-pencil questionnaire, we must recognize that we are dealing primarily with opinion and belief. Knowledge about attitudes and ideology is a level removed from the questions of opinion and belief, and such knowledge must be inferred from the more direct responses.

In dealing with ideology of youth, the construction of the questionnaire begins with an analysis of the opinions and beliefs related to that ideology. The general concept of ideology must first be analyzed into the specific aspects with which this study will deal. Of the many possible aspects of ideology, the topics must be limited so that the data can be collected by means of a questionnaire administrable in a classroom period.

24

The selection of specific aspects of ideology was guided by judgments as to the social importance of the values concerned, and by the findings of previous research in this area. The aspects of ideology selected for study in this research are: freedom as defined by the Bill of Rights, general fascistic tendencies, patriotism, the economic ideology of Marx, and anti-communist attitudes. The specific meanings or operational definitions of these aspects of ideology are discussed in the next section.

Constructing the Questions. Beginning with the area of freedom, questions were constructed by paraphrasing statements of the freedoms (or violations of freedoms) with which the Bill of Rights deals. The specific statements which formed the stem of the item were phrased in common, easily understood language so that the pupils would have little trouble interpreting the question. Many statements deal with exceptions to the freedoms; i.e., one commonly hears persons expressing their general belief in freedom of speech, "except for. . . ." There is little doubt that a broad question, "Do you believe in freedom of speech?" would receive widespread, unqualified approval. Everyone is "for virtue and against sin"; many persons who are essentially anti-democratic are heard to pay lip-service to the socially approved values. The questions were purposely constructed so as to evoke easy agreement from those who like to feel that they generally believe in freedom but would make exceptions in a number of cases. The point is that freedom of speech, for example, also means freedom for minorities or unpopular opinion, not merely freedom to express the majority view.

Each of the questions could be discussed in turn, but this general rationale underlies most of them, and little emphasis should be placed upon the individual question. As McNemar (1946) has pointed out, the single question is subject to many limitations, and since the major analyses will be based upon summated responses to a number of questions, we shall not attempt to justify in detail each aspect of question wording. There are several reasons, aside from the required space, for not discussing each item in detail. These reasons find expression in the three major kinds of information about each item.

First, each of the original, larger number of items was judged by a group of graduate students and staff members in psychology, all of whom were qualified in the area of opinion research.

Second, evidence from the respondents in a pre-test of the questions was used in improving the items and in demonstrating that the items were clear to the respondents.

Third, the items are evaluated statistically, through accepted procedures of item analysis, and the results are presented in the next section.

In the construction of the questions, the Bill of Rights served as the source of item ideas for one scale.

The items concerned with general fascistic ideology were based primarily upon previous research in this area. As early as 1936, Stagner (1936) constructed a scale for measuring fascist attitudes; Edwards (1944) published research on "the signs of incipient fascism" shortly thereafter. Fromm (1941), Maslow (1943), and Adorno *et al.* (1950) were the first to systematize the concept of "authoritarianism." The items dealing with general fascistic ideology in the present research were based upon these earlier viewpoints.

The items on Marxian economics were constructed by paraphrasing some of the basic elements of the Communist Manifesto (Marx, 1932). The content of the items was not explicitly identified as Marxian, and the scale is best described as a measure of "latent acceptance of Marxian principles." It should be noted that these items deal with the theoretical communism of Marx, not with life in the Soviet Union today nor with any of the varied "party lines" of recent years. As such, these items are nearly indistinguishable from the elements of other economic theories, e.g., Fabian socialism. There are a number of emotionally-loaded terms for describing the values inherent in these items. Either socialism or communism might be used to describe them, since these elements are common to both. But some elements of Marx, such as the graduated income tax or the federal post office system, are even common to the United States government. One relatively neutral way of describing the items might be as "a scale of attitude toward the role of central government in economics." It is hardly necesary to point out that a high score on these items does not necessarily demonstrate that a person is a com-

26

munist, since other information must first be known about the person's value system.

The items on patriotism might more accurately be described as "super-patriotism." The items are expressions of the more chauvinistic kind of patriotism, along with a generalized ethno-centrism and distrust of "foreigners." Based upon an informal content analysis of the most salient characteristics of the out-spoken patriot, these items provide an indication of the extreme self-declared patriotism. Many of us would regard these aspects of patriotism as the more superficial aspects of true patriotism, but the purpose of the scale is to identify the "super-patriot" who declares his Americanism most vociferously.

The general questions on civil liberties were also based upon an analysis of the literature, and represent the more salient issues in this area. Some of the items included had been previously used in polls of the *Purdue Opinion Panel,* thus data for analysis of trends in recent years would be available. Five of these items explicitly referred to "communism" or "communists," and are best described as a measure of "manifest anti-communism."

The questions in the preceding areas, dealing with opinion or belief in each scale, are all worded as statements to which the pupil responds with "agree," "disagree," or "uncertain." The items on general civil liberties issues, which deal with more heterogene-ous topics, are provided with different response alternatives.

The poll questionnaire included a test of knowledge or in-formation, in both U. S. History and current events, consisting of multiple choice and true-false questions.

A large number of items were constructed in each area out-lined above. The number of original items ranged from 12 in the economic area to 40 in the general fascistic ideology area. The items in each area were submitted to a panel of experts for judg-ment as to (a) relevance of the item—the extent to which its content is appropriate to the area as defined, and (b) clarity of question wording—lack of ambiguity, suitability of vocabulary level, etc. On the basis of these preliminary judgments, the best items were retained, other items were improved, and some items were dropped. The items were then assembled, in random order except for the personal data questions, into a preliminary form of the questionnaire. This form was again judged by faculty members in the area of the social sciences, and by the *Purdue Opinion Panel Advisory Committee.*

Pre-Test and Revision. The questionnaire was then administered to 105 high school pupils in a local rural school. The polling procedure and instructions were identical with the nationwide operation, except the pupils had the opportunity to comment orally or in writing about the questions, after taking the poll. They were specifically instructed to indicate any questions that were not clear, or any words of whose meaning they were not certain. On the basis of the pre-test experience, a few minor changes in wording were made, but the questionnaire was essentially unchanged. An item analysis of the five scales and the knowledge test, using the responses of the pre-test group, demonstrated the positive discriminatory power of each item, as measured by the relationship with the criterion of total score for each respective scale.

The Final Questionnaire. All available evidence indicated that the questionnaire was now in satisfactory form for nationwide use. The final questions are presented in the next section, with the items grouped by area of content. In the actual questionnaire, the questions of opinion and belief were randomly arranged and unidentified as to the area of ideology (see Appendix A).

In summary, the table of specifications for the final questionnaire of Poll 30 is shown in Table 3.

The personal data questions, all of which had been used in

TABLE 3

TABLE OF SPECIFICATIONS
FOR THE QUESTIONNAIRE

Personal Data Questions	10 items
Belief in the Bill of Rights	15 items
General Fascist Ideology	8 items
Latent Acceptance of Marxian Economics	8 items
Super-Patriotism	8 items
Manifest Anti-Communism	5 items
General Civil Liberties Issues	8 items
Knowledge Test	10 items
Total	72 items

previous polls, established the pupils' sex, grade, rural or urban residence, political party preference, education of mother, religious denomination, intensity of religious belief, "race," socio-economic status, and whether the pupil had completed a school course in Civics or U. S. Government. The rural-urban distinction follows that of the U. S. Census (1953). Socio-economic status is measured by the House-Home Scale, an unidimensional scale of demonstrated validity (Remmers, 1953).

A PRELIMINARY ANALYSIS OF THE SCALES

Purpose of the Analysis: Problems of Validity

The purpose of the preliminary analysis of the scales, before undertaking a more complete study of the ideological variables included in this research, is to explore the characteristics of the items with reference to their validity. How well do the items actually measure what they purport to measure?

Validity of a measuring device, as Cureton (1951) has pointed out, may be considered as having two major aspects. To be valid for a particular purpose, the test content must be *relevant,* and the test must yield *reliable* scores when used with the group for whom it is designed.

In addition to validity, measuring devices used in the area of attitude and ideology should meet certain other requirements. From a theoretical standpoint, one of the desiderata closely related to validity but not identical with it is that of unidimensionality or homogeneity of content. In other words, the items in a scale should all measure the same thing, and only one thing.

Let us consider first the problem of validity, and at this point the determination of relevance. The relevance of a measuring device may be established in either of two major ways: statistically or logically. In the statistical analysis of relevance, test *scores* are correlated with criterion scores. In the logical analysis of relevance, test *content* is compared with a criterion. In much research in the area of ideology and attitudes, the investigator finds it difficult—if not impossible—to use quantitative scores on some criterion performance for validation of measures. It is true that scores (responses) on measures of ideology and attitude, if valid, should bear some relationship to other behavior; if not, then those measures would be of little practical importance. Consider, for example, a paper-and-pencil test of "citizenship attitudes" for high school students (Drucker, 1950). Presumably, a valid test of citizenship attitudes would be related to the behavior of "good citizens." Yet, we are often unable to obtain scores of criterion performance in such classroom evaluation of pupils. The behavior may be inaccessible to systematic observation; it may be of such a nature that unbiased observation or evaluation is impossible; one might find that experts do not agree on which behavior consti- tutes "criterion" performance. Yet, educators and others nonethe- less feel it is important to try to measure attitudes and knowledge pertaining to citizenship; it is regarded as an important objective of education. Similarly, the aspects of ideology and attitudes that are included in the present research may not always be validated against criterion scores of performance.

From one viewpoint, having defined *beliefs* as the subject of research—beliefs that in some cases have no observable behav- ioral manifestation—the question of validity might be considered as being resolved into the question of reliability alone (Remmers, 1954).*

Eighteen judges were used in the analysis of logical relevance of the items. The judges were qualified for the task by one of two criteria: they were either doctoral candidates or professors in the social sciences. In either case, they were familiar with the methods of research and the literature pertaining to this topic of study. Given the rationale of the study and a brief statement of the ob- jectives with which the items were concerned, the judges evalu- ated the items as to the extent to which they were appropriate or relevant. A copy of the Bill of Rights was provided in evaluating the items purporting to measure "Belief in the Bill of Rights." For the items appearing in the final questionnaire, the judges agreed that the content of the items was relevant. If the items pro-

* (But in the pre-election polls in the Presidential campaigns, responses in the North versus the South on questions of school integration, differential concerns of the well-to-do versus the poor, these polls provide much in the way of both external and internal evidence of their general validity. H. H. Remmers.)

vided reliable scores, then the validity of the measures would be demonstrated. Let us now turn to the statistical analysis of the items and the estimation of reliability.

THE SAMPLES FOR THE PRELIMINARY ANALYSIS

Actually, two preliminary analyses of the items were made before undertaking the detailed analysis of the national sample. The preliminary tryout of the questionnaire, conducted on 105 pupils in a rural Indiana high school, has already been described. From this first pre-test, two kinds of data were used: the informal comments of the pupils, and the responses as used in the item analysis. The results of the item analysis demonstrated the positive discriminatory power of each item retained in the final questionnaire.

TABLE 4

COMPOSITION OF THE SAMPLES USED IN ANALYSES
AS COMPARED WITH POPULATION CHARACTERISTICS [a]

| | | Per cent present in: | | |
| | | Population | Sample for preliminary analysis | Sample for detailed analysis |
Characteristic	Group	N = 1,123,000	N = 300	N = 1,000
SEX [b]	Boys	48%	48%	48%
	Girls	52%	52%	52%
REGION [b]	East	27%	27%	27%
	Midwest	32%	32%	32%
	South	27%	26%	27%
	Mountain-Pacific	14%	15%	14%
COMMUNITY [b]	Rural	38%	39%	38%
	Urban	62%	61%	62%
MOTHER'S EDUCATION [c]	Grade School	56%	56%	53%
	High School	36%	34%	37%
	College	8%	10%	10%
FAMILY IN-COME LEVEL [d]	Low	no	18%	19%
	Middle	data	63%	61%
	High		19%	20%

[a] Population is defined as U. S. high school seniors (12th grade).
[b] Population data from the *Biennial Survey of Education* (op. cit.).
[c] Population data not separately available; mother's education data from U. S. Census reports for all females over twenty-five years of age (op. cit.).
[d] Family Income Level is based upon an arbitrary division of House-Home Scores (op. cit.) for purposes of analysis.

The need remained for a second preliminary analysis, which would provide cross-validation of the items and data for further analysis on a wider sample. From the 4,054 twelfth graders responding to the poll in the nationwide administration, a sample of 300 was randomly selected for this second preliminary analysis. A sample size of 300 was selected as large enough to yield reliable results in the kinds of preliminary analysis planned, yet small enough for convenience in handling. The composition of the sample was controlled or stratified on certain relevant variables, but cases were randomly selected within the strata being controlled. The sample composition was controlled by region of the country, sex, and rural-urban residence, so that the proportions in the sample were the same as the corresponding proportions in the population sampled. Table 4 shows the characteristics of the samples used in detailed analysis, as compared with the population.

GUTTMAN SCALING

The first analysis undertaken was a Guttman scale analysis,[2] using the "Cornell technique," or scalogram (Guttman, 1947; Stouffer, 1950), to determine the reproducibility of each scale and to test the hypothesis of unidimensionality.

None of the five attitude areas yielded scales meeting Guttman's criteria of unidimensionality. Failure to meet Guttman's stringent requirements for a "scale" is not necessarily damaging to one's research. The Guttman scale model is concerned primarily with *consistency* among patterns of response for the individuals studied. Inconsistencies in patterns of response may arise through error variance attributable to persons as well as items. Jahoda (1949) and Hyman (1949) have discussed some of the sources of inconsistency and the problems of inconsistency in attitude measurement. Attitude areas in which feelings are relatively unstructured or not sharply "crystallized" by individuals, or in which inconsistent cultural norms and value systems exist, would be expected to yield less consistent response patterns when measured, as compared with, say, religious orthodoxy—structured by institutions and dogma—which yields a unidimensional scale of Christian belief.

Guttman himself points out (Stouffer *et al.*, 1950) that quasi-scales are a promising method of research into complex areas. Furthermore, a quasi-scale has the full mathematical advantages of a scalable area.

Research by Kriedt and Clark (1949) is relevant to the general problem of "scales" versus "quasi-scales." They compared Guttman scaling with three methods of item analysis, and concluded that methods of item analysis yielded scores more reliable (i.e., with a higher coefficient of internal consistency) than did Guttman scaling. They conclude that non-scalability, in the Guttman sense, is not necessarily a "bad" characteristic. For some uses, scalability may be irrelevant or even undesirable.

In the present study, the variables of ideology, such as acceptance of the Bill of Rights, were judged to be of sufficient importance and meaningfulness, in and of themselves, that the failure to meet Guttman's criteria was not considered a severe blow in the research. The attitudes and ideology relating to acceptance of the Bill of Rights are sufficiently complex that one would not expect them to constitute an unidimensional scale, yet a score on such a variable is quite meaningful and significant in our society.

ITEM ANALYSIS OF THE MEASURES

Using the sample of 300 cases selected for preliminary analysis, scores were obtained for each pupil on each of the five attitude areas and the knowledge test. The procedure of scoring should be considered in detail with regard to the measures used in the complete analysis of the data; the problem is whether differential weighting of item responses or simple unitary weights will yield scores of maximal reliability. For the present, however, a simple scoring scheme will be adequate for determining high and low criterion groups for analysis of items in each area.

Knowledge scores were obtained simply by summing the number of correct responses. No correction for guessing formula is considered necessary when pupils have been instructed to answer every item and have sufficient time to attempt every item, since corrected scores under those conditions correlate perfectly with the number right (Gulliksen, 1950).

Scores on the attitude items were based upon the three re-

TABLE 5

ITEM STEMS FOR THE SCALE OF
"BELIEF IN THE BILL OF RIGHTS"

Item Number	Item Stem
9	Newspapers and magazines should be allowed to print anything they want except military secrets.
13	Religious belief and worship should not be restricted by laws.
17	The government should prohibit some people from making public speeches.
19	In some cases, the police should be allowed to search a person or his home even though they do not have a warrant.
22	Some criminals are so bad that they shouldn't be allowed to have a lawyer.
25	Some religious groups should not be allowed the same freedom as others.
27	If a person is accused of a crime he should always have the right to know who is accusing him.
29	Certain groups should not be allowed to hold public meetings even though they gather peaceably and only make speeches.
32	Foreigners in this country should always be allowed the same basic freedoms that citizens have.
34	Local police may sometimes be right in holding persons in jail without telling them of any formal charges against them.
36	In some criminal cases, a trial by jury is an unnecessary expense and shouldn't be given.
39	In some cases, the government should have the right to take over a person's land or property without bothering to go to court.
41	The police or F.B.I. may sometimes be right in giving a man the "third degree" to make him talk.
44	Persons who refuse to testify against themselves (that is, give evidence that would show that they are guilty of criminal acts) should either be made to talk or severely punished.
47	Some of the petitions which have been circulated should not be allowed by the government.

sponses of "agree," "uncertain," and "disagree" by assigning "2," "1," and "0" for the respective answers. Items that were reversed, i.e., worded in negative form, received reverse scoring. The direction of scoring is indicated by the name of the scale; thus a high score on "Belief in the Bill of Rights" means agreement with paraphrased freedoms included in that document; disagreement, with reversed statements that deny freedoms.

Items in each of the five attitude quasi-scales were analyzed as follows. For each scale, in turn, high and low criterion groups were selected on the basis of total score. The top one-third and

TABLE 6

ITEM ANALYSIS DATA FOR THE SCALE OF
"BELIEF IN THE BILL OF RIGHTS"

Item No.	Gist of Item	Per cent Marking the Response Scored "2" in Each Group			t ratio	"p" is less than:
		Total N = 300	"High" N = 100	"Low" N = 100		
9	Newspapers print	45	64	29	5.0	.001
13	Religious belief	82	91	71	3.5	.001
17	Some public speeches	54	79	28	7.5	.001
19	Police search	77	92	53	6.5	.001
22	Criminals allowed lawyer	85	97	67	6.0	.001
25	Religious groups	88	96	76	4.3	.001
27	Right to know accuser	81	91	69	4.0	.001
29	Hold public meetings	64	88	43	7.0	.001
32	Foreigners same freedoms	50	61	34	3.8	.001
34	Police hold persons	78	94	60	6.1	.001
36	Trial by jury unnecessary	80	94	63	5.6	.001
39	Gov't. take person's land	91	97	85	3.3	.001
41	Third degree permitted	26	48	15	5.1	.001
44	Testify against self	23	83	29	8.0	.001
47	Petitions not allowed	43	76	11	10.0	.001

bottom one-third were used as criterion groups, providing 100 cases in each group. The per cent of each group marking each of the keyed responses was then tabulated.

In the present study, the discriminatory power of each item is indicated by using the "t ratio"[3] to test the significance of the difference between percentages of the high and low criterion groups marking the keyed response. The choice of the "t ratio" was based primarily upon the facts that t is widely known and understood as a significance test, that more is known about the sampling distribution of t as compared with lesser known indices, and that the Lawshe-Baker nomograph (1951) facilitates computation.

Tables 5 to 16 on the following pages summarize the items by area. For each attitude area and the knowledge test, a table pre-

TABLE 7

ITEM STEMS FOR THE SCALE OF
"GENERAL FASCIST IDEOLOGY"

Item Number	Item Stem
11	Obedience and respect for authority are the most important virtues that children should learn.
15	Whatever serves the interests of government best is generally right.
21	Most children these days need more discipline.
26	Most criminals and some other persons, like the feeble-minded, should be prevented from having children.
31	What this country needs most is a few strong, courageous, tireless leaders in whom the people can put their faith.
33	A large mass of the people are not capable of determining what is and what is not good for them.
35	There will always be strong groups and weak groups, and it is best that the strong continue to dominate the weak.
40	The right of some working groups to call a strike should be abolished, as it is a threat to democracy and not in the general interest of society.

TABLE 8

ITEM ANALYSIS DATA FOR THE SCALE OF
"GENERAL FASCIST IDEOLOGY"

Item No.	Gist of Item	Per cent Marking the Response Scored "2" in Each Group			t ratio	"p" is less than:
		Total $N = 300$	"High" $N = 100$	"Low" $N = 100$		
11	Obedience and respect for authority	73	91	46	7.3	.001
15	Whatever serves best	20	33	5	5.4	.001
21	More discipline	69	84	39	6.7	.001
26	Most criminals and others	44	68	20	7.0	.001
31	Faith in strong leaders	59	72	28	6.3	.001
33	Large mass incapable	51	68	32	5.3	.001
35	Strong dominate weak	19	36	2	7.0	.001
40	Abolish right to strike	37	63	5	9.6	.001

36

TABLE 9

Item Stems for the Scale of
"Latent Acceptance of Marxian Ideology"

Item Number	Item Stem
12	The government should have control of the railroads and airlines.
16	The government should abolish all rights of inheritance to insure equality of opportunity.
20	Most basic industries, like mining and manufacturing, should be owned by the government.
24	Our modern society is moved chiefly by the desire for profit.
30	Most history is the story of the fight for power between different classes: master and slave, landowner and peasant, management and labor.
37	The price of goods we buy should depend only upon the cost of making them.
42	All banks and all credit should be run by the government.
46	Large estates, on which the land lies idle and unused, should be divided among the poor for farming.

sents the item stems as actually used in the questionnaire. A second table for each area shows the results of the item analysis. The significance tests presented were made by comparing the proportions marking the response scored "2" on the attitude questions.

Reliability Estimates for the Measures

Method of Analysis. In addition to demonstrating the positive discriminatory power of each item in the respective scales and the knowledge test, it is also desirable to compute an estimate of the "reliability coefficient" of each measure.

The method requiring the least stringent assumptions appears to be the analysis of variance approach, as proposed by Hoyt (1941). As the extent to which the content of a scale is complex and heterogeneous increases, the obtained internal consistency coefficient will be an *under-estimate* of the actual reliability. A test or scale of heterogeneous content might yield a very high test-retest correlation, but be low in internal consistency. The reliability of the scales in the present study, if measured by test-retest correlation, would probably be significantly higher than any internal consistency coefficient we might obtain.

TABLE 10

ITEM ANALYSIS DATA FOR THE SCALE OF
"LATENT ACCEPTANCE OF MARXIAN IDEOLOGY"

Item No.	Gist of Item	Total $N = 300$	"High" $N = 100$	"Low" $N = 100$	t rdtio	"p" is less than:
		Per cent Marking the Response Scored "2" in Each Group:				
12	Government should control railroads, airlines	19	46	0	10.5	.001
16	Government abolish all rights of inheritance	4	9	0	4.4	.001
20	Government own basic industries	14	31	3	5.8	.001
24	Society moved by the desire for profit [a]	68	70	65	.7	not signif.
30	History the story of class struggle for power	61	71	37	4.8	.001
37	Price depend only upon cost of manufacture	36	50	7	7.2	.001
42	All banks and credit run by government	24	47	10	6.0	.001
57	Idle estates divided among the poor	49	74	17	8.6	.001

[a] Item 24, the only item in any of the scales not discriminating at better than the .001 level, was dropped from the final scoring. Further analysis revealed a curvilinear relationship between score on the item and total score on the scale; a large percentage at each extreme agreed to the statement about the profit motive, with a significantly smaller percentage in the center range agreeing. The data suggest the hypothesis that the two extremes, while agreeing in the same numbers, do so for different reasons; those "high" in acceptance of Marx making a negative evaluation of "profit," while those at the other extreme make a positive evaluation of "profit."

Problems of Weighting. Gulliksen (1950) and Guttman (in Horst, 1941) have considered the problem of weighting items in detail, and each has shown that in most cases, elaborate weighting systems with fractional weights should be avoided; the use of "0" and "1," or "0," "1," and "2," is quite adequate. Under very general assumptions, the correlation between scores derived from arbitrary constant weights, and scores derived from fractional differential weights, is near unity. The assumptions made are (1) that the arbitrary weights are in the right direction, and (2) that the scores (in this case, items) are moderately inter-correlated.

TABLE 11

Iᴛᴇᴍ Sᴛᴇᴍs ꜰᴏʀ ᴛʜᴇ Sᴄᴀʟᴇ ᴏꜰ
"Mᴀɴɪꜰᴇsᴛ Aɴᴛɪ-Cᴏᴍᴍᴜɴɪsᴍ"

Item Number	Item Stem
51	Should or should not teachers in our schools and colleges be required to sign a special non-communist oath?
55	Some cities have passed laws against printing or selling any communist literature. Should or should not such laws be passed?
56	In peacetime, do you think that members of the Communist party should be allowed to speak on the radio?
57	Do you think that a person suspected of being a communist should be fired from his job even if there is no proof that he is actually a communist?
58	Do you think that our schools should or should not compare and contrast democracy as it works in the U. S. with communism as it works in Russia?

TABLE 12

Iᴛᴇᴍ Aɴᴀʟʏsɪs Dᴀᴛᴀ ꜰᴏʀ ᴛʜᴇ Sᴄᴀʟᴇ ᴏꜰ
"Mᴀɴɪꜰᴇsᴛ Aɴᴛɪ-Cᴏᴍᴍᴜɴɪsᴍ"

Item No.	Gist of Item	Per cent Marking the Response Scored "2" in Each Group:			t ratio	"p" is less than:
		Total N = 300	"High" N = 100	"Low" N = 100		
51	Teachers sign special oath	74	91	50	6.7	.001
55	Pass laws against communist literature	71	94	33	10.0	.001
56	Communists not speak on radio	69	97	34	10.8	.001
57	Fire suspected communists without proof	6	14	2	3.4	.001
58	Schools not compare communism and democracy	16	31	3	6.0	.001

For the scales in the present research, the results of the item analyses have demonstrated that the arbitrary weights are in the right direction.

Although coefficients of item inter-correlation within a scale were not computed, cross-sorts demonstrated the moderate inter-

TABLE 13

ITEM STEMS FOR THE SCALE OF
"SUPER-PATRIOTISM"

Item Number	Item Stem
10	The greatest threat to democracy in the U. S. comes from foreign ideas and foreign groups.
14	In these days, patriotism and loyalty to established American ways are the *most* important requirements of a good citizen.
18	Immigration of foreigners into this country should be greatly restricted, since it may mean lowering national standards.
23	Foreign countries have very little to contribute to American progress.
28	We should firmly resist any attempts to change the American way of life.
38	The American way of life is superior in nearly all respects to any other.
43	Some important organizations in the U. S. have objected to flying the United Nations flag above the U. S. flag. Do you agree or disagree with them?
45	The average citizen does not show enough respect for the U. S. flag.

TABLE 14

ITEM ANALYSIS DATA FOR THE SCALE OF
"SUPER-PATRIOTISM"

Item No.	Gist of Item	Per cent Marking the Response Scored "2" in Each Group:			t ratio	"p" is less than:
		Total N = 300	"High" N = 100	"Low" N = 100		
10	Greatest threat to democracy is foreign ideas	39	67	14	8.1	.001
14	Patriotism and loyalty to established ways	74	84	48	5.5	.001
18	Greatly restrict immigration of foreigners	42	61	13	7.4	.001
23	Foreign countries have little to contribute	10	21	1	5.4	.001
28	Resist change in American way of life	42	74	14	9.2	.001
38	American way superior in all respects	70	85	42	6.6	.001
43	Object to U. N. flag	31	48	13	5.6	.001
45	Not enough respect for U. S. flag	67	81	43	5.6	.001

40

TABLE 15

ITEMS OF THE "KNOWLEDGE TEST"

Item Number	Item Stem
61	Bernard Baruch is: (a) a member of the U. S. cabinet, (b) a member of Congress, (c) a Supreme Court judge, (d) none of these.
62	The present Secretary of Defense is: (a) Robert Lovett, (b) George Marshall, (c) General Eisenhower, (d) Dean Acheson.
63	The U. S. has signed a peace treaty with Germany. (T-F)
64	The federal government has made it illegal to be a communist in the U. S. (T-F)
65	The Constitution of the U. S. provided for the President's Cabinet. (T-F)
66	Women gained the right to vote about the year: (a) 1791, (b) 1880, (c) 1902, (d) 1920.
67	All thirteen of the original states had ratified the Constitution by the year 1787. (T-F)
68	Congress has recently passed a universal military training law. (T-F)
69	Communism was relatively unheard of before the year 1930 or so. (T-F)
70	The Constitution of the U. S. drew many ideas about the rights of man from early English writers. (T-F)

TABLE 16

ITEM ANALYSIS DATA FOR THE
"KNOWLEDGE TEST"

Item No.	Gist of Item	Per cent Marking the Correct Response in Each Group:			t ratio	"p" is less than:
		Total $N = 300$	"High" $N = 100$	"Low" $N = 100$		
61	Bernard Baruch	50	75	23	7.7	.001
62	Secretary of Defense	35	64	9	8.7	.001
63	German peace treaty	46	77	19	8.6	.001
64	Illegal to be communist	54	77	31	6.6	.001
65	Constitution provided	40	62	17	6.8	.001
66	Women gained vote	44	73	19	8.1	.001
67	Original states ratified	46	66	29	5.3	.001
68	Universal military law	38	63	18	6.7	.001
69	Communism unheard of	52	58	39	2.6	.01
70	Early English writers	67	77	54	3.4	.001

relationships among items, as required by the second assumption.

The present investigator therefore concluded that the arbitrary constant weights used in item analysis would be satisfactory for the final scoring. Dichotomizing of responses on the attitude items was considered, and even used in analysing scores on one scale for comparison of the two scoring procedures. As one might expect, considering the relationship between test length and reliability, decreasing the number of scored alternatives from three to two resulted in lower reliability. Scoring on the original trichotomy was therefore retained for all attitude items.

Results of the Reliability Analyses. Table 17 summarizes the reliability estimates for each measure. Because of the lack of homogeneity of content within each area, the reliability coefficient obtained should be considered as an *underestimate* of the actual reliability that would be obtained by test-retest correlation.

If the purpose of the scales were prediction for *individuals*, the reliabilities would be much too low to be acceptable, even considering that they are underestimates. However, the remaining analyses being concerned with discrimination among *groups* or classifications of individuals, the reliabilities are sufficiently high for such analyses.

TABLE 17

RELIABILITY ESTIMATES FOR THE MEASURES
AS COMPUTED BY ANALYSIS OF VARIANCE

Measure Analyzed	Reliability Estimate ("r")
Scale of "Belief in the Bill of Rights"	.576
(15 items)	
Scale of "General Fascist Ideology"	.494
(8 items)	
Scale of "Latent Acceptance of Marxian Ideology"	.439
(7 items)	
Scale of "Super-Patriotism"	.504
(8 items)	
Scale of "Manifest Anti-Communism"	.474
(5 items)	
"Knowledge Test"	.518
(10 items)	

ANALYSIS OF RESULTS FOR THE NATIONAL SAMPLE

Hypotheses to be Tested

The major hpotheses to be tested are concerned with the relationships among the variables measured. These relationships fall into two classes: the correlations among the attitudes measured by the five scales, and the relationships among attitudes and other characteristics of the respondents. Specific hypotheses are stated at the beginning of each section dealing with separate analyses.

The Sample Used in Analysis

The composition of the sample used in these analyses has already been described. The sample of 1,000 does not include the preliminary sample used for item analysis and scaling attempts.

Following the random selection of cases for the national sample, scores were obtained for each respondent on each of the five attitude scales and the knowledge test, using the scoring procedures described in the previous section. Scores were gang-punched into each respondent's IBM card, and much of the analyses was carried out with IBM equipment.

The Correlational Analysis

Specific hypotheses to be tested with regard to correlations among the measured variables are as follows:

1. Belief in the Bill of Rights will be positively correlated with knowledge scores, but negatively correlated with authoritarianism (general fascist ideology), "super-patriotism," acceptance of Marxian ideology, and manifest anti-communism.
2. Feelings of "super-patriotism" will be negatively related to knowledge scores, but positively related to authoritarianism and anti-communism. There will be no significant relationship between "super-patriotism" and latent acceptance of Marxian ideology.
3. Authoritarianism (general fascist ideology), in addition to the previously mentioned relationships, will be negatively related to knowledge scores, but positively related to manifest anti-communism and latent acceptance of Marxian ideology. The relationship between acceptance of Marx and authoritarianism

43

may well be curvilinear; persons extreme in acceptance of Marx and extreme in rejection of Marx will tend to be more authoritarian than those with moderate Marxian scores.

4. Latent acceptance of Marxian ideology, in addition to the previously mentioned relationships, will have *no* significant correlation with feelings of anti-communism and with knowledge scores.

5. Manifest anti-communism will be negatively related to knowledge scores, in addition to the relationships hypothesized above.

Table 18 presents the inter-correlations of the measured variables with which the preceding hypotheses are concerned. Shown in the table are the uncorrected Pearson product-moment correlation coefficients and the coefficient as corrected for attenuation (in parentheses). Correcting the coefficient for attenuation due to unreliability of the respective measures provides information of theoretical interest, indicating the probable magnitude of the relationship if the measures were perfectly reliable.

With only one exception, all of the uncorrected coefficients are statistically significant at better than the one-tenth of one per

TABLE 18

INTER-CORRELATIONS AMONG THE MEASURED VARIABLES [a][b]

N = 1,000 [c]

	1	2	3	4	5	6
1. Belief in the Bill of Rights ("B-R")	.58	−.36 (−.67)	−.22 (−.41)	−.23 (−.46)	−.34 (−.66)	.18 (.33)
2. General Fascist Ideology ("F")		.49	.26 (.52)	.30 (.64)	.27 (.56)	−.12 (−.24)
3. Super-Patriotism ("P")			.50	.11 (.24)	.27 (.56)	−.08 (−.16)
4. Latent Acceptance of Marxian Ideology ("M")				.44	.21 (.45)	−.20 (−.43)
5. Manifest Anti-Communism ("A-C")					.47	−.23 (−.45)
6. Knowledge Scores ("K")						.52

[a] Reliabilities of the respective scales are shown on the diagonal.
[b] The first correlation given is uncorrected; the one below it, in parentheses, is the coefficient corrected for attenuation.
[c] For testing the null hypothesis, the standard error of a correlation coefficient computed for this sample is: S.E. = 0.03. All of the uncorrected coefficients are significantly different from zero at better than the .001 probability level, with the exception of $r_{3.6}$, which is significant at better than the .01 level.

44

cent level. The single exception, the relationship between knowledge scores and "super-patriotism" scores, is significant at better than the one per cent level.

Discussion of the Correlational Analysis. In general, the hypotheses are substantiated; most of the relationships are in the predicted direction.

Belief in the Bill of Rights, high knowledge scores, rejection of fascist ideology, rejection of the chauvinistic ideas of "super-patriotism," and rejection of Marxian ideology all tend to vary concomitantly. The significant relationship between belief in the Bill of Rights and rejection of general fascist ideology (authoritarianism) might be taken as further evidence for the validity of the "F Scale" and the usefulness of the concept of authoritarianism as a more general trait. Or conversely, one might interpret the evidence as pointing to the validity of the quasi-scale devised in the present research for measuring acceptance of the Bill of Rights.

The positive correlation between "super-patriotism" and authoritarianism, and the negative relationship between "super-patriotism" and knowledge scores are not surprising, in view of the extremely chauvinistic nature of the statements in the "super-patriotism" scale. Similarly, the positive relationship between such patriotism and manifest anti-communism is to be expected. Perhaps unexpected is the positive correlation between "super-patriotism" score and acceptance of Marxian ideology. Considering that the Marxian ideology was not explicitly identified as such, the acceptance, by extreme patriots, of concentrated power in the federal government is currently "reasonable."

The relationship between acceptance of Marxian ideology and adherence to fascist values (authoritarianism) is positive as predicted. This finding is contrary to the assertions by Adorno *et al.* (1950) that authoritarianism is associated with political-economic conservatism, or the ideology of the political "Right Wing." Shils (in Christie *et al.*, 1954) has suggested that there is an authoritarianism of the far "Left" as well as the far "Right." That authoritarianism is more likely to be associated with extreme views, regardless of direction, has been substantiated by Eysenck in his studies of British political groups (Eysenck, 1951).

In the present research, it was hypothesized that the extreme

45

high scorers and the extreme low scorers on the economic (Marxian) ideology scale would both tend to be more authoritarian than those receiving moderate scores on that scale. Inspection of a "scattergram" revealed a tendency toward curvilinearity of regression between authoritarianism and acceptance of Marx, as predicted. Using analysis of variance technique to investigate the relationships and to test for linearity of regression, it was concluded that the tendency toward curvilinearity is not statistically significant. With eta $= .321$ and $r = .297$, the hypothesis of curvilinearity of regression is rejected. Had the measure of economic ideology been expanded to cover a wider range, from the conservatism of the far "Right" to the radicalism of the far "Left," the scattergram would have resembled a U-shaped curve, considering the findings of Adorno *et al.* (1950), and the departure from rectilinearity probably would have been statistically significant.

Further theoretical insight into the relationship between authoritarianism and economic ideology is suggested by the writing of Fromm (1941). He deals with man's "escape from freedom"—the attempt to avoid the feelings of isolation, doubt, and anxiety that he describes as concomitants of new-found freedom and independence. With regard to economic freedom, it is apparent that the subordination of the individual is accomplished by *either* the far "Right" or the far "Left," politico-economically speaking. Contrary to the assertions of Adorno *et al.* (1950), "authoritarianism" may be allied with economic views of the "Left" as well as the "Right." "Submission to authority," for example, may involve the authority of a communist, state-controlled economy as well as the authority of monopolistic capitalism.

Shils (in Christie *et al,* 1954) has pointed out that classification of political, social, and economic philosophies on a "Right-Left" continuum is a gross oversimplification, and that not all political and social attitudes can be so dichotomized. Evidence from the present research shows that there is no unidimensional continuum usable for such purposes. Eysenck (1951) has demonstrated that more than one factor is necessary to distinguish British political parties; one factor is closely related to the "Radical-Conservatism" dimension, while the second necessary factor is identifiable as a close approximation to general fascist ideology (Eysenck identifies the factor with William James' terms: "tough-minded" versus "tender-minded").

The positive correlation between acceptance of Marxian ideology and anti-communist feelings is of interest. The scattergram again revealed a tendency toward curvilinearity of regression, with those extremely high in acceptance of Marx and those extremely low in acceptance of Marx being lower in expression of anti-communist feelings than those with moderate acceptance of Marx. The departure from rectilinearity is not statistically significant, however. The anomalous relationship, which may appear to be logically inconsistent, may be explained in any of several ways. One probable reason for the relationship is that subjects may be responding to the label "communist" in the items of the manifest anti-communism scale, while the items of latent Marxian ideology were not explicitly identified as such. A second possible explanation lies in the "logic-tight compartments" into which a person's beliefs are frequently organized. A third factor may be sheer ignorance on the part of the respondents as to the nature of communism.

The only other relationships showing any tendency toward curvilinearity, when scattergrams were plotted, was the regression of "super-patriotism" upon latent acceptance of Marxian ideology. It was noted that those persons extremely high in acceptance of Marx and those extremely low in acceptance of Marx both received lower scores on the patriotism scale. A test for curvilinearity of regression, again rejected the hypothesis of curvilinearity. None of the other regressions showed any tendency to deviate from rectilinear regression.

The Analysis of Variance Designs

General Description. To test additional relationships between the measured variables of attitude and ideology, and the other characteristics or attributes of the respondents, four basic designs were planned for analysis of variance. The independent or classificatory variables included in the designs are: sex, rural or urban residence, region of the country, education completed by pupil's mother, family income level (House-Home Scale), religious denomination, intensity of religious belief, political party preference, and whether the pupil had or had not completed a high school course in U. S. Government or Civics.

Including all of the classificatory variables in one design would have involved more than two thousand cells in the design. Because of the impossibility of filling all of the cells in such a complex design, the variables were grouped into four separate designs, each a three-way classification. The grouping or selection of variables to be included in any one design was guided by specific hypotheses as to the effects of certain interactions. Thus religious denomination and religious intensity, for which we have a hypothesized interaction, are included in the same design, rather than including religious intensity in a design with political party, for which we would have less rationale for hypothesizing a significant interaction effect.

After planning the four designs, each analysis of variance design was completed with each of the five attitude measures, in turn, serving as dependent variables. Thus 20 analysis of variance problems, in all, were completed.

In selecting the samples for the analysis of variance problems, the distribution of cases was determined for each variable. The variables were dichotomized or trichotomized in some cases, depending upon the distribution and the frequencies available. For religious preference, only two categories were included, Protestants and Catholics, since the frequencies for "Jewish," "Other," and "None" were too small for analysis.

After determining the distribution of cases for each variable within a particular design, cell frequencies were established with either equal N's or proportional N's. Cases were then randomly selected in each cell to obtain the desired frequency, and the sums for the dependent variables were obtained on IBM equipment. When the sums were obtained for a given design, the cards for that analysis were returned to the original deck of 1,000 respondents, and the procedure begun anew for the next design.

The results presented on the following pages are organized in terms of the dependent variables. All of the tests and conclusions dealing with "Belief in the Bill of Rights" are first presented, then results for analysis of the other attitude measures are presented in turn.

Hypotheses to be Tested. The major hypotheses, which are generalizable for all of the attitude measures, since the same designs were used for each in turn, are as follows:

It is hypothesized that attitude and ideology measured by the quasi-scales of the present research are significantly related to:

1. The sex of the respondent.
2. The respondent's home environment, as indicated by family income level and education of the mother.
3. The respondent's religious affiliation and intensity of religious belief.[4]
4. The political party preference of the pupil.
5. Whether the pupil has completed a high school course in U. S. Government or Civics.
6. The region of the country in which the respondent lives, and whether he resides in a rural or urban community.

It is further hypothesized that the interaction effects of certain variables, in addition to their main effects, will be significant. Particularly, it is hypothesized that, in relation to attitudes and ideology, there may be double or triple interaction effects as follows:

7. There will be significant interactions among the sex of the respondent, rural or urban residence, and region of the country in which he resides.
8. There will be significant interactions among the pupil's political party preference, the region of the country in which he resides, and the family income level.
9. There will be significant interactions among knowledge score, completion of a course in U. S. Government or Civics, and education completed by the pupil's mother.
10. There will be significant interactions among religious affiliation, intensity of religious belief, and knowledge score.

DISCUSSION OF THE ANALYSIS OF VARIANCE PROBLEMS.

General. Table 19 summarizes the significance tests for all of the analysis of variance problems. The following discussion will elaborate upon the significant relationships found.

"Belief in the Bill of Rights" Analyzed. In summarizing the significant results of the analyses of the scores on "Belief in the

49

TABLE 19

SUMMARY OF THE SIGNIFICANCE TESTS IN THE ANALYSIS OF VARIANCE
PROBLEMS FOR THE FIVE ATTITUDE MEASURES

| Source | Attitude Measure: | | | | |
	BR	F	M	AC	SP
Region (R)	—	—	.10	.05	—
Rural-Urban (RU)	.05	—	.05	—	—
Sex (S)	—	.02	.001	—	.005
Income (I)	—	—	—	—	—
Party (P)	—	—	.10	.005	.001
Knowledge (K)	.001	.05	.005	.001	—
Civics (C)	—	—	—	—	—
Mother's Education (ME)	.05	.05	.01	.05	—
Religious Denomination (RD)	.10	.10	—	.10	—
Religious Intensity (RI)	—	.10	—	.10	—
R × S	.05	—	—	—	—
R × RU	—	—	—	—	.05
R × I	—	.10	—	—	—
K × RI	—	—	.05	—	—
RD × RI	—	.02	—	—	—
R × S × RU	.005	.01	.10	—	—
R × P × I	—	—	—	.05	—

Note: The following interactions, which were *not* significant at the .10 level or better, are
omitted from the table: S × RU, R × P, I × P, K × C, K × ME, C × ME,
K × RD, K × ME × C, K × RD × RI.

Bill of Rights," we find that greater acceptance of the Bill of
Rights is characteristic of urban pupils, of pupils with higher
knowledge scores, and of pupils whose mothers had completed
more years of school. The significant interaction of sex with region
of residence (see Table 18) reveals that girls more often accept
the Bill of Rights than do boys, for all regions of the country except the Midwest. In the Midwest, the sex difference is in the
opposite direction.

Inspection of the cell means, in order to give meaning to the
significant second order interaction (R × S × RU), shows that
the first order interaction (R × S) is differentially related to rural-
urban residence. In other words, the second order interaction,
R × S × RU, is best understood as the R × S effect interacting
with RU. Specifically, the reversal of sex differences in the Midwest is attributable to the atypical responses of the Midwestern
rural girls, for whom the mean score on "Belief in the Bill of

Rights" is significantly *lower*. The writer has no explanation for these findings; he can only speculate as to possible differences in the acculturation of Midwestern rural females.

"General Fascist Ideology" Analyzed. Higher "F" scores or authoritarian attitudes have been found to be significantly related to other variables as follows: High scores on the items of "General Fascist Ideology" are more characteristic of girls, of pupils with low knowledge scores, and of pupils whose mothers had completed little education. There is a tendency for persons with greater religious intensity scores to be more authoritarian, and Protestants tend to be more authoritarian than Catholics when religious intensity is controlled. These main effects of "Religious Intensity" and "Religious Denomination" approach, but do not reach, the .05 level of significance. The interaction of "Religious Intensity" and "Religious Denomination" is significant at better than the .02 level. The results show that for Protestants, the higher "F" score is obtained by those of high religious intensity; but for the Catholics, the higher mean score is obtained by those of low religious intensity.

The triple interaction of region, sex, and rural-urban residence is statistically significant. Inspection of the cell means reveals that the triple interaction is due to the following differences: Rural girls of the Midwest and South score higher in authoritarianism than do rural boys in those regions, while in the East and the Mountain-Pacific regions, the rural girls score *lower* than do rural boys.

"Latent Acceptance of Marxian Ideology" Analyzed. The significant results of the analyses show that acceptance of Marxian ideology is greater among girls, among rural pupils, among those with low knowledge scores, and among those pupils whose mothers completed only grade school education.

The interaction effect of "Knowledge" and "Religious Intensity" shows the following relationship. For pupils of high religious intensity, knowledge is inversely related to acceptance of Marxian ideas; but for pupils of low religious intensity, knowledge tends to be directly related to acceptance of Marxian ideology. High knowledge and strong religious feelings are characteristic of those who most firmly reject Marxian socialism.

High knowledge and more indifferent religious beliefs are characteristic of those pupils scoring highest in acceptance of Marxian socialism.

"Anti-Communism" Analyzed. The findings of the analyses are that feelings of anti-communism are significantly related to a number of variables. By region, the greatest expression of anti-communism is found in the Midwest and the South. Analysis by political party preference shows that the Democrats are highest in mean anti-communism scores,[5] followed by the Republicans and "no party preference" group, in that order. Extreme feelings of anti-communism on the items of this poll were highest for those pupils with low knowledge scores, and among those whose mothers completed fewer years of education.

Religious denomination and intensity of religious belief as related to "anti-communism," while approaching the .05 level of significance, fell just short of that point. In general, Catholics tend to score higher on the anti-communism scale than do Protestants, with or without controlling the effects of religious intensity in the analysis. Religious intensity is related to feelings of anti-communism—regardless of religious denomination—so that pupils with more intense religious beliefs score higher on the anti-communism items.

"Super-Patriotism" Analyzed. Significantly higher scores on the "Super-Patriotism" items were obtained by boys and by pupils with low knowledge scores. By political party preference, highest scores in "Super-Patriotism" were obtained by the Republicans, followed by Democrats and those of "no party preference," in that order.

The significant interaction of region and rural-urban residence reveals that urban pupils had higher "Super-Patriotism" scores in all regions except the Midwest. In the Midwest, the rural pupils again were the exception and scored significantly higher in "Super-Patriotism."

OTHER ANALYSES

Statistical analysis of the data, as reported in this section, has been based upon total scores in each of the five areas of attitude and ideology. Analysis of responses to each item was not presented because of the greater unreliability of responses to individual items, as compared with summated scores, and because of the space required for such presentation.[6]

Since the analyses in the present research have been based only upon twelfth-grade pupils, the analyses in the Report for Poll Number 30 by grade in school are of particular interest. In general, we find that the comparisons of twelfth-grade pupils with pupils in the lower grades yield a number of significant differences. The higher the grade level in school, the greater the acceptance of the Bill of Rights, the lower the proportions marking agreement with fascist ideology, the greater the rejection of Marxian ideology, and the lower the agreement with chauvinistic patriotism. Feelings of anti-communism increase with grade in school on three of the five items.

Single poll questions of interest, which were not considered in the analyses reported in this section, include questions about "McCarthyism," loyalty oaths, the banning or censorship of books, and depriving conscientious objectors of their right to vote. In the fall of 1951, when these data were collected, the majority of the students approved of Senator McCarthy and his methods. Since that time, a later poll, No. 40, of high school youth has shown that the majority in 1954 disapproved of McCarthy's methods. With regard to the other items, it is of interest to note that 65% of the high school seniors believe that "police and other groups . . . should have the power to ban or censor certain books and movies." Persons who refuse to serve in the Army "should be deprived of their right to vote" according to 63% of the high school seniors.

Poll Report No. 30 also presents the comparisons on certain individual poll items over a period of time, whenever the item has been previously asked. These comparisons show, in general, a trend toward much stronger feelings of anti-communism in recent years. The proportion of high school pupils saying that members of the Communist party should not be allowed to speak on the radio has increased from 36% (in 1947) to 65% (in 1951).

SUMMARY AND CONCLUSIONS

PURPOSE

The major purposes of this research were: (1) to measure certain aspects of youth's attitudes and ideology related to freedom, specifically belief in the Bill of Rights, general fascist ideology, acceptance of Marxian ideology, expression of anti-communist feelings, and chauvinistic patriotism; (2) to evaluate the adequacy of the scales for measuring these variables; (3) to determine the relationships among these attitudinal measures; (4) to investigate the correlates of the attitudes measured, such as other personality characteristics and environmental factors.

PROCEDURE

Data were obtained by administering a 72-item questionnaire to more than 15,000 pupils in 103 high schools. The schools were randomly selected from a directory of U. S. secondary schools, and were widely scattered geographically to provide a sample representative of the nation's high school youth. Analyses of the data were based upon stratified-random samples selected from the total returns. The analyses in the present study were limited to twelfth graders, making the high school seniors the focus of the research. From the high school seniors represented in the total returns, two samples were drawn for analysis: a sample of 300 used for a preliminary analysis of the scales, and a sample of 1,000 used for more detailed analysis of the relationships among variables.

GENERAL RESULTS

The preliminary analysis of the measuring devices revealed that none of the five attitude measures met Guttman's criteria for a unidimensional scale, although several closely approached the requirements. Technically, the instruments of the present study are "quasi-scales," a result to be expected in view of the complex nature of the variables being studied. The reliabilities of the respective measures, although not sufficiently high for prediction

54

for individuals, are adequate for discrimination of group differences.

Two major kinds of analyses were made on the responses of the larger sample. For the measured variables, inter-correlations of scores on the quasi-scales revealed the existing relationships; for the classificatory variables, analysis of variance techniques were used to test relationships among attitudes and other variables.

The correlational analysis demonstrated that belief in the Bill of Rights is negatively related to acceptance of fascist ideology, to chauvinistic expression of "super-patriotism," to acceptance of Marxian ideology, and to extreme feelings of anti-communism. Acceptance of the Bill of Rights is positively related to knowledge score.

"General Fascist Ideology" (authoritarianism) is positively correlated with acceptance of Marx, with "Super-Patriotism" score, and with anti-communism score; it is negatively related to knowledge score. The positive correlation between fascist ideology and acceptance of Marx lends support to the assertion that there is an authoritarianism of the politico-economic "Left" as well as the "Right." Adorno *et al.* (1950) have asserted that authoritarianism is characteristic of the "Right"—the politico-economic conservative. The possibility of an authoritarian "Left" is largely overlooked in their book, *The Authoritarian Personality,* partly due to the nature of the measuring instruments used. The present research has demonstrated the positive correlation of fascist ideology with acceptance of Marx, suggesting that authoritarianism is more likely to be characteristic of extreme views, regardless of direction.

Disguising the statements of Marxian ideology by not explicitly identifying them as such, while including the word "communist" in the items purporting to measure "Manifest Anti-Communism," led to the anomalous finding that acceptance of Marx is positively correlated with feelings of anti-communism. Several hypotheses are suggested to explain this relationship. The positive correlation of both variables with authoritarianism suggests further research; an investigation of the factorial structure of the items included in these variables would be of interest.

None of the relationships tested by correlational analysis deviated significantly from rectilinear regression.

The principal findings of the analysis of variance problems, carried out with each of the five attitude measures as dependent variables, are as follows: For purposes of this summary, let us characterize as "liberal" the attitudes and ideology which consist of high agreement with the Bill of Rights, rejection of fascist ideology, low score on acceptance of Marx, less extreme feelings of anti-communism, and disagreement with the chauvinistic statements of "super-patriotism." A word of explanation is in order with regard to the characterization of the Marxian score; we have seen that there is an authoritarianism of the far "Left" as well as the far "Right." With the measure used in the present research, a low score on Marxian ideology is more "liberal" than a high score—for the latter is more authoritarian. Evidence for considering all of the measures together in this way is found in the substantial positive inter-correlations of the variables as just described.

1. More liberal responses are most significantly related (positive correlations) to the amount of education completed by the pupil's mother, and to the knowledge score of the pupil.
2. More liberal responses are characteristic of pupils in the East and the Mountain-Pacific regions of the country. The least liberal scores are obtained by pupils in the Midwest and South, and significant interactions revealed the rural pupils of the Midwest and South as least liberal in several analyses.
3. More liberal responses are more frequently characteristic of pupils who have no political party preference; Democrats are next in order, and Republicans tend to be least liberal.
4. More liberal attitudes tend to be associated with lower intensity of religious belief, although the relationship depends, in part, upon other variables such as knowledge and religious denomination, as revealed by the significant interactions of those variables.
5. Of interest is the finding that completion of a high school course in Civics or U. S. Government *is not related* to any of the attitude measures in the present study. No significant effect appears in the analysis of variance of belief in the Bill of Rights (nor for other variables); the item by item analysis shows, in

56

fact, that pupils who have completed such a school course are *less* in agreement with the Bill of Rights than those who have not had such a course—approximately three times in four. There is no evidence of any positive effects of such courses upon the beliefs of the pupils so far as freedoms guaranteed by the Constitution are concerned.

6. More liberal attitudes are significantly more characteristic of urban pupils than of rural pupils.

7. While girls score higher on agreement with the Bill of Rights, they also score higher in agreement with items of general fascist ideology. This finding is somewhat unexpected, in view of the negative correlation between the two variables in the total sample. Several explanations might be offered, which suggest hypotheses for further research. The pattern of response for the girls suggests that they might be more likely to constitute the "authoritarian liberal" as described by Adorno *et al.* (1950). Furthermore, the items of the Bill of Rights scale are such that the "correct" or socially approved responses are more apparent to the respondent, as compared with the items of the F Scale. This characteristic of the scales leads to the hypothesis that girls may be more "conforming" than boys on items for which the socially approved response is apparent. An additional hypothesis, related to the preceding one, is that a response set may be operating differentially for boys and girls, in terms of a tendency to agree with poll items in the questionnaire.

IMPLICATIONS OF THE FINDINGS

The results of this research have indicated that a significant proportion of the nation's high school seniors does not agree with the freedoms guaranteed by the Bill of Rights. Specifically, about one student in five does not agree with the freedoms stated in the Bill of Rights, and on some issues, the proportion is even greater. Our analyses show that these same students who reject the freedoms tend to accept the tenets of fascism. At the same time, these students who manifest the symptoms of authoritarianism are likely to declare themselves to be the "best" Americans and the most loyal supporters of American democracy.

The implications for education are clear, if one accepts "good citizenship" as an important educational goal. In our society, "good citizenship" certainly requires the acceptance of the democratic way of life, including tolerance of others and respect for the rights of minorities. The acceptance of the totalitarianism of either fascism or communism is incompatible with our democratic goals, and the totalitarianism that passes in the guise of "super-patriotism" is equally undesirable.

The analysis of belief in democratic values, in terms of having taken a school course in U.S. Government or Civics, showed no constructive effect attributable to such school courses. In fact, when differences in response do occur on the items dealing with the freedoms guaranteed by the Bill of Rights, those who have had a course in Civics tend to be *less* in agreement with the Bill of Rights. One fairly consistent difference between the groups is that those who have had a course in Civics are less uncertain about their beliefs; their attitudes might be said to be more "crystallized." The lack of evidence for any positive effects of such school courses upon the pupils' belief in democratic values may give us pause. It may well be that courses in civics or government concentrate more upon the *mechanics* of government than upon the *values* of democracy. In considering the teaching of "good citizenship," one may well question the value of instructional objectives that consist of certain dates, names, etc., to be committed to rote memory. From the results of this research, it seems that a need exists for greater emphasis upon the basic values of freedom upon which the existence of our democratic society depends.

The implications for education are even more apparent when we consider the comparisons of ninth graders with twelfth graders. While the acceptance of the Bill of Rights increases slightly with grade, such change is equivocal evidence for the benefits of education. The changes may be the result of greater maturity regardless of the intervening school experiences. And, since a considerable proportion of those entering high school will "drop out" before graduation, the difference between ninth graders and twelfth graders may be one of *selection* rather than *education*. For the majority of the "drop outs" come from families of lower income level and lower level of parental education, and, as we have seen, it is precisely those pupils of such background who are least likely to believe in the Bill of Rights.[7]

Further comparison of the ninth grader with the twelfth grader shows that the proportion of "uncertain" or "undecided" responses decreases considerably with an increase in grade in school. The ninth-grade pupil is less certain of his attitudes in nearly all areas measured; the attitudes of the twelfth-grade pupil are more highly "structured" and he is more certain of his beliefs. How the uncertainty is resolved during this four-year period of secondary education must certainly depend, to a large extent, upon the experiences which occur in this interval. The role of the educator may well be crucial in preparing youth for better citizenship, and whether democracy is strengthened or weakened in the future may well depend upon the extent to which sensitive educators perceive the needs of youth and respond to them. It is hoped that studies such as this one may help reveal some of those educational needs.

NOTES

1. To reduce technicalities and to save space considerable detail has been omitted. The full details are given in the author's doctoral dissertation on file under the above title in the Purdue University Library. (H. H. R.)

2. The Guttman Scale analysis or Cornell technique is a technique for determining empirically whether attitude toward a specified attitude object is unidimensional, i.e., whether the attitude measured is a single or a multiple variable. (H. H. R.)

3. When t has a value of 2.58 the difference is reliable at the .01 level of significance; i.e., the chances are 99 to 1 that further similar sampling will yield differences in the same direction.

4. "Intensity of religious belief" was determined by response to the question: "Regarding your religious beliefs and practices, how do you feel about them? (a) very strongly, (b) somewhat strongly, (c) mildly, (d) indifferent." Because of the infrequent response to alternatives (c) and (d), those categories were combined with (b) in dichotomizing the variable into "High" and "Low."

5. This is to at least some extent a function of Southern Democrats. See Dr. Corder's study in Chapter VI. (H. H. R.)

6. The mimeographed report of Poll Number 30 includes analysis of each item response in relation to the following variables: sex, grade in school, rural or urban residence, region of the country, political party preference, mother's education, family income level, knowledge score, and whether the pupil has taken a school course in Civics or U. S. Government.

7. In view of this restriction of range in the attitude scores it is clear

that the relational statistics are necessarily lower than they would be if all four grades had been included in the sample (See Table 1 *re* attrition). Dr. Horton's conclusions are, therefore, conservative and understatements with respect to the true relationships in teenagers among the attitudes and their correlates. (H. H. R.)

III SWEET LAND OF LIBERTY

H. H. Remmers and Richard D. Franklin

> *Congress shall make no law respecting an establishment of religion or prohibiting the free exercise thereof; or abridging the freedom of the press; or the right of the people peaceably to assemble, and to petition the government for a redress of grievances.*
> —Article I of Amendments to the Constitution

Possibly because applications of the First Amendment of the United States Constitution are "controversial," they are not well taught by the agencies primarily responsible—the home and the school—for its meaning is rejected by many who will shortly be voting citizens, i.e., teenagers. A very reasonable inference is that this general proposition holds for the adult population, too, as will appear below.

Beginning early in the McCarthy era (1951) the *Purdue Opinion Panel* in its regular operations has at various times polled a nationally representative sample of high-school students regarding their attitudes toward relevant current applications of the Bill of Rights. The results have not been reassuring.

Before presenting them, however, perhaps in view of fairly wide spread suspicions of polls and their results, a bit of legitimizing of such results is in order.

Perhaps most convincing evidence of the validity of adult poll results are predictions of election results based on pre-election polls. Here our poll results in predicting the popular vote in presidential elections, based on representative samples of 2,000 to 3,000 individuals, have come off at least as well as have pollsters of adults such as Gallup, Roper, and a number of others. By asking about mid-October: "If the coming election were being held

61

today and you could vote in it, for whom would you vote?" our results predicted the winners and the popular vote with less than one per cent error. For example, our figures in the 1960 election (Franklin and Remmers, 1960) were:

Kennedy–Johnson	47.1%
Nixon–Lodge	46.6%
Some other candidate	1.0%
I wouldn't vote	4.0%
No response	1.3%

Our pre-election polls of 1952 and 1956 were similarly accurate. These youngsters, therefore, apparently faithfully reflect their parents' political orientation. Further evidence of close correspondence between many parents' and childrens' attitudes has been presented elsewhere.[1]

Abridgment of the freedom of the press is by no means abhorrent to many if not most of our young citizens. In fact, it is less so now than it was ten years ago, as these figures show in response to the statement:

"Newspapers and magazines should be allowed to print anything they want except military secrets."

	1951	1960
Agree	45%	29%
Disagree	41%	51%
Undecided	14%	19%
No response	0%	1%

This is clearly a very general statement of the meaning of "freedom of the press." When the issue is made more specific, only 11 per cent vote for no limitation on "the sale and distribution of 'objectionable' printed matter." "Objectionable" was defined as material that many or most people consider "sexy, profane, obscene, immoral, filthy, etc." How should it be limited?

	Total	Boys	Girls
Prohibited entirely	40%	27%	52%
Limited to adults	27%	31%	23%
Limited to adults and teenagers	19%	25%	13%
Not prohibited or limited at all	11%	13%	8%
No response	3%	4%	4%

"Objectionable" movies fare about the same as printed matter. Only eight per cent vote for no prohibition or limitation.

More than three-fourths (77%) say that the U. S. Post Office should continue to prosecute "persons who use the mails to send obscene materials." Further probing the issue of who should censor printed matter, movies, TV programs, etc., revealed that the federal government is the clear favorite:

A federal board or committee set up by Congress	41%
Public opinion	32%
A national committee of religious leaders from all faiths	27%
A state group	23%
A local citizens committee	23%
Parents	20%
Whoever publishes or produces the material	13%
No one	6%

Since instructions were to "Mark as many as you wish," the percentages add to more than 100. Obviously in the eyes of the teenager the federal government is much more trustworthy in defining and limiting what is objectionable than are parents. Fears of federal thought control through censorship are evidently not very salient.

Reasons for limiting or prohibiting printed matter, movies, etc. come as no surprise since the advent of Freud. Frequency of choice:

Sex–perversion, sexual promiscuity, pornography, etc.	63%
Irreligion–profanity, atheism, etc.	43%
Political–un-Americanism, radicalism, etc.	35%
Violence–assault, sadism, gore, etc.	28%
They shouldn't be limited or prohibited for any reason	15%

It seems clear that controversy concerning issues of censorship will continue and that freedom of the press is not likely to be the absolute that a strict construction of the First Amendment language appears to make it. The psychological mechanism of projection ("It won't influence me, but think of all those with less character!") will continue to ensure such controversy. As the late Heywood Broun once observed: "To the pure all things are rotten." Thus Anthony Comstock, responsible for most of the federal statutes on use of the mail for obscene purposes, shortly after the turn of the century was active in attempting to obtain federal legislation to prohibit the exposure to view of unclothed wooden mannikins used in store window displays!

Further specific probing of attitudes toward freedom of the press yields no comfort to those who would protect this right guaranteed in the first amendment. The typical teenager believes that "police and other groups" should have the power to impose censorship as shown in the following item:

"Police and other groups have sometimes banned or censored certain books and movies in their cities. Should they or should they not have power to do this?"

	1951	1960
Should	60%	60%
Should not	27%	24%
Uncertain	13%	15%
No response	0%	4%

Obviously there has been no significant change with respect to this issue over the ten year period from 1951 to 1960.

Still another question aimed at another facet of attitudes toward freedom of the press is the following:

"Some cities have passed laws against printing or selling any communist literature. Do you think such laws should or should not be passed?"

	1951	1960
Should	66%	61%
Should not	21%	21%
Uncertain	13%	14%
No response	0%	2%

Obviously if this attitude, again substantially unchanged over a ten-year period, were to be implemented, we should indeed be "cutting off our nose to spite our face," for we should then be unable to do what retired Harvard university president, J. B. Conant, suggested. "We study cancer in order to learn how to defeat it. We must study the Soviet philosophy . . . for the same reason."

Freedom of speech also is not necessarily and always to be protected, according to the mid-century teenager. At three different times over a ten-year period the *Purdue Opinion Panel* polled a national sample on the proposition:

"The government should prohibit some people from making public speeches."
Our results:

	1951	1958	1960
Agree	34%	20%	25%
Disagree	53%	54%	51%
Uncertain	13%	23%	22%
No response	0%	3%	2%

Perhaps the most noteworthy aspect of these results is the great increase in uncertainty in the two later periods. Although the decrease in "agree" is both statistically and socially significant, the "disagree" response change is neither.

A similar proposition concerning group meetings yielded a similar result.

"Certain groups should not be allowed to hold public meetings, even though they gather peaceably and only make speeches."

	1951	1958	1960
Agree	25%	15%	15%
Disagree	60%	61%	64%
Uncertain	15%	23%	17%
No response	0%	1%	4%

Here the reduction over time of "agree" is significant, though hardly a cause for jubilation for those who agree with the Founding Fathers on the rights of free speech and assembly.

Three additional questions first asked in 1951 and repeated in 1960 further bear on freedom of speech.

"Some of the petitions which have been circulated should not be allowed by the government."

	1951	1960
Agree	34%	30%
Disagree	34%	34%
Uncertain	32%	34%
No response	0%	1%

"Should or should not a foreigner visiting this country be permitted to criticize our government?"

	1951	1960
Should	56%	52%
Should not	33%	31%
Uncertain	11%	13%
No response	0%	4%

"In peacetime, do you think that members of the Communist party in this country should be allowed to speak on the radio?"

	1951	1960
Should	20%	18%
Should not	65%	63%
Uncertain	15%	16%
No response	0%	3%

On one of the freedoms guaranteed by the first amendment, religious belief and worship, there is, happily, agreement by four out of five teenagers.

"Religious belief and worship should not be restricted by laws."

	1951	1960
Agree	79%	83%
Disagree	13%	9%
Undecided	8%	6%
No response	0%	2%

Another proposition polled four times during the four year interval, also strongly corroborates this freedom and shows that ideologically it is safe with our young citizens.

"Some religious groups should not be allowed the same freedom as others."

	1951	1956	1958	1960
Agree	7%	6%	5%	4%
Disagree	87%	86%	84%	90%
Uncertain	6%	6%	8%	5%
No response	0%	2%	3%	1%

No person shall . . . be deprived of life, liberty or property without due process of law; nor shall private property be taken for public use without just compensation.

A series of poll items asked two or more times over the ten-year period show that the right to trial by jury, protection against arrest without formal charge and protection against search without a warrant are reasonably safe.

"In some cases, the police should be allowed to search a person or his home even though they do not have a warrant."

	1951	1958	1960
Agree	26%	29%	33%
Disagree	69%	58%	57%
Uncertain	5%	13%	8%
No response	0%	0%	2%

"Some criminals are so bad that they shouldn't be allowed to have a lawyer."

	1951	1960
Agree	15%	6%
Disagree	79%	88%
Uncertain	6%	5%
No response	0%	1%

"Foreigners in this country should always be allowed the same basic freedoms that citizens have."

	1951	1960
Agree	54%	42%
Disagree	32%	32%
Uncertain	14%	23%
No response	0%	3%

"Local police may sometimes be right in holding persons in jail without telling them of any formal charge against them."

	1951	1958	1960
Agree	17%	17%	13%
Disagree	76%	66%	73%
Uncertain	7%	16%	8%
No response	0%	0%	6%

"In some criminal cases, a trial by jury is an unnecessary expense and shouldn't be given."

	1951	1960
Agree	12%	10%
Disagree	76%	78%
Uncertain	12%	7%
No response	0%	5%

"In some cases, the government should have the right to take over a person's land or property without bothering to go to court."

	1951	1958	1960
Agree	8%	6%	6%
Disagree	88%	82%	86%
Uncertain	4%	11%	5%
No response	0%	1%	3%

"The police or F. B. I. may sometimes be right in giving a man the "third degree" to make him talk."

	1951	1958	1960
Agree	58%	37%	42%
Disagree	27%	33%	32%
Uncertain	15%	28%	23%
No response	0%	2%	3%

"Persons who refuse to testify against themselves (that is, give evidence that would show that they are guilty of criminal acts) should either be made to talk or severely punished."

	1951	1958	1960
Agree	33%	16%	14%
Disagree	47%	55%	61%
Uncertain	20%	28%	23%
No response	0%	1%	2%

It is not reassuring, however, that while in 1951 only one in four (26%) would forego the right of search without a warrant, ten years later one of every three (33%) would yield this right.

The attitude toward the rights of foreigners in this country, in the light of constitutional guarantees, has clearly deteriorated over the ten-year period. Xenophobia appears to be significantly on the increase with 54% in 1951 and only 42% in 1960 willing to allow "the same basic freedom that citizens have" to foreigners.

The right of private property is in no danger, as shown by the disagreement with the proposition that the government should have the right to dispossess persons without due legal process.

. . . nor shall be compelled in any criminal case to be a witness against himself . . .

Physical and psychological torture via the "third degree" fortunately is significantly less favored in 1960 than in 1951, but the proportions who would condone this practice—from more than a third in 1958 (37%) to more than a half in 1951 (58%) is cause for serious concern. Doubtless the revulsion against "McCarthyism" accounts for the very significant change in the attitude concerning refusal to testify against oneself; while less than half (47%) in 1951 disagreed with the proposition that such individuals should "either be made to talk or severely punished," in 1960, 61% disagreed.

No state shall make or enforce any law which shall abridge the privileges or immunities of citizens of the United States; nor shall any state deprive any person of life, liberty, or property without due process of law; nor deny to any person within its jurisdiction the equal protection of the law.

A series of items aimed at exploring attitude relevant to the protection of the rights of minorities are the following:

"Pupils of all races and nationalities should attend school together everywhere in this country."

	1956	1958	1960
Agree	41%	52%	49%
Undecided; probably agree	20%	13%	18%
Undecided; probably disagree	9%	9%	8%
Disagree	29%	26%	24%
No response	1%	0%	1%

"There should be laws against marriage between persons of different races."

	1958	1960
Agree	38%	35%
Undecided; probably agree	12%	13%
Undecided; probably disagree	12%	15%
Disagree	36%	36%
No response	2%	1%

"People who have wild ideas and don't use good sense should not have the right to vote."

69

	1958	1960
Agree	31%	28%
Undecided; probably agree	16%	13%
Undecided; probably disagree	14%	15%
Disagree	38%	43%
No response	1%	1%

"People should not be allowed to vote unless they are intelligent and educated."

	1958	1960
Agree	22%	18%
Undecided; probably agree	11%	8%
Undecided; probably disagree	17%	11%
Disagree	50%	60%
No response	0%	3%

"Do you think that a person suspected of being a communist should be fired from his job even if there is no proof that he is actually a communist?"

	1951	1960
Should	9%	11%
Should not	79%	68%
Uncertain	12%	18%
No response	0%	3%

"Do you think that some racial or religious groups should be prevented from living in certain sections of cities?"

	1956	1958	1960
Agree	21%	24%	18%
Undecided	15%	21%	22%
Disagree	63%	55%	56%
No response	1%	0%	4%

"Would you favor a law in your state which requires employers to hire a person if he is qualified for a job regardless of his race, religion, or color?"

	1956	1958	1960
Would	65%	64%	63%
Undecided	7%	16%	12%
Would not	22%	17%	22%
No response	6%	3%	3%

Nationally we are fairly clearly in favor of desegregation of schools as shown by the fact that approximately two-thirds over a five-year period, agree or probably agree that "pupils of all races and nationalities should attend school together every where in this country." Here, however, to no one's surprise, one finds large regional differences "in the East, 90%; Midwest, 78%; West, 85%; but South, only 29%. Laws against marriage between persons of different races again show regional differences: East, 39%; Midwest, 44%; West, 33%; but the South, 67%.

Restriction on the right to vote gets agreement of about one-fourth or one-third (1958, 33%; 1960, 26%) for the unintelligent and uneducated to nearly half (47%, 41% respectively in 1958, 1960) for those who have "wild ideas and don't use good sense."

Protection of a person suspected of being a communist in his right to a job is fairly staunchly supported. These teenagers would not presumably approve of the kinds of blacklists for what in a recent unhappy period of our history came to be labelled "fifth amendment communists," particularly by the late junior senator from Wisconsin, Joseph McCarthy.

Segregation in housing—perhaps even a more basic problem than segregation in education—is definitely disapproved by a majority and shows little change over time. The same holds for attitude toward a proposed fair employment practices law.

In summary, teenagers—and inferentially the adult population from whom they descend—accept the Bill of Rights with respect to religious freedom, trial by jury, and rights of property. Refusal to testify against oneself has lost much of its odiousness over a decade beginning in 1951.

On the debit side of the ledger are attitudes toward the constitutionally guaranteed rights of foreigners and minorities in general. The world's "image" of the world minority in skin color (only about a fourth of the world population is white) needs much improvement. Supreme Court Justice William O. Douglas has phrased it succinctly:

"We cannot glorify Little Rock, anti-Semitism, supremacy of the police, downgrading of education at home, and at the same time be strong abroad. We are the same people in Guinea as we are in Boston. We cannot be leaders of people abroad unless we honor at home the democratic ideal in race relations, in labor relations, in community development."

NOTES

1. Remmers, H. H. Chapter 4, "Early Socialization" in *American Political Behavior*. Burdick and Brodbeck (Editors) Free Press of Glencoe, 1959.

IV   SOCIAL DISTANCE AND SOME RELATED VARIABLES IN VOTING BEHAVIOR

Arthur D. Kirsch

INTRODUCTION

Social Distance: The Method of the Proposed Study

The concept of Social Distance dates back to 1925 when R. E. Park suggested the concept. He contended that:

1. Groups develop a sense of distance toward other groups with whom they come in contact.
2. Such terms as in-group, ethnocentrism, race consciousness, class consciousness, and the like suggest a state of mind within the group which determines the distance that separates it from the other groups.
3. This in-group feeling and/or state of mind interferes with, modifies, and qualifies the nature of intergroup relations.
4. Every individual, by virtue of his group identification, along with the supporting group ritual, etiquette, and expectancies, learns his 'place' and develops appropriate attitudes regarding the proper distance he must observe in his interpersonal relations with individuals outside of his own group (Park, 1924).

The following year this concept was further extended when E. S. Bogardus stated that:

Social Distance refers to the degrees and grades of understanding and feeling that persons experience regarding each other. It explains the nature of a great deal of their interaction (Bogardus, 1933).

He goes on to say that "the smaller the range of contacts accorded a race, the less, presumably, the opportunities for accommodation and assimilation." To obtain ratings regarding the range of contacts that one group would accord another, he

73

assumed that he could average the ratings given to each group and use these means as indices of accorded contacts. He assigned

arbitrary values to . . . the seven classifications, namely a value of 7 for grouping one, . . . and so on, by which it is possible to work out what may be called a social contact quality.

In other words, the order of the seven-fold classification from left to right seems to constitute (further experimentation is needed) a gradation in social contact distance.

Following the work of Thurstone in 1929, Bogardus developed a new *Social Distance Scale* in 1933. This scale was constructed by means of the method of equal-appearing intervals a la Thurstone. He collected 60 items and scaled them using 100 judges. Social Distance was defined:

in this instance for each judge as the degree of sympathetic understanding that exists between two persons or between a person and a group . . . The judgments, ranging from one to seven . . . were added and the arithmetic mean taken. In order to obtain a series of equal social distance situations, the statements having means nearest 2.00, 3.00, . . . were selected, which together with the statements having means of 1.00 and 6.98, constitute the series of seven nearly equidistant Social Distance situations (Bogardus, 1933).

As will be seen in the scale below, the items do not fall in any one domain by content. The aim of the present study is to delimit the area of the scale to the area of voting behavior. The 1933 scale follows (Bogardus, 1933):

> Would marry
> Would have as regular friends
> Would work beside in an office
> Would have several families in my neighborhood
> Would have merely as a speaking acquaintance
> Would have live outside my neighborhood
> Would have live outside my country

Many investigators have used either the original scales or constructed scales of their own. But in all but one case reviewed, that of Paisios (1954), no one has split the concept of social distance into various areas. The trend is to develop an overall scale much as the original scale and modify the list of referent groups. Such studies were the ones of Hoult in 1954, Prothro and Miles in

74

1953, Tuberville in 1950, Sartin and Bell in 1949, Bogardus in 1933, 1947, 1948, and 1926, Papuchis in 1948, Gurnee and Baker in 1938, Runner in 1937, and Dodd in 1935.

Hoult repeated the 1933 Bogardus study with but slight modifications. He used the adult population of Portales, New Mexico, and the referents: Negroes, Jews, Japanese-Americans, Mexican-Americans, American Indians, and Canadians. His rankings did not differ significantly from the rankings of the Bogardus study. His further breakdown of respondents showed that there tended to be "more distance in the lower classes" (Hoult, 1954.)

Tuberville used the 1933 version of the Bogardus scale on eight groups of students from the fifth-grade through college. He found that the differences due to the sex of the respondents were negligible; the differences due to religious preference and nationality background significant; and the differences due to education suggestive but with too many reversals to establish the significance of one set trend (Tuberville, 1950).

Sartin and Bell evaluated the 1925 scale of Bogardus by taking the original items and placing them in a collection of other items and then subjecting the whole batch to Thurstone scaling. The results are quite similar to the 1933 version of Bogardus (Sartin and Bell, 1949).

Gurnee and Baker (1938) attempted to use the method of paired comparisons to investigate the concept of Social Distance. They used 200 undergraduate students and had them rate several relationships, such as:

Members of family through marriage
Members of same fraternity
Persons having same hobbies
Persons engaged in same occupations
Persons of same religious sect
Persons living in same neighborhood
Persons at same economic level
Persons with same political convictions
Persons of same race

They stated:

That relationship has the least social distance which provides the strongest feeling of mental nearness . . .

S. C. Dodd constructed "A Social Distance Test in the Near East." In selecting the five statements that he used in the test, he used the criteria of

a. Equal attitudinal distance (by Thurstone's method)
b. Minimal ambiguity
c. Maximal agreement between two panels of judges

Although most social distance scales have used Thurstone's method of equal-appearing intervals, we shall not do so here. Rather we shall assign arbitrary weights to the response categories. These weights will be only temporary and will not necessarily be the final weights given to the response categories. Rather, the final weights will be determined by scalogram analysis [1] using the latest IBM methods (Riley *et al.*, 1954). There are great differences in rationale between the technique of equal-appearing intervals and scale analysis. While the technique of equal-appearing intervals rests on the decisions of judges, Guttman scale analysis has no concern with the behavior of judges. Rather, the entire concern is with the behavior of the ultimate respondents. Several studies have found no necessary relationship between the weights assigned by judges and the pattern of behavior of the respondents. From a score obtained by the method of equal-appearing intervals the response pattern of an individual cannot usually be determined. That is, the selection and weighting of items by the equal-appearing interval method does not, of necessity, yield a scale in the sense of reproducibility of responses (Stouffer, 1950).

Hypotheses to Be Tested

Once the three scales have been developed, we shall subject the data to various multi-variate analyses. We shall test the following null hypotheses to establish construct validity for these scales.

1. Each of the following personal data variables is not significantly related to the variables measured by any of the three scales.
   a. Region of the country
   b. Rural-urban residence
   c. Sex
   d. Grade

    e. Mother's education

    f. Religion

    g. Social status by House-Home Scale

    h. Race

    i. Political party preference

    j. Mixed or segregated schools

2. Attitudes toward civil liberties are not significantly related to the variables measured by any of the three scales.

3. Attitudes toward segregation are not significantly related to the variables measured by any of the three scales.

4. The level of knowledge of democratic principles is not significantly related to any of the variables measured by any of the three scales.

DESCRIPTION OF THE SAMPLE

In October of 1956, the *Purdue Opinion Panel* conducted a poll (No. 47) entitled *Knowledge of Democracy, Current Events, and Segregation.* In addition to various items of personal data, 10,000 high school students in grades 10, 11, and 12, gave their opinions of the 1956 presidential elections and current events, including civil rights, Middle East problems, and school segregation. They were also asked to answer a "short but highly refined test of knowledge of democratic principles" (Heath *et al.*, 1956).

From those 10,000 high school students, a stratified, representative national sample of 1,989 students was selected. The schools participating in this poll were located in the following thirty-one states: Alabama, Arizona, Connecticut, Florida, Georgia, Illinois, Indiana, Iowa, Kentucky, Louisiana, Maryland, Massachusetts, Michigan, Minnesota, Mississippi, Montana, Missouri, Nebraska, Nevada, New Hampshire, New York, North Carolina, North Dakota, Ohio, Oregon, Pennsylvania, Tennessee, Utah, Washington, West Virginia, and Wyoming. This sample was stratified on region of the country, rural-urban residence, grade, and sex. The model for this stratification was set up from statistics from the 1953–1954 Biennial Survey of Education and the 1950 U. S. Census (Heath *et al.*, 1956).

Included in this poll were questions whose analysis would be of interest to researchers in many of the social sciences.

This report gave percentage breakdowns of the various items

by sex, grade, religion, social stratification, mother's education, region of the country, and rural-urban residence. We shall develop the alternatives of three of the items given in this poll into unidimensional Guttman scales and relate them to personal data variables and to other items in the poll which will provide a matrix in which these scales will become more meaningful. Such other items are those dealing with segregation, religion in the schools, knowledge of government and democratic principles, and civil liberties. The items to be scaled by the Guttman techniques are the following:

Would you vote for a Negro for any of the following offices? If so, mark which ones.

> President
> Vice President
> Senator
> Congressman
> Governor
> Mayor
> State Legislator
> City government office holder

The same question was repeated for "a Catholic" and "a Jew."

These items, basically social distance scales, will be subjected to Guttman scale analysis as suggested by Stouffer (Stouffer, [1950], p. 13).

It is often possible to find items which have an intrinsic cumulative character. The prototype is perhaps the social distance scale . . .

Thus we shall provide information about the attitudes of American high school youth by integrating the techniques of attitude surveys, scale analysis, and the concept of social distance to "get at the cultural, societal, and psychological orientations of the individual characterized by his total configurational mobilization with reference to the whole situation towards which he behaves" (Hill, 1953). This concept of social distance, integrated with the above-mentioned data, will be used to carry out multivariate analyses as a means of testing the null hypotheses given above.

78

ESTABLISHING THE THREE SCALES

BACKGROUND

In October of 1956, the *Purdue Opinion Panel* Poll 47 was sent out to high school students across the country. At the same time, the writer served as poll director for the administration of a modified form of Poll 47 to a sample of West Lafayette adult registered voters. This survey was performed on a personal interview basis under the supervision of Dr. H. H. Remmers, Professor of Psychology and Education, at Purdue University. When the West Lafayette survey results were tabulated, the items dealing with social distance in voting behavior did, indeed, form a Guttman scale. The present writer, with the aid of Mr. J. Norton of the Purdue University Statistical Laboratory, subjected the following item to the IBM scale analysis procedure described by Riley, Riley, and Toby (1954).

Would you vote for a Negro for any of the following offices? If so, mark which ones.

President
Vice President
Senator
Congressman
Governor
Mayor
State Legislator
City government office holder

This procedure led to a Guttman scale with a reproducibility of .92. Notably, the items did not maintain the a priori ranks as shown in the question above. Instead the rankings were:

President
Vice President
Governor
Mayor
Senator
Congressman
State Legislator
City government office holder

79

with the office of the President being the most socially distant.

The method of Riley, Riley, and Toby worked well for the West Lafayette sample of 256 but was not suited for analysis of the national poll sample of 1,989 high school students. Therefore, it was decided to sort-scale the items to see if the national poll would yield the same pattern as the West Lafayette sample and to see if this pattern was the same for all three scales. That is, to see if the changing of order of the offices would hold for the two scales for "a Catholic" and "a Jew" as well as for the Negro scale illustrated above.

The method developed by the writer is only appropriate if a pre-test sample such as the West Lafayette sample mentioned above is first used to establish the scale pattern. The test of the acceptability of the procedure is the comparison of the re-producibilities of the original small sample scaling and the final sample scaling. In all cases the reproducibilities of the national sample scales were above .96. This is acceptable evidence that the correct scale pattern was obtained.

THE SCALE PATTERNS

The patterns for the Negro scale are shown in Table 20. The patterns for Catholic and Jew are highly similar. These patterns are shown with the original frequencies of perfect response patterns and the final frequencies of response patterns after shifting each individual into that pattern in which he exhibited the least number of "errors." These non-perfect types meet the criteria stated in the Introduction of having the error patterns random. The decision of which scale pattern to place an individual in so as to minimize the number of response errors was clear-cut in only about one-third of the cases. In the other two-thirds of the cases the individual could have been classified in any of two, or sometimes three patterns and still have had the same number of errors. The decisions were made by use of an unbiased random procedure, the flipping of a coin.

REPRODUCIBILITY

It will be recalled that reproducibility is defined as repro-

$$\text{ducibility} = 1 - \frac{\text{number of errors}}{\text{number of responses}}.$$ Guttman states that re-

TABLE 20

SCALE PATTERNS OF SOCIAL DISTANCE IN VOTING
BEHAVIOR TOWARDS A NEGRO

Scale Value	City Govt. Office	State Legislator	Congressman	Senator	Mayor	Governor	Vice President	President	Orig. freq.	Final freq.
1	−	−	−	−	−	−	−	−	555	593
2	+	−	−	−	−	−	−	−	251	268
3	+	+	−	−	−	−	−	−	65	106
4	+	+	+	−	−	−	−	−	111	155
5	+	+	+	+	−	−	−	−	104	190
6	+	+	+	+	+	−	−	−	75	115
7	+	+	+	+	+	+	−	−	54	85
8	+	+	+	+	+	+	+	−	26	33
9	+	+	+	+	+	+	+	+	409	442

producibility is a lower bound of the average test-retest reliability coefficients of the scaled items (Guttman, 1950). This is true since:

From general considerations of scale theory, it should be clear that if a set of items has high reproducibility, then the items must necessarily have high test-retest reliability. If there was a substantial unreliability factor operating in the responses to the items, this would create appreciable scale error; there would be more than a single factor present. Hence, if scalogram analysis shows that essentially only a single factor is operating in the responses, this must mean that there cannot be any additional factors, including unreliability . . . For the case of the scale scores then, as well as for the qualitative responses to the separate items, we have assurance that if the items are approximately scalable, then they necessarily have very substantial test-retest reliability. Scalogram analysis provides as an automatic byproduct the assurance that responses . . . to total scores have relatively little error of measurement if the reproducibility is high.

For our three scales of Social Distance in Voting Behavior towards a Negro, Catholic and Jew, the reproducibilities are .966, .969, and .973 respectively.

ANALYSES OF THE SCALE SCORES

Although the three scales have the same format except for the different referents, there are significant differences in the level

81

of social distance for the three referent groups. The means of the three scales are Negro 4.30, Catholic 5.59, and Jew 4.49, with the social distance decreasing with increasing score. The analysis of variance of these three scales showed significant differences well beyond the .01 level of confidence. The analysis of variance table and the means and variances are shown in Table 21.

TABLE 21

ANALYSES OF THE THREE SCALES OF SOCIAL
DISTANCE IN VOTING BEHAVIOR

Source of Variation	d.f.	M.S.S.	F
Between	2	964.00	93.78 **
Within	5964	10.28	
Total	5966		

Classification	N	$\bar{X}$	S^2
Negro Scale	1989	4.30	9.736
Catholic Scale	1989	5.59	10.579
Jewish Scale	1989	4.49	10.551

* signifies .05 level of confidence.
** signifies .01 level of confidence.

The three scales in every case are significantly correlated with each other beyond the .01 level of significance. The highest correlation is between attitudes toward Catholics and Jews, .623. The correlations are presented in Table 22.

TABLE 22

INTERCORRELATIONS OF THE THREE SCALES [a]

	Negro	Catholic	Jew
Negro	(.966)		
Catholic	.437	(.969)	
Jew	.499	.623	(.973)

[a] Reproducibilities indicated by parentheses. All correlations are significant beyond the .01 level of confidence.

The first order partial correlations were also computed and are shown in Table 23. These coefficients are all significant beyond the .01 level of significance. The largest correlation is be-

TABLE 23

First Order Partial Correlations Among the Three Scales

Negro-Catholic · Jew = .186
Negro-Jew · Catholic = .323
Catholic-Jew · Negro = .520

Note—All partial correlations are significant beyond the .01 level of
confidence.

tween the attitudes toward Catholics and Jews, with the effect
of social distance toward a Negro held constant. This correlation
is .52.

Thus, there are both significant differences and likenesses.
The three scales would seem to have some general factor underlying them while also tapping some very specific areas. The
fact that the partial correlation of attitude toward Catholics
and Jews was so much higher than either of the other partials
might be indicative of a religious factor in social distance as
distinct from a minority factor. This implies, of course, a
"racial" factor as well.

In the following sections, each scale will be investigated separately.

ANALYSES OF THE THREE SCALES *RE* PERSONAL DATA

As mentioned previously, various personal data variables were
collected along with the attitude items on Poll 47. These variables
include:

1. Region of the country
2. Rural-urban residence
3. Sex of respondent
4. Grade in school
5. Mother's education
6. Socio-economic status by *House and Home Scale*
7. Race
8. Religion
9. School attendance in mixed or segregated schools
10. Political party preference

To test the hypotheses concerning their relations to the three
scaled attitude measures, each of these variables will be used as

83

the classificatory variable for one-way analyses of variance of each scale separately. The writer is aware of possible interactions but has decided to treat these by other means. For example, the mean scale values for the total group of respondents are ranked with the Catholic, Jewish, and Negro scales in this order. However, it will be noted that for the lower socio-economic level, the Negro scale mean is higher than the Jewish scale mean. The writer immediately thought of a race-by-socio-economic interaction. He investigated this by means of a frequency count of Negros in the lower socio-economic classification and found a disproportionately high number of Negroes. The difference was tested by χ^2 and found to be significant at the .01 level of significance. Thus, the reversal of scale values by socio-economic classifications are seen to be contaminated by a racial loading of the responding population. The other interactions of interest will also be investigated as they arise.

In every case, a test for homogeneity of variance was performed before any analyses of variance was carried out. In the few cases of heterogeneity of variance, the χ^2 test suggested by Norton in his *Tests of Equality of Means When the Estimators Possess Unequal Variances* was used (Norton, 1955). This is indicated in each instance.

1. *Region of the Country.* The three scaled attitude variables were investigated as to the effect of the region of the country as specified by the U. S. Bureau of the Census. Significant differences well beyond the .01 level of confidence were found for each scale. In all cases the East evinces the least social distance (highest mean value) with the West next, the Midwest next, and the South last (greatest social distance). The means of the scale scores in the various regions consistently ranked, from high to low, Catholic, Jew, Negro. This uniform ranking of the regions of the country comes as no surprise. The South does not like Catholics, but likes Jews less and Negroes still less.

2. *Rural-Urban Residence.* When the three scaled attitudes were analyzed by rural-urban residence, significant differences beyond the .01 level were found in each case, with the urban residents exhibiting the least social distance in every case. The usual Catholic, Jewish, Negro ranking of means was found in all

cases. (Unless otherwise noted, the comparison of the rankings will be omitted hereafter when they follow this order.) A possible interaction of rural-urban by region of county was investigated by inspection of the joint frequencies. No reversals were noted which would have indicated an interaction.

3. *Sex of Respondent.* In no case was there a significant effect due to the sex of the respondent. This agrees with the results of the sex breakdowns on the various attitudinal questions given in the poll. Tuberville in the previously cited study also found no sex differences. His instrument was the 1933 Bogardus Social Distance Scale.

4. *Grade in School.* This poll was conducted on students in grades 10, 11, and 12. The effect of grade was not significant on the attitude toward the Negro, was significant at the .05 but not .01 level for attitude towards the Catholic, and was significant at the .01 level for attitude toward the Jew. In these two scales exhibiting significance, the means were higher as the grade level increased, i.e., social distance decreased. This might well be due in part to the fact that the children from the higher socio-economic levels tend to stay in school longer. (We shall see later that the mean values increase significantly as socio-economic status increases.)

5. *Mother's Education.* One of the classification variables which also reflects socio-economic status is the educational level of the mother of the student. The three classifications used were:

1. Did not graduate from high school
2. Graduated from high school but not from college
3. Graduated from college

All three scaled attitudes significantly related beyond the .01 level in the direction of decreased social distance with increased mother's education. The connection with socio-economic status is too obvious to need further clarification.

These results are in agreement with the question asked by the Gallup Poll, June 24, 1956.

If your party nominated a generally well-qualified man for president this year, and he happened to be a Catholic, would you vote for him?

Of those adults who themselves had a college education, 79 per cent said yes, of those with a high school education, 77 per cent said yes, and of those with a grade school education, 63 per cent said yes.

6. *Social Status by the Purdue Opinion Panel House-Home Scale.* Socio-economic status was measured by means of the Purdue Opinion Panel's unidimensional House and Home Scale (Remmers and Kirk, 1953).

As previously mentioned, the higher the socio-economic level, the higher the mean attitude scale value. This holds for all three scales. However, the rankings of the three scales do not exhibit the usual Catholic, Jewish, Negro pattern uniformly. The low status group has less social distance from Negroes than Jews. When a frequency count was taken and tested, it was found that there was a disproportionately high number of Negroes in the lower status. This was tested by a x^2 and found to be significant beyond .01 level of confidence. This explains the reversal of the usual rank ordering.

These results are in accord with the study of Hoult in 1954 in which he found more social distance in the lower economic areas of the city of Portales, New Mexico. His instrument was the 1933 Bogardus scale.

7. *Race.* As might be expected, the Negro scale showed significant differences beyond the .01 level when the respondents were classified by race. The Negroes in the sample exhibited significantly less social distance than did "whites" or "others." However, there were no significant differences due to race in either the Catholic social distance or Jewish social distance scales although the "other" classification did have a noticeably, but not significant, higher mean value on the Catholic social distance scale than did the Negroes or Jews.

8. *Religion.* The results of the analysis of this classification are what the writer would have predicted from past experience with the *Purdue Opinion Panel* polls. On the *Social Distance Scale Toward a Negro,* the Jews in the sample have the least social distance, then the Catholics, then the Protestants and others.

When we analyze the Catholic social distance scale, we naturally find the Catholic respondents having significantly smaller variance. Therefore, the previously mentioned x^2 test was performed in place of the usual analysis of variance and was significant as well beyond the .01 level. The ranking of the responding groups within this Catholic scale were, from high to low, Catholics, Jews, Protestants, and others.

When we analyze the Jewish social distance scale, we find a much smaller variance for the Jews than for the other responding groups. However, the sample included only ten Jews, which was not a large enough group to produce significant heterogeneity to necessitate using the x^2 test. The analysis of variance showed significance at the .01 level.

It is interesting to note that out of a possible scale score of 9.00 (indicating the least social distance) the Catholics gave a Catholic a value of 7.98 and the Jews gave a Jew the value of 8.20.

9. *Mixed and Nonmixed School Attendance.* The question asked in the Poll was: "Do both whites and Negroes attend your school?" Unfortunately, this phrasing does not tell us whether the school is segregated or whether there are just no Negroes and whites attending the school together. Even so, there was significantly less social distance shown on all three scales by those students who attended mixed schools.

10. *Political Party Preference.* When the scores on the three scales were analyzed by political party preference, no significant differences were found for the Negro social distance and Catholic social distance scales, but differences significant at the .05 but not at the .01 level were found for the Jewish social distance scale. In all cases the Republicans exhibit the least social distance, with the Democrats next, the undecideds next, and the others showing the most. A card sort showed that the ten students who answered "other" were all Southerners; this would explain their greater social distance in light of the preceding regional analyses.

ANALYSIS OF THE SCALES *RE* CIVIL LIBERTIES ITEMS

The authors of the Poll tried to tap the broad aspect of civil liberties by asking a very limited number of questions. This was supplemented by several other questions on segregation. The authors and the present writer are aware of the overlap of the two classifications; however, they provide a useful, if hazy, distinction for the purpose of analyses.

When the question "Do you think that classes in religion should be taught in the public schools?" was asked, no significant differences were found for any of the three scales. Although this item was hypothesized by the writer to be able to discriminate among attitudes towards Catholics, it failed to do so.

When asked: Which of the following do you think would be most likely to become a member of the Communist party?

A poor person
A wealthy person
A person with average income
Income makes no difference
Undecided

the high school students showed no significant differences on the Negro social distance scale as classified by these alternatives. However, there were significant differences at the .05 but not at the .01 level for the Catholic social distance scale, and significant differences at the .01 level for the Jewish social distance scale. There are interesting comparisons in the means of these two scales. On the Catholic scales, those students who thought that wealthy persons were most likely to become communists had the highest mean value, while on the Jewish scale those who thought that wealthy persons were most likely to become members of the Communist party had the lowest mean value. This group did not contain an unusually large proportion of Catholics.

To the question "Do you think that some racial or religious groups should be prevented from living in certain sections of cities?" the respondents showed significant differences in their scale values for all three scales. The three alternatives to the question were "should," "should not," and "undecided." Within the Negro scale those who felt that the groups should be prevented from living in certain sections of cities had significantly less variance in their social distance toward Negroes. This necessitated using the previously mentioned χ^2 test which showed a significance well beyond the .01 level. The "should" group had the smallest mean, the "undecided" group the next, with the "should not" group the highest. This order was the same for all three scales.

The statement that "Some religious groups should *not* be allowed the same freedom as others," had the possible alternatives of "agree," "disagree," and "undecided." When the scores on the three scales were analyzed by this breakdown, those on the Negro social distance scale analysis showed differences significant at the .05 level but not significant at the .01 level. The Catholic social distance and Jewish social distance scales both had differences significant at .01 level. These differences were in the expected direction with the "agree" respondents having lower mean values than the "disagree" respondents. Notably, the lowest mean values for all three scales were exhibited by the "undecided" respondents.

ANALYSIS OF THE SCALE SCORES *RE* SEGREGATION ITEMS

This section contains 11 items dealing with segregation. Of these, nine fall into a subgroup. These nine items all had the alternatives "agree," "undecided, probably agree," "undecided, probably disagree," and "disagree," which were dichotomized, putting the first two together and the last two together. Responses to all nine items exhibit differences significant beyond the .01 level of significance for all three scales. All the means go in the expected direction, with those students answering in the pro-segregation direction exhibiting the most social distance (lowest mean). The nine items follow.

1. Even if segregation were ended everywhere, Negroes would never make good citizens.
2. When white students and Negro students attend the same school, it does *not* lower the health standards of the total group.
3. In a school which white and Negro students both attend, the cultural level of the whites is sure to be lowered.
4. The morals of white students would not be lowered if they went to the same schools as Negroes.
5. The scholastic achievement of the white students in segregated schools is higher than those in integrated schools.

89

6. Most Negroes in the South do not want to attend the same schools as whites.
7. To make our country truly democratic, we must eventually end segregation in public schools.
8. Negroes are unable to master many school subjects and should be trained to do physical work.
9. Negro teachers should be allowed to teach white students.

The tenth question, "Do you think that eventually children of all races and nationalities will go to the same public schools together everywhere in this country?" had the alternatives: "eventually all will go together," "this will never happen," and "undecided." Differences were significant beyond the .01 level for all three scales. Those who thought that this "would eventually happen" had the least social distance from the three referents; those who were "undecided" had the next largest social distance; while those who thought that it would "never happen" exhibited the largest amount of social distance.

The eleventh statement; "The press, radio, and television present a one-sided case in favor of integration," failed to differentiate the students' social distance on any of the three scales. Whether or not the students agreed with the statement, made no difference as to the amount of social distance in voting behavior they displayed towards a Negro, Catholic or Jew.

SUMMARY AND CONCLUSIONS

SUMMARY

Three scales of *Social Distance in Voting Behavior* were established as Guttman scales using a nationally representative sample of 1,989 high school students. The intercorrelations of the three scales were computed. The three scale means were analyzed.

Responses on the three scales were investigated in relation to the various personal data variables of: region of the country; rural-urban residence; sex of respondent; grade in school of respondent; mother's education; socio-economic status by the *House and Home Scale;* race of respondent; mixed or unmixed racial school attendance; and political party preference.

The respondents' scaled attitudes were investigated in relation to the responses to several items about civil liberties and several other items concerning segregation.

The relationships of the three scales to the test of knowledge of democratic principles were investigated by analyses of variance and rank order correlations.

Conclusions

The three scales of *Social Distance in Voting Behavior* had the same format except for the referents, which were Negro, Catholic, and Jew and had reproducibilities above .96. The computed intercorrelations were found to be significant beyond the .01 level of confidence. The highest correlation (.62) was between scores on the Catholic social distance scale and the Jewish social distance scale. The scale patterns established were the same for all three scales. The order of the offices was, from most socially distant to least socially distant: president, vice president, governor, mayor, senator, congressman, state legislator, and city government office holder. The three scale means were significantly different beyond the .01 level of confidence. The least social distance was evinced towards Catholics, then Jews, and lastly, Negroes. The less the social distance, the higher the scale value.

Region of the country is significantly related to scores on all three scales. The regions rank from least social distance to most social distance: East, West, Midwest, and South.

Rural versus urban residence also has a significant effect on all three scales. In all cases, the urban students exhibit less social distance than do the rural students.

Mother's education and socio-economic status by the *House and Home Scale* both show significant effects in the direction of less social distance with increase in mother's education and socio-economic status.

Those students who attended mixed high schools showed significantly less social distance than those who attended unmixed schools.

The respondents' grade in school had an effect on his social distance only towards Catholics and Jews, with a decrease in social distance with an increase in grade.

91

The sex of the respondents had no effect on their social distance on any of the three scales.

The political party preference of the respondents had a significant effect on only their social distance towards a Jew. The Republicans had the least social distance, followed by the "undecided," the Democrats, and the "others," in that order.

Race and religion had differences in the expected directions with Negroes being least socially distant from Negroes, Catholics from Catholics, and Jews from Jews.

The question as to whether religion should be taught in the public schools had no discriminatory power for any of the three scales.

A question about income and propensity to become a communist brought out the interesting feature that those who thought a wealthy person would most likely become a communist had the highest attitudes towards Catholics and the lowest attitudes towards Jews.

To a question on preventing some racial or religious groups from living in certain sections of cities, the students exhibited social distance towards all three referent groups in the expected direction.

The respondents showed significant differences in their social distance to all three referents when classified by their responses to whether they thought some religious groups should *not* be allowed the same freedom as others.

In this and the item as to whether race prejudice is inborn the interesting thing to note is that those students who were undecided had the most social distance towards all referents.

Those who thought race prejudice inborn had more social distance towards all three referents than did those who thought it was not inborn. However, the most social distance was displayed by those who were undecided.

When the scales were analyzed by means of 11 segregation items, ten of the items were found to discriminate in the expected direction. That is, those who answered om the pro-segregation direction showed the most social distance while those who answered in the anti-segregation direction had the least social distance.

The statement that the press, radio and television presented a one-sided case in favor of integration failed to discriminate among students on any of the three scales.

When tested on knowledge of democratic principles, the students' social distances were found to correlate highly with the total test scores. The rank order correlations between test scores and scale means were found to be: .85 for test and Negro scale; 1.00 for test and Catholic scale; 1.00 for test and Jewish scale. The mean differences within each scale as classified by test scores were significant.

DISCUSSION

The three scales have been investigated from internal considerations of the scales as scales and considerations of their relationships to other variables. Let us first look at the scales per se.

The three scales produced exactly the same scale patterns; that is, the most socially distant office was that of the president, followed by vice president, governor, mayor, senator, congressman, state legislator, and finally city government office holder. This pattern is not what the writer had predicted, namely, that of president, vice president, senator, congressman, governor, mayor, state legislator, and finally, city government office holder. Why the change? The writer had reasoned that many mayors become governors, many governors become congressmen or senators, and many congressman become senators. The pattern seems to be one of wider duties and sphere of influence. To the respondents, however, the progression seems to be in the order of personal importance; that is, importance to the respondent himself. Much publicity is given to the president and vice president; everyone is aware of who they are and what they do. And within any given state, the next office to have personal prestige value to the respondents, as indicated by the publicity received, is that of governor. Every state has its governor and the people know who he is and what, in general, he does. Next comes the mayor. People realize he is an important person in his home town. Then come senators. People know they are important but there are two of them in each state. Lots of people are not too sure of who their senators are. As for congressmen, there are many in each

93

state and are constantly being replaced. Who knows exactly what their congressmen do? The upper house state legislators are called "Senator," but they don't go to Washington. And everybody knows the local officials.

The above, of course, is at best a testable hypothesis, plausible to the extent of being logically consistent.

When the intercorrelations of the three scales were investigated, scores on the Negro social distance scale correlated far less with either the Catholic or Jewish social distance scales than did the Catholic and Jewish social distance scales with each other. The zero order correlation of .623 for the Catholic-Jewish correlation only shrank to .520 when considered with the social distance in voting behavior toward a Negro held constant. This means that for any value in the whole range of social distance towards Negroes, 27 per cent of a person's attitude towards a Catholic is explained by his attitude toward a Jew. This led the writer to postulate the "religious" and "racial" factors mentioned earlier. The additional considerations of the other smaller but significant correlations led to a postulation of a "general" factor. Consideration of the analyses of which income groups the respondents thought most likely to become communists showed us that those who thought that the "wealthy" were the most likely exhibited the least social distance from Catholics and the most social distance from Jews. Here is an example of specific factors within the overall "religious" factor. This is also shown by the significantly higher mean social distance scale value for a Catholic as compared to the scale value for a Jew.

When we look at the scales in their relationships to the various classifications, we notice what at first appear to be very hopeful signs. Increases in education bring decreases in social distance; increases in the educational level of the mothers of the respondents bring decreases in social distance; going to school with both whites and Negroes decreases social distance; knowledge of democratic principles decreases social distance. All very encouraging findings; but also all very possibly contaminated by extraneous influences.

Increased education is known to be influenced by social status (Bendix and Lipset, 1953; Gage, 1947). Only those students with more than ordinary motivation can stay in school if financial and social pressures argue for dropping out.

Increases in the educational level of the mother is even more influenced by socio-economic status.

Attending school with both Negroes and whites appears to indicate what we would prefer to state: namely, that contact with minorities tends to decrease social distance. Unfortunately, we must temper the generalizations made from this study by pointing out that one extraneous reason that those students who did not go to mixed schools displayed such large social distances is that all the Southerners in the sample were in this group. The writer found differences for the rest of the country, but they were considerably reduced.

Also to be taken into account is the following statement from Sherif in his *The Psychology of Social Norms* (Sherif, 1936).

Social attitudes that are common in the members of a group are more or less established psychological processes that are formed on the basis of standardized values; the values towards persons and things *do not necessarily* arise from personal experiences with these persons and ideas.

Increase in knowledge of democratic principles also showed a regional effect. Whenever the percentage of correct answers showed a regional effect, the South had the lowest percentage. This is most striking in the display of correct percentages for the questions, "Which one of the following is characteristic of a democratic form of government?" The correct answer to this question is "Respect for the rights of minorities." Seventy per cent of the Easterners got this correct, 62 per cent of the Midwesterners, 70 per cent of the Westerners, but only 50 per cent of the Southerners. The socio-economic status of the respondents also affects this item strongly. Of those in the "high" group, 69% had the correct answer; of the middle group, 68%; of the low group, only 43%.

However, the trends are strong enough in spite of the possible limitations just pointed out that the writer still feels that these are hopeful signs that education may have some not insignificant effects on prejudices and may help lessen the social distances of various groups towards other groups. And he also hopes that integration will show that contact of Negroes and whites in schools will really reduce social distance.

As far as the civil liberties items and their relations to the measured attitudes are concerned, the writer wishes to point out that those who think that a wealthy person is most likely to become a communist are the students with the greatest social distance from Jews. It would appear that the stereotype of the wealthy subversive Jew is still operating. This is in direct agreement with the recent research of the Anti-Defamation League of B'Nai B'rith (Forster and Epstein, 1952).

It had been pointed out previously that those who were "Undecided" as to whether or not race prejudice is inborn exhibited the most social distance, even more than the respondents who thought that it was. This means that education should have both the goals of teaching the facts and of having these facts interiorized by the high school students. Some students knew the right answer; others thought they did. But those who didn't have an opinion were the least tolerant of minorities.

The segregation items followed the predicted pattern in their relations to social distance. The pro-segregationists showed the most social distance towards all three minorities. The item which gave unexpected results was the statement that the various means of communication gave a "one-sided case in favor of integration." The respondents' answers to this statement showed no relationship to their scale values. This could either indicate a lack of interest or that the students think their side is being presented fairly, whichever that side might be.

Thus, the purpose of this study has been fulfilled: namely, three unidimensional Guttman scales have been developed and related to personal data variables and other items dealing with segregation, civil liberties, and knowledge of democratic principles. A certain degree of construct validity has been established.

IMPLICATIONS OF RESULTS FOR FUTURE RESEARCH

We have seen the fruitfulness of approaching the concept of social distance by means of Guttman scaling and the analyses of the established scales by means of various other items. This is the method by which the writer established his construct validity.

This approach might well be extended to cover other areas such as recreation, social activities, job situations, etc. Such items as:

> Would have as my business partners
> Would have as my supervisors
> Would have as my co-workers
> Would have as workers under my supervision

could well form the core of a social distance towards authority-on-the-job scale. This could be investigated and related to all those factors which are functionally related to attitude towards the job authority situation.

The writer would like to end with the criticism made by Smith, Bruner, and White (1956) of the objective group approach to attitude measurement.

A third general conclusion concerns the complexity of opinions and the implications of this complexity for attitude measurement . . . It is our conviction that the task of arraying them in terms of basic likeness of attitudes will be more readily accomplished after we have developed a surer setting of an opinion within the individual and its functional significance for him.

NOTES

1. For a brief and relatively non-technical explanation of this technique—also often called the Cornell technique—see Appendix.

V SOCIAL DISTANCE IN VOTING BEHAVIOR IN TWO PRESIDENTIAL ELECTIONS

H. H. Remmers

That socially discriminatory attitudes function in voting behavior is generally believed. The belief has some validity. For example, Franklin and Remmers (1960) in a nationally representative pre-election poll of high school students which predicted the popular adult vote with less than ½ of 1% error, obtained the following percentages in response to the question:

"If the coming election were being held today and you could vote in it, for whom would you vote?"

	For Kennedy and Johnson	For Nixon and Lodge
Protestants	38%	56%
Catholic	72%	24%
Others	45%	42%

Incidentally, in the last three presidential elections the *Purdue Opinion Panel* results have predicted the popular vote with less than one-half of one per cent error—a rather better batting average than the pollsters of adults achieved.

The same study also showed significant relationships of "voting" to mother's education and family income. The psychological dimensionality of voting behavior is obviously an interesting social-psychological problem.

Just before the 1956 election (See Chapter IV) and again in the 1960 election, we measured social distance in voting behavior via the *Purdue Opinion Panel* by including in each poll the following question:

"Would you vote for a ——— for any of the following offices? If so, mark which ones."

For the blank the words Negro, Catholic, Jew, were used, the

TABLE 24

GUTTMAN SCALING RESULTS OF TEENAGERS' VOTING BEHAVIOR
IN THE PRESIDENTIAL ELECTIONS OF 1956 AND 1960

Coefficient of Reproducibility

	1956 N = 1986	1960 N = 200
Negro	.97	.95
Catholic	.97	.94
Jew	.97	.95

question thus being repeated four times. Table 24 gives the Guttman scaling results for eight different elective offices for each of the two years.

From the 1956 data Kirsch (1957) found that with respect to the three minority groups, Negro, Catholic and Jew, social distance was unidimensional a la Guttman with reproducibilities of each of three scales approximately .97. To quote him: ". . . the scale patterns established were the same for all three scales. The order of the offices was, from most socially distant to least socially distant: president, vice-president, governor, mayor, senator, congressman, state legislator and city government office holder." (Kirsch, 1957, p. 31)

The results of a replication with our 1960 data of Kirsch's 1956 scaling results are also shown in Table 24. It is clear that the dimensionality of the attitudes involved has not changed appreciably, even though the rank order of preference for Catholic candidates changed sharply from 1956 to 1960, as shown in Table 25.

Inspection of Table 25 reveals that the referent "Catholic" meant something considerably different in 1960 than it did in 1956.

While the hypoethetical vote for President in 1956 had a rank of seven, in 1960 it had a rank of two.

The rank order correlations—a kind of coefficients of stability—indicate little or no change in the relative social distance of voting behavior for Negroes and Jews over the four-year period with coefficients of .98 and .99 respectively. For Catholics, however, the coefficient of .52 clearly indicates considerable

TABLE 25

PERCENTAGES SHOWING HOW HIGH SCHOOL STUDENTS
WOULD HAVE VOTED FOR CANDIDATES IN THE FOLLOWING CATEGORY

| | Negro | | Catholic | | Jew | | Protestant |
	1956	1960	1956	1960	1956	1960	1960
President	24	23	41	58	27	35	84
Vice President	22	25	39	50	27	35	74
Senator	36	41	46	56	36	45	71
Congressman	41	48	48	56	38	48	69
Governor	26	28	43	53	32	41	70
Mayor	31	34	48	57	36	47	69
State Legislator	37	42	48	55	40	48	64
City Official	50	54	56	61	50	55	68
$\bar{X}$	33.4	36.9	46.1	55.6	35.6	44.3	71.3
Difference	3.5		9.5		8.7		

lack of stability in this social-psychological dimension as shown in Table 26.

Table 26 shows the rank order intercorrelation for both 1956 and 1960. Here again it is obvious that the instability of the attitude toward Catholic candidates has decisively lowered the correlations with the attitude values for Negro and Jew.

The mean percentages of Table 25 may properly be labeled toleration indices for the various categories. They indicate a definite trend in the direction of greater tolerance in 1960 with gains of 3.5%, 9.5%, and 8.7% respectively for Negro, Catholic and Jew. At face value they indicate, for example, that the Negro in 1960 somewhat exceeds the status of the Jew in 1956 and the Jew in 1960 closely approaches the status of the Catholic in 1956. Attitudes toward all three obviously also must undergo considerable change before they will equal the index of 71.3% for Protestants in 1960.

There can be little if any doubt that these results of teenagers'

TABLE 26

RANK ORDER INTERCORRELATIONS, 1956 AND 1960

	1956	1960
Negro versus Catholic	.93	.29
Negro versus Jew	.96	.96
Catholic versus Jew	.96	.50

"voting" hold for the actual adult voting population as well. *Purdue Opinion Panel* pre-election poll data in previous presidential elections in 1952, 1956, and 1960 predicted the actual popular vote with remarkable accuracy—at least as accurately as the polls of adults by Gallup, Roper, Crosley, and others. A number of important characteristics of voting behavior of American teenagers coincide with those of adults (Remmers, 1958).

As a sidelight, it is interesting to note that in 1960 when the public for the first time in over 30 years had a real opportunity to vote for a Catholic for president, 20 students or 10% said that they would vote for a Catholic for president but for no other office. It may well be that many of the students responded to these particular items not as hypothetical situations but rather relate them to the actual candidates for the various offices. For example, if no Catholic were a candidate for governor of a particular state, a student may say that he will not vote for a Catholic for governor, not because he wouldn't vote for a Catholic but because no Catholic is a candidate. It may be more enlightening to rephrase the items to read, "If a Catholic (Negro, Jew) were a candidate would you vote for him for president, vice-president, etc.?" Another possible procedure to avoid error would be to list the offices from least socially distant to most socially distant as opposed to the present listing which is from most socially distant to least socially distant.

Another item in the 1960 Poll which appeared to lend itself to scaling was also investigated. The item was as follows:

Should books, movies, etc. be limited or prohibited if they are objectionable for any of the following reasons? (Mark as many as you wish.)

    A. Irreligion–profanity, atheism, etc.
    B. Violence–assault, sadism, gore, etc.
    C. Sex-perversion, sexual promiscuity, pornography, etc.
    D. Political–un-Americanism, radicalism, etc.
    E. They shouldn't be limited or prohibited for any reason.

Ignoring category E, the items ranked in popularity as follows:

Sex—63%
Irreligion—43%
Political—35%
Violence—28%

From this, we chose the scale pattern Violence, Political, Irreligion, Sex. The Guttman reproducibility coefficient obtained for this pattern was .926. From this we would conclude that we have a reliable scale for the measurement of attitude toward censorship.

SUMMARY AND CONCLUSIONS

The "votes" of nationally representative samples of high school students in grades 10–12 for eight different elective offices support the following conclusions:

1. Social distance in voting behavior is clearly demonstrated and across offices is unidimensional.

2. Attitude toward Negroes and Jews as candidates for elective office shows a high degree of stability.

3. The Catholic faith of Kennedy in the 1960 election apparently introduced a strong element of instability in the attitude of potential candidates for elective office.

4. A definite trend toward an increase in tolerance for candidates of minority groups over the four-year period is shown.

5. Attitude toward censorship as measured with poll items concerning irreligion, violence, sex and political deviation is a single psychological dimension.

VI SOME DIMENSIONS OF ANTI-DEMOCRATIC ATTITUDES OF HIGH SCHOOL YOUTH

Robert F. Corder

INTRODUCTION

A FACTORIAL APPROACH TO ANTI-DEMOCRATIC ATTITUDES

For many years the problems of minority group relations have been the subject of wide study by social scientists in this country. The extent and diversity of theories that have been advanced and the number of experimental investigations carried out are attested to by the mountainous literature which has accumulated over the past decades. Research approaches to minority group prejudices have varied greatly with respect to theoretical orientation and purpose. Consequently, the results of many such studies are no longer applicable as background material for current research. Notable exceptions to this are those investigations which have approached the problems of prejudice broadly in terms of the personality traits and attributes associated with it.

STATEMENT OF THE PROBLEM

The purpose of this research is:

(1) To investigate the factorial interrelationships among the attitude patterns of social discrimination, ethnocentrism, and authoritarianism of a national sample of teenagers.
(2) To investigate and develop a technique for meaningfully combining the measures of these attitude patterns so that they may be interpreted in terms of total scores.
(3) To determine whether differences in these attitude patterns exist with reference to certain items of personal data.

Survey of the Literature

(Dr. Corder's extensive review of the theoretical literature—48 books, monographs and articles—is omitted here in the interests of saving space. The review of the literature in all of the studies in this book would obviously overlap very much, since they were originally written as separate and independent dissertations. A summary of Dr. Corder's review of the literature in his own words appears below. H.H.R.)

The results of this research have revealed that the authoritarian individual is a supreme conformist to middle-class ideas, ideals, and to authority. His conformity is compulsive and irrational and is an attempt to find security by merging with the herd, or by submitting to some higher power or authority. He sees the world as menacing and unfriendly. Threatened and anxiety-ridden, he must seek security somewhere, and the best security is to surrender to a powerful authority. To him life is a power system into which he must fit. He doesn't have to wield power himself so long as he can be near it.

The authoritarian is rigid and shows limited imagination. He reacts to only a limited number of ideas and is inclined to remain in channels in which he has been conditioned to operate. This does not mean that he is a person of low intelligence, but it does mean that his personality restricts his intelligence and imagination.

The authoritarian is herd-minded and feels that people who are different from himself are strange and threatening, although they may be few in number and unimportant in influence. He tends to exalt his own group and reject members of other groups. He is inclined to categorize people rigidly and outside his own group sees only masses or types.

The authoritarian is a pseudo-conservative who attempts to convince those about him that he is a patriot, while at heart he hates the traditions and institutions he professes to love. In his most rabid form he is the anti-democratic agitator who is more destructively radical than the radicals he claims he is attacking. He is also a moral purist and frowns on anything he considers as sensuality, a trait he is ready to find in members of other groups.

Christie and Garcia (1951) repeated portions of the California studies on a Southern sample using the scales of ethnocentrism, political and economic conservatism, and fascism. This samples showed significantly higher acceptance of items on the ethnocentrism and fascism scales indicating greater prejudice and acceptance of authoritarian ideology. These investigators describe their sample as more homogeneous than the California sample, and point out that they had been subjected to life in an environment characterized by a narrower range of expressed ideology which was fairly conservative.

This presentation of several of the more recent studies serves to emphasize the increasing interest in prejudice as a function of personality attributes. Although the approaches have been varied, the results have generally tended to confirm one another. Many of the studies have shown that prejudice is associated with personality rigidity, suspicion with the tendency to view the environment as hostile and threatening, compulsive conformity, and stereotyped thinking. At the same time the prejudiced individual is inclined to hold a disciplinarian or authoritarian outlook on life with a strong need for belief in some supernatural determinant of his fate. Other studies have demonstrated differences in prejudice in terms of such variables as education, religious denomination, socio-economic status, and geographic location of residence. Certainly not all investigations have been equally good in methodological approach, but it seems apparent that social scientists are becoming increasingly aware of the necessity for careful research design in this area.

THE SOURCE OF THE DATA

In many of the recent studies of attitudes the investigators have failed to specify the manner in which the data were collected and the representatives of the samples used. While the present study was primarily concerned with methodology in attitude and opinion analysis, its merit as a contribution must rest, at least to some degree, on a consideration of these factors.

The Purdue Opinion Panel

The data for this study were collected through the mechanism of the *Purdue Opinion Panel,* which has been described in detail by Remmers (1945) and Gage (1947). This organization invites the participation of high schools all over the nation and is partly supported by subscription fees charged the schools on a per-pupil basis for the service.

The Questionnaire

In October, 1952, the *Purdue Opinion Panel,* Poll 33, contained 36 items dealing with the areas of social discrimination, ethnocentrism, and authoritarianism. The items in the area of social discrimination (Nos. 22 through 33) were written especially for this poll. The areas of ethnocentrism (Nos. 16, 34, 45, 46, 47, 48, 49, 50, 51, 52, 53, and 56) and authoritarianism (Nos. 35, 36, 37, 38, 39, 40, 41, 42, 43, 44, 54, and 55) were composed of items that had appeared previously in other studies mainly the California studies by Adorno *et al.* (1950). Mention should be made that several of these items were rephrased to reverse the direction of the responses. In addition, appropriate items were included in the poll for personal data such as sex, grade, religious preference, etc.

Prior to the poll the questionnaire was administered to a group of approximately 200 students in a small Midwestern high school. The students were invited to make comments concerning the clarity of the items and their reactions to being asked to participate in this procedure. On the basis of these data certain items of the questionnaire were altered to remove ambiguities and to increase discriminatory power.

The Sample

The sample covered in Poll 33 consisted of approximately 9,000 students from 44 high schools in 27 states. The possible indeterminate biases operative in such a sample as this have been stated by Gage (1947). This sample was representative of high schools financially able to pay for the polling service, and inclined, either by interest or progressive outlook, to seek the benefits of this type of educational device.

The results of a complete analysis of the poll responses to single questions have been reported by Remmers, Horton, and Mainer (1952). This report was based on a sample of approximately 3,000 cases, drawn randomly from the national sample and stratified on region and grade. The report shows the overall percentages as well as breakdowns of the responses by sex, economic status, political party preference, religious preference, rural or urban residence, grade, and region.

ANALYSIS OF THE DATA

The present experiment was in many respects similar to the research of Gage (1947) which sought to develop a technique for the investigation of anti-Negro attitudes and related variables. In his study Gage combined the results of a centroid factor analysis and the Cornell scaling technique to arrive at a meaningful total score on tolerance toward the Negro. After determining this score for each individual subject, he carried out a factorially designed analysis of variance with six personal data variables. In the present study the main point of departure from the work of Gage lies in the method by which this total score was obtained.

FACTOR ANALYSIS OF THE DATA

The application of factor analytic methods is not new in attitude research. Carlson (1934), Eysenck (1944, 1947), Ferguson (1939, 1940), Johnson (1942), Kahn (1950), Lorr (1951), Stagner (1944), and Thurstone (1934) have employed either the centroid analysis or the Hotelling principal component analysis in what have been largely general studies of attitudes. Sanai (1951) in reviewing certain of these studies has criticized them on the grounds that they have not formulated and tested specific hypotheses. He insists that it is aimless experimentation to place variables in an intercorrelation matrix and factor them "merely to see what happens." This reasoning might lead one to believe

107

that the setting up of specific hypotheses concerning the variables, prior to factoring, is the only legitimate means by which psychological meaning may be attached to the emerging factors. This point of view ignores the hypothesis implicit in the formulation of any factor problem, that common factors will emerge, and that these factors will reveal the structure of the variables from their observed covariation. In this sense, Cattell (1952) regards factor analysis as "the ideal method of open exploration in regions unstructed by present knowledge."

The present research employed the centroid method of factor analysis to ascertain the number of common factors required to explain the interrelationships found among the items. As previously stated, these items were believed to represent the areas of social discrimination, ethnocentrism, and authoritarianism. The area of social discrimination was very well defined by its title in that it was concerned with minority group prejudices in social situations. Ethnocentrism was restricted to items concerning chauvinistic nationalism and distinctions between American ideas and "foreign ideas." The area of authoritarianism or pre-fascist ideology was defined in a manner similar to that of Adorno *et al.* (1950). This included items intended to reveal disciplinarian ideology, irrational suspicion, submissiveness to authority figures, etc.

When the data had been collected and analyzed in percentages, as reported in Remmers, Horton, and Mainer (1952), the items for inclusion in the factor analysis were selected. This was achieved by choosing items that had relatively the highest discriminatory power within their respective areas. Item analyses were carried out to determine the discriminatary power of the groups of items. One other consideration in the selection of an item was whether it seemed, from the percentages of responses, to be tapping the same thing as another item. In such cases the item with the higher discriminatory power was chosen. This procedure yielded 27 items, 10 social discrimination, 8 ethnocentrism, and 9 in the area designated as authoritarianism.

The response categories for each item as it appeared in the questionnaire were: agree; undecided, probably agree; undecided, probably disagree; and disagree. In order to compute tetrachoric correlation coefficients the responses were dichotomized between the two "undecided" categories.

The sample of respondents chosen for this study was taken from the stratified random sample on which the report of Poll 33 (Remmers *et al.* 1952) was based. From this stratified sample all eleventh and twelfth grade students were selected who had responded to each of the 27 items mentioned above, and who had not responded in more than one response category for each item. This selection yielded a sample of 867 respondents. For this sample the 351 tetrachoric r's were computed using the cosine-pi formula which Guilford (1950) has shown to accurately approximate the results of the graphic methods of estimation to the second decimal place.[1]

The diagonal cell values which appear in parentheses in Table 1 were the communality estimates used in the analysis. These estimates were computed by a method in which the intercorrelations of small clusters of variables are taken into account. In this case four variables were used to compute each communality estimate. The method is discussed in some detail along with others in Cattell (1952) and Thurstone (1947).

The centroid factoring process was carried out until eight common factors had been extracted. At this point the standard deviation of the residuals from the eighth factor became smaller than the standard error of a correlation coefficient of zero with a sample of 867. This criterion was accepted as evidence of completeness of factor extraction.[2]

The Multiple Correlation Technique

The multiple correlation technique was chosen as a means by which appropriate weights could be assigned to the variables in each of the isolated factors that was meaningful. The items for this procedure were chosen on the basis of the magnitude of their loadings and their degree of complexity as factor variables. This meant that for the multiple R to be large, the factors would have to appear as fairly well-defined clusters whose centroid values were relatively high. When the factors had been chosen on this basis, a multiple correlation solution was carried out for each of the factors. In these solutions the factor appeared in each case as the dependent variable and the items as independent variables in each solution, and these were treated as component parts that could be totaled to give an appropriate factor score.

The Analysis of Variance

A factorially designed analysis of variance was employed in studying the effects of four personal data variables with reference to the previously described factor scores. In each analysis the factor score of the subjects was the dependent variable, while the personal data were the independent variables. This design permitted the study of all combinations of all variables at each of their respective levels.

Definitions of Personal Data Variables

The personal data variables included in this study were religious affiliation, mother's education, rural or urban residence, and geographical region of the country.

Religious Affiliation. Information concerning this variable was obtained by means of the item:

5. My religion is
———Protestant
———Catholic
———Jewish
———Some other
———None

The sample was limited to those who responded to Protestant or Catholic, because the number of responses to the other categories was negligible.

Mother's Education. Information on this variable resulted from the item:

6. Schooling of my mother. My mother:
(a) ———did not finish the eighth grade.
(b) ———finished the eighth grade but did not go to high school.
(c) ———had some high school but did not graduate.
(d) ———finished high school but did not go to college.
(e) ———had some college but did not graduate.
(f) ———graduated from college.

Inasmuch as the frequency of response to each of these categories varied appreciably with respect to the other personal data, this variable was dichotomized between categories (c) and (d).

Rural-Urban Residence. The data for this variable were obtained by the item:

3. I live in an area which is chiefly (the person giving you these sheets will tell you which to mark)
———Rural
———Urban

For this item the individuals administering the questionnaire were asked to instruct the respondents to check "rural" if they lived in the country, or in a town of 2,500 or less in population. Exceptions to this were made where the place of residence was near a large city and was essentially suburban rather than rural.

Geographical Region. Information concerning this variable was available by merely noting the location of the school which each respondent attended. Four regions were determined as follows: The South included the seventeen states in which racial segregation is enforced in the public schools. The East was made up of all states east of Ohio that were not included in the Southern region. The West was defined as all states west of the eastern boundaries of Montana, Wyoming, and Colorado, and not included in the Southern region. The remaining states were designated as the Midwest.

Selection of the Experimental Sample

The factorial design made up of the variables described above consisted of 32 cells. This required that the national sample of approximately 9,000 respondents be broken down into 32 groups. First, the eleventh- and twelfth-grade respondents were selected. This group was then divided into the 32 groups described by the various cell combinations of the experimental design. The smallest group found was for the cell combination South, rural resident, Catholic, and mother's education as high school graduate or higher. This group consisted of 12 cases. The remaining groups were then randomly selected from their

111

parent groups so that each cell in the design had a frequency of 12 cases.

When the sample of 384 cases had been selected, factor scores for each of the individual respondents were computed. This procedure consisted of adding the beta weights assigned to each variable on each factor. A separate analysis of variance was carried out for each of the isolated meaningful factors. In each

TABLE 27

ROTATED FACTOR MATRIX *

Item	I	II	III	IV	V	VI	VII	VIII	h^2
22	87	24	−02	−01	12	17	−04	−11	87
24	82	22	03	05	07	12	−09	02	75
25	34	29	−47	20	−49	07	06	−04	71
26	74	27	−04	06	−14	−14	−03	25	73
27	42	52	17	12	−15	02	21	−11	57
28	66	13	−24	03	−02	−28	−10	−16	63
29	86	31	−08	13	02	−09	02	07	87
30	56	22	−25	10	−01	−32	−20	−14	60
31	85	30	03	14	12	04	00	−05	85
32	22	46	−14	13	16	−21	13	17	41
34	21	−16	−21	−03	02	17	13	08	17
35	10	48	07	22	17	10	−11	16	37
36	02	51	−13	−03	−06	−14	−18	−03	33
37	01	52	−21	28	−47	44	01	−17	84
38	−01	51	−32	−05	01	17	−27	06	47
39	−01	46	−09	17	21	05	−14	17	34
41	12	55	19	09	12	13	02	−21	44
43	−07	43	−34	02	−01	10	07	12	34
44	01	−01	−09	10	08	02	29	−03	11
45	14	56	38	−38	−27	02	01	10	70
46	18	−14	−22	−25	18	06	15	−09	23
49	03	55	−03	−30	06	−11	14	13	45
50	26	−07	−25	−09	13	19	02	27	27
51	38	−12	−02	−23	−05	15	−11	10	26
52	03	43	07	−30	−15	−13	05	11	33
54	−02	52	−18	−16	17	04	04	−13	38
56	29	55	14	01	14	−21	22	−04	52
Sum of Squares	4.95	4.15	1.09	0.78	0.86	0.75	0.48	0.47	13.54
% Variance	36.6	30.6	8.1	5.8	6.4	5.5	3.5	3.5	100.0

* Decimal points have been omitted in main body of table.

analysis F-tests were made on each main effect and on all of the possible interaction combinations.

RESULTS

In the two previous sections the nature of the data, the sample, and the techniques of analysis have been discussed. The present section presents the final results and an attempt to evaluate them with reference to this method of analysis of inter-group attitudes.

The rotated loadings of all factors is presented in Table 27.

The interpretation of Factors I and II can perhaps be aided by a listing of the variables which formed the factor clusters. The Factor I cluster consisted of seven items from the area of social discrimination. These items were as follows:

22. Pupils of all races and nationalities should attend school together everywhere in this country.
24. Swimming pools should admit people of all races and nationalities, to swim in the same pool.
26. Hotels are right in refusing to admit people of certain races or nationalities.
28. People of different races and nationalities should be allowed to live in the same neighborhoods.
29. Public eating places should serve people of all races and nationalities, even at the same table if the customers want it that way.
30. Property owners or their agents should prevent people of some races or nationalities from living in the better neighborhoods.
31. All theatres should admit people of all races and nationalities, and allow them to sit anywhere they want.

The cluster of items on Factor II consisted of three ethnocentrism items and eight items from the area on authoritarianism. These items were:

Ethnocentrism:

45. We should have as little as possible to do with the foreign countries of the world.
49. It's a mistake to trust any nation until we are completely sure of them.

113

52. Foreign countries have very little to contribute to American progress today.

Authoritarianism:

35. The true American way of life is disappearing so fast that force may be necessary to preserve it.
36. People who complain about things in the U. S. should be sent out of this country if they don't like it.
37. People without a deep and unquestioning faith in Almighty God should not be trusted in public office.
38. There is hardly anything lower than a person who does not feel a great love, gratitude and respect for our flag.
39. Americans are getting soft; most people need stricter discipline and the will to defend their interests.
41. Most people don't realize how much our lives are controlled by plots hatched in secret by others.
43. Obedience and a proper respect for authority should be the very first requirements of a good citizen.
54. An insult to our honor should always be punished.

From the content of the items composing these two factor clusters, the meaning of the factors is fairly clear-cut. Factor I contains a majority of the social discrimination items placed in the matrix. Factor II consists of eight of the nine authoritarianism items placed in the matrix in addition to three items which are related in that they are all statements of chauvinistic, in-group glorification. The fact that a separate factor of ethnocentrism did not emerge was probably due to the complexity of the items in that area. It may be noted that many of the items in this area were paraphrased "foreign policy" statements which were perhaps, relegated to the status of the cliche during the 1952 election campaign.

A very interesting doublet consisting of variables 25 and 37 is as follows:

25. There should be laws against marriage between persons of different races.
37. People without a deep and unquestioning faith in Almighty God should not be trusted in public affairs.

Although such a doublet has little meaning either psychologically or from the standpoint of prediction, the magnitude of the loadings of these two variables in this plane indicates that they represent something more than a graphic curiosity.

THE MULTIPLE CORRELATION TECHNIQUE

Of the eight factors resulting from the factor analysis, Factors I and II together accounted for 67 per cent of the matrix variance and were considered to be the only factors satisfactory for the application of the multiple correlation technique. The variables included in these solutions were those described above as composing these factor clusters.

The multiple correlation coefficients for Factors I and II, respectively, were 0.93 and 0.90. This indicated that the two arrays of items studied had high predictive value in the areas of which the factors were representative. The beta weights computed in the multiple R solutions are given in the original thesis. Statistically the beta weights are standard partial regression coefficients, because they would apply if standard measures were used in all variables and, as in the case of coefficients of partial correlation, the effects of other variables are held constant.

THE ANALYSES OF VARIANCE

After computing scores for the sample of 384 cases on each of the two factors, the two sets of data were tested for homogeneity of variance. Bartlett's test as described by Lindquist (1953) was used for this purpose. This procedure revealed that no significant departure from homogeneity existed in either set of data.[3]

In the analysis of Factor I, the factor of social discrimination, the F-tests indicated that two main effects were significant at the 1 per cent point. The values of F in these tests were: for geographical regions, 38.08, and for rural-urban residence, 8.69.

The interaction between geographical regions and rural-urban residence was also significant at the 1 per cent point as indicated by an F of 8.22.

Another significant interaction was that between geographical regions and the two levels of mother's education. The F of 3.30 was significant at the 1 per cent point.

The most outstanding characteristic of the significant variance of scores on social discrimination is the recurrence of the regional effect in two interaction variances. This analysis reveals that the Southern sample was probably so much higher in this factor than the other regions that these scores alone are the source of most of the significant interaction variance. The significant variance due to rural-urban differences was also largely accounted for by the rural-urban difference in the Southern region.

In the analysis of Factor II, the factor of authoritarianism and ethnocentrism, all of the main effect variances were significant. In this case, the effect due to geographical regions was significant at the 5 per cent point with an F of 3.18.

Once again the rural-urban residence differences were significant at the 1 per cent point as indicated by an F of 9.82. While the rural-urban differences were noticeably larger on Factor II scores in other regions, the difference in the South was still the source of the major portion of this variance. The importance of the large difference in this single region is clear when it is compared to the means for the two groups in the four regions combined.

By far the largest F, 33.53, was obtained when the difference between religions was tested. This difference was significant at the 1 per cent point. On this factor the difference due to the levels of mother's education yielded an F of 9.19 which was significant at the 1 per cent point.

The analysis of scores on Factor II showed a significant interaction variance between religious preference and level of mother's education. The F for this difference was 6.92, and it was significant at the 1 per cent point. In this case the interaction variance is due largely to the difference in the mean scores of the two levels of mother's education for the Catholics. The mean scores for the two levels of mother's education for the Protestants were practically identical.

The foregoing discussion of the results of the two analyses of variance has concerned only those variances that proved significant at the 5 per cent point or better. In consideration of this fact, it was judged that very little, if any, consequence could be attached to variances which did not yield values of F that were significant at the 5 per cent point. In passing, however, it is perhaps worth noting that for the interaction between regions, rural-urban residence, and religion, the value of F is 2.49. The value of

F required for significance at the 5 per cent point is approximately 2.65. The interaction variances for regions and rural-urban residence, and for regions and religious preference yielded values of 2.41 and 2.15 respectively in their F-tests. The value of F required for significance is the same as that mentioned above. All other values of F are so small as to be safely attributed to chance variation.

SUMMARY AND CONCLUSIONS

PURPOSE

The purpose of this research was to determine the factorial relationships of social discrimination, ethnocentrism, and authoritarianism as areas of a broad pattern of anti-democratic attitudes. The method employed was chosen as a means of relating the measures of these areas in a manner that would produce meaningful total scores. A further aim of the study was to establish the relationships between these attitude patterns and certain personal data variables.

SOURCE OF THE DATA

An opinion poll was administered through the facilities of the *Purdue Opinion Panel* to approximately 9,000 high school students in all areas of the nation. These students were attending 44 schools in 27 states. With the exception of the possibility that a bias was present due to the high schools' financial ability to pay for the polling service, the sample was representative of the nation's high school population.

The questionnaire contained 36 items concerning the three areas under investigation. Certain of the items were written especially for this poll, while the others were adapted from previous related research, primarily the California studies (Adorno *et al.*, 1950).

ANALYSIS OF THE DATA

A sample of 867 eleventh- and twelfth-grade respondents were selected from a random sample of 3,000 cases, stratified on region and grade. From the 36 items used, 27 were selected by an item analysis technique. Item intercorrelations were computed for these 27 items, and a centroid factor analysis carried out on the resulting intercorrelation matrix. Eight statistically significant common factors emerged, and these were rotated to yield a meaningful psychological structure.

Of the eight common factors, two were found to yield fairly well-defined clusters of variables with relatively low complexity. These two factors were observed to account for approximately 67 per cent of the factor matrix variance, and to represent the areas of social discrimination and a combination of authoritarianism and ethnocentrism.

Accepting these two factors as the most meaningful, multiple correlation coefficients were computed using factors as criteria and the items as predictors. This yielded beta weights for each of the variables in the two factor clusters, and made possible the calculation of factor scores through the summation of the weights on each factor.

A factorially designed analysis of variance was then carried out for each of the two factors. The factor score in each case was the dependent variable, while four items of personal data (geographical region, rural or urban residence, religious preference, and mother's education) were the independent variables. This sample was randomly selected from the national sample of approximately 9,000 cases. Tests of significance were made on all main variables and on all possible interaction combinations.

This analysis showed that for Factor I, the factor of social discrimination, two of the personal data variables, geographical region and rural-urban residence, were associated with group differences so great that they could have occurred by chance in only 1 per cent of samples similarly selected. The interaction between these two variables was also significant at the 1 per cent point. The regions-by-levels of mother's education interaction was shown to be significant at the 5 per cent point. The differences for the other variables and interactions were no greater than could be expected from chance variation.

In the second analysis using the scores derived from Factor II, the factor of authoritarianism and ethnocentrism, three of the personal data variables, rural-urban residence, religious preference, and mother's education, revealed group differences so great as to be significant at the 1 per cent point. The fourth main variable, geographical region, showed a difference which was significant at the 5 per cent point. Once again, a two variable interaction, that between religious preference and levels of mother's education, was significant at the 1 per cent point.

IMPLICATIONS FOR FURTHER RESEARCH

The results of this study have indicated the prevalence of unfavorable minority group attitudes in our teen-age population. The attitude patterns demonstrated by the factors which emerged from these techniques could have been predicted from the results of the California studies of Adorno, *et al.* (1950). The failure to find a high relationship between discrimination and authoritarianism, as would have been predicted by the latter, was undoubtedly due to the specificity of the items in the area of social discrimination. On the other hand, the presence of several ethnocentrism items in the authoritarianism cluster, tends to confirm the findings of the California studies.

While this study has emphasized methodology rather than exploration of "causal" effects, consideration of the results obtained with reference to the material used suggests several points which should be observed in planning research or action programs in the improvement of inter-group relations. There is little doubt that at present, education provides the most hopeful long-term approach for the mitigation of minority group prejudices. However, to the present time education has largely consisted of the dissemination of facts and rational appeals for tolerance. For very young children, certainly, correct information concerning minority groups may be the essence of education in ethnic relations. But counter-measures with prejudiced adults should take into account the whole structure of the prejudiced outlook. Before factual information can serve its purpose, a frame of reference must exist in the minds of the persons to be educated which is in line with that of the educator. For example, the argument that personality characteristics such as willingness to serve others or to live by correct moral values are equally common among all groups will have little effect if the values of the intolerant are based chiefly or solely on economic success. The argument will only convince the intolerant that the educator does not understand what is really important and will tend to cause all further statements to be discounted.

Education for ethnic tolerance should, perhaps, place its major emphasis not upon discrimination against particular minority groups, but upon such phenomena as stereotypy, emotional coldness, destructiveness, and lack of personal insight. The educator must realize that he is dealing with essentially irrational phenomena and that rational argument will produce little ameliorative effect. When such patterns of prejudiced attitudes are present, closer association with minority group members can hardly be expected to influence these people, because they are largely characterized by the inability to have experience. An effective approach, however, may be made by showing intolerant persons how they are exploited because of their prejudices. All such efforts should acquaint individuals with the manner in which subtle propaganda in mass media has served to perpetuate the fiction that minorities are the mysterious forces behind social problems. Ultimately, all education should aim toward discouraging the semi-respectability of using minority groups as outlets for discharging hostility.

Future research can perhaps be intensified to determine the salience of prejudiced attitudes, especially with reference to their expressed intensity. Some clarification of this relationship has been offered by Hartley (1946). Determination of these relationships should be preceded by rather exacting validation of an instrument in terms of clinical interviews and possibly projective devices. A useful approach here might be the use of content analysis of the responses to appropriate open-end questions or other projective stimuli.

A further suggestion would include the investigation of the complex relationship between the degree of internalization of prejudiced attitudes and the structure of value systems. One orientation might approach this problem through a system of typologies such as those of Adorno (1950). Another approach could be made through an extensive study of perceptual processes as has been done to some extent by Rokeach (1948, 1950, 1951).

120

Finally, some effort should be made to ascertain the nature of the situational determinants of attitude response patterns (for example, the nature of the determinants of the responses by individuals who are aware of their prejudices, but who respond as though they hold no prejudice, even though their responses are anonymous). One means of exploration would provide for multiple responses to each attitude item to determine the group with which the respondent identifies. This information if combined with data on the salience and intensity of the attitude should allow some conclusion as to the nature of the determinants of individual item responses. If highly correlated direct and indirect measures of the attitude pattern can be constructed, a comparison of the two scores should provide even more conclusive data as to situational determinants.

NOTES

1. The completed intercorrelation matrix is presented as Table 1 in the original thesis.

2. The final residual matrix is presented as Table 2 in the original.

3. Summaries of the two analyses of variance are presented in Tables 7 and 8 of the original thesis.

VII ATTITUDE CHANGE IN INTER-GROUP EDUCATION PROGRAMS

Robert E. Mainer

INTRODUCTION

In the fall of 1951, the editors of *The Purdue Opinion Panel* published a report entitled "Does Youth Believe in the Bill of Rights?" (Remmers *et al.*, 1952). This report presented evidence from the poll responses of a nationwide sample of high school youth to indicate that there was a marked tendency for teenagers to reject certain civil rights guaranteed by our Constitution, and to endorse some principles advocated by Marx, some that are implicit in totalitarianism and others that are generally regarded as "un-American."

To the editors of this report, such findings represented a challenge to American education. Publication of the essential material from this report in a popular magazine (*Look*, 1952), brought a deluge of correspondence, telegrams and telephone calls to *The Purdue Opinion Panel*, and it was evident in the public's response that they, too, were disturbed by the attitudes of high school youth.

It was in this way that the editors of the panel came to propose an intensive study that would yield information about how anti-democratic attitudes can best be combatted as well as provide data on their correlates and factorial structure.

Several major problems made it impossible to carry out the proposed research during 1952–53. Certainly the greatest deterrent was the matter of cost. It would have required a budget of several thousands of dollars to secure a nationwide sample of schools, to provide experimental materials, and to collect the data. Apart from the important problem of cost, however, were the further problems of developing the necessary instruments for evaluating the success of measures designed to modify attitudes, and of selecting and measuring the variables that would be necessary to provide controls and correlative data.

For such reasons, the proposed study was postponed. In its place, a program of more modest proportions was undertaken for the purpose of developing the instruments and selecting the variables to be included in later studies. In this program, four polls were planned and administered during the 1952–53 school year.

While planning the 1952–53 program, it was recognized that an opportunity would exist to conduct a preliminary study of attitude change in a situation where no intentional modification of attitudes would be made. In this situation, it was hoped it would be possible to make a coarse examination of the effect of exposure to five months of public education upon a particular social attitude. Furthermore, it seemed possible that something of the characteristics of those who do change their attitudes could be determined.

It was obvious from the beginning that the plans for the study left much to be desired in the way of experimental design and analysis. It was known, for example, that some schools gave more attention to their students' attitudes than others, and that comparable school environments probably would be difficult to find in all regions of the country. Also, it was recognized that the very process of conducting a poll and sending reports back to the schools for pupil discussion would influence the attitudes measured by the poll.

However, despite shortcomings and limitations, it was felt that useful information could be obtained from such a study. The problem of this study is the systematic description and evaluation of the procedures, instruments and results of the preliminary study which made up the research program of *The Purdue Opinion Panel* for 1952–53.

PROCEDURES AND INSTRUMENTS

Construction of questionnaires. The editors elected to focus the investigation of anti-democratic attitudes on three areas that had received wide attention by other investigators: (1) attitudes toward the rights of minority groups; (2) authoritarian-fascistic attitudes, especially as defined by Adorno *et al.* (1950); and (3) ethnocentrism, "in-group" preoccupation, and chauvinistic patriotism. This selection was made in the belief that the large body of information about these areas that has come from previous research would be of great assistance in intrepreting the findings of this study and in drawing conclusions from them.

Since 1952 was an election year, and since civil rights, fair employment practices and similar topics appeared as hotly debated issues in the campaigns, it was decided to remove some of the abstractness of anti-democratic attitude questions by placing them within the context of political issues. It was judged that what might be lost in the students who would parrot the platforms of their favorite political party would be more than compensated by the gain from their increased interest in the polls. Thus, the schools were informed that the *Panel* intended to sound out the nation's high school youth on their political preferences and their stands on the issues of the election.

Poll 33 of The Purdue Opinion Panel. This first poll of the school year was administered during late September and early October, 1952 (Remmers *et al.*, 1952). The major areas of personal data, presidential candidate choice, election issues, attitude toward social discrimination, authoritarianism and ethnocentrism were included in the poll.

The information collected in the personal data section of Poll 33 included sex, grade, rural or urban residence, political party preference, religion, amount of mother's education, socio-economic status, as given by the House-Home scale (Remmers and Kirk, 1953); and intensity of religious belief. The questions used to obtain this information had been used often in previous polls.

Questions nine through 20 of Poll 33 tapped the areas of candidate choice and opinions on election issues. These questions were developed from the issues most widely discussed in news sources at that time.

The area of attitude toward social discrimination was tapped by a group of 12 items in Poll 33. These items reflect a decision by the editors to approach this area through proposed actions toward minority groups rather than by asking pupils to report directly their attitudes toward these groups.

The response alternatives used with these and subsequent items in Poll 33 are believed to be unique in opinion measurement. It has been the experience of the *Panel* editors that respondents object to alternatives which do not include an "Undecided" response. On the other hand, when "Undecided" responses are included, they are used indiscriminately by respondents as an easy "out" from having to take a position. As a compromise that seems both acceptable to respondents and effective in separating various degrees of opinion, the following four alternatives were used when an item was presented as a statement requiring agreement or disagreement:

(a) Agree
(b) Undecided; probably agree
(c) Undecided; probably disagree
(d) Disagree

The twelve items measuring attitude toward social discrimination in the final form of Poll 33 were selected and revised on the basis of pre-test information, including distribution of item responses and evidence of the items' discrimination ability. For pre-testing purposes, the questionnaire was administered to the pupils of a rural Indiana high school. These pupils were instructed to call attention to any difficulties encountered in understanding the poll's directions or items.

Table 28 presents the item stems from the Scale of Attitude toward Social Discrimination as administered in Poll 33 and the proportions of the sample choosing this anti-discrimination responses. For convenience, this scale will be referred to as the "D Scale."

Note that in the wording of the item stems in Table twenty-eight, half of the D Scale items are pro-discrimination statements while the other half are anti-discrimination statements. This alteration in direction of meaning was introduced intentionally to counteract possible response sets.

Twelve items in Poll 33 were included to measure authoritarianism or tendencies toward fascistic thinking. These items are 12 of a much larger pool of items that was subjected to pre-test

125

TABLE 28
Item Stems for the Scale of
Attitude toward Social Discrimination

Item Number Poll 33	Poll 35	Item Stem	Per cent choosing Anti-dis-criminatory Response (N = 3,000)
22	14	+ Pupils of all races and nationalities should attend school together everywhere in this country.	74
23	15	− People of different races should not dance together.	62
24	16	+ Swimming pools should admit people of all races and nationalities, to swim in the same pool.	54
25	17	− There should be laws against marriage between persons of different races.	57
26	18	− Hotels are right in refusing to admit people of certain races or nationalities.	67
27	19	− Our armed forces should not have officers of some races and nationalities.	82
28	20	+ People of different races and nationalities should be allowed to live in the same neighborhoods.	63
29	21	+ Public eating places should serve people of all races and nationalities, even at the same table if the customers want it that way.	74
30	22	− Property owners or their agents should prevent people of some races and nationalities from living in the better neighborhoods.	71
31	23	+ All theaters should admit people of all races and nationalities, and allow them to sit anywhere they want.	71
32	24	− There are people of some races and nationalities who are by nature less capable of advancement.	34
33	25	+ Any kind of people—no matter what their race or national origin—can become 100% Americans.	84

trial and revision. The original item pool for this scale represented a collection of items and ideas from several sources. Publications by Adorno *et al.*, (1950), and Sanford (1950) provided much material, and personal correspondence from Else Frenkel-Brunswik provided a group of items that had been used with children. To this basic group, the editorial staff added some original material. The 12 items selected from this group to form the Scale of Authoritarianism, or A Scale, are presented in Table 29.

TABLE 29

ITEMS STEMS FOR THE SCALE OF AUTHORITARIANISM

Item Number Poll 33	Poll 35	Item Stem	Per cent choosing Authoritarian Response (N = 3,000)
35	28	+ The true American way of life is disappearing so fast that force may be necessary to preserve it.	46
37	30	+ People without a deep and unquestioning faith in Almighty God should not be trusted in public office.	41
39	32	+ Americans are getting soft; most people need stricter discipline and the will to defend their interests.	60
40	33	− Even people who have wild ideas or don't use their heads should still have the right to vote.	35
41	34	+ Most people don't realize how much our lives are controlled by plots hatched in secret by others.	88
42	35	− Criminals, especially those guilty of sex crimes, should have mental and medical help rather than severe punishment.	19
43	36	+ Obedience and a proper respect for authority should be the very first requirements of a good citizen.	87
44	37	+ Strict and forceful leaders who demand an unquestioning trust are not desirable in this country.	31
47	40	− In its relations with other countries, the U. S. should depend more upon a discussion of problems than upon "get tough" actions.	19
51	44	− Despite what people say about human nature, all the people of the world will someday live peacefully together.	46
54	47	+ An insult to our honor should always be punished.	49
55	48	− We should encourage more new ideas rather than always keeping to the old, tried and established ways of doing things.	8

Note: The plus signs indicate items which if chosen, are scored 1, the minus signs, zero, since the scale is designed for authoritarianism.

127

TABLE 30

ITEM STEMS FOR THE SCALE OF ETHNOCENTRISM

Item Number Poll 33	Item Number Poll 35	Item Stem	Per cent choosing Ethnocentric Response ($N = 3,000$)
16	27	+ Some politicians place too much emphasis upon the principle, "America for Americans."	38
34	26	+ One can't tell much about a person's character by his appearance.	31
36	29	+ People who complain about things in the U. S. should be sent out of this country if they don't like it.	25
38	31	+ There is hardly anything lower than a person who does not feel a great love, gratitude and respect for our flag.	80
45	38	+ We should have as little as possible to do with the foreign countries of the world.	27
46	39	− The U. S. should be willing to give up some of its national power and independence to the United Nations in the interest of a better world.	41
48	41	− Foreign countries have contributed a great deal to the *past* development of the American way of life.	20
49	42	+ It's a mistake to trust any nation until we are completely sure of them.	81
50	43	− We should not limit and control immigration of foreigners into this country as much as we do now.	73
52	45	+ Foreign countries have very little to contribute to American progress *today*.	41
53	46	− There is too much concern about danger to democracy from foreign ideas within this country.	46
56	49	− Most foreigners have annoying habits.	39

Note: The plus signs indicate items which, if chosen, are scored 1, the minus signs, zero, since the scale is designed for ethnocentrism.

Half the items in the A Scale are opposite in direction of meaning to the other half, to reduce the possibility of response set.

Table 30 contains the twelve items used in Poll 33 to measure ethnocentrism. The Ethnocentrism Scale, or E Scale, borrows many ideas from other similar attitude measurement devices reported widely in the literature, but also contains a substantial amount of original material. Pre-test information provided the basis for the selection of the twelve items included in the final scale from among the items in a larger item pool. Again, half the items in this scale are opposite in direction of meaning to the other half to offset response set.

Table 31 presents results from the national sample of pupils who responded to the E Scale in Poll 33, and contains item analysis data collected from a sub-sample of the nationwide group.

Poll 34. The second of the 1952–53 polls was administered in early December, 1952 (Remmers *et al.,* 1953A).

The first ten items of Poll 34 were personal data items, many of which duplicated those used in Poll 33. Items 4 and 5, which asked about siblings, Item 9, which asked about father's occupation, and Item 10, which inquired about future plans, were items which had not been used in Poll 33.

Items 11 through 18 were intended to tap peer orientation; i.e., the extent to which a pupil sought the judgment of members of his own age group in preference to that of his elders on a number of topics. Question 19 was asked to discover how the pupil felt about tackling new and untried problems.

Items 20 through 39 comprise a selection of teen-age problems taken from earlier polls or, in a few instances, developed for this poll. These items were included as a means of inferring the existence of various felt insecurities as manifested in such problems.

Items 40 through 46 were included to gauge the extent to which the pupil's parents had followed an authoritarian child rearing philosophy. In these items, the pupil was to indicate how he thought his parents would answer each item as well as to give his own response.

The items of Poll 34 * that have been discussed thus far were given pre-tests to check their readability and to note the interpretations given to them by teenagers. However, no effort was made to refine the items by the techniques described for Poll 33.*

On the other hand, the vocabulary test—items 47 through 62 —did receive extensive refinement before inclusion in the poll questionnaire. This test was used in Poll 34 to make possible

---

* To save space these three poll reports are not included here. They are included in Dr. Mainer's original dissertation. (H. H. R.)

statistical controls of verbal ability if desired in later analyses of data. When used with college freshmen, the final set of 16 items in the vocabulary test correlated .90 with the L score of the *ACE Psychological Test* after corrections for restriction in range of talent in the sample and for attenuation in the group intelligence test.

*Poll 35.** The third poll in the 1952–53 series was administered to the panel members in the middle of March, 1953B (Remmers *et al.*). Except for minor changes in personal data items and in items concerning issues from the 1952 campaign, the questionnaire was a repetition of the one used for Poll 33.

ASSEMBLING THE DATA

To enable students to be traced through the year while guaranteeing anonymity, an envelope containing four ballot cards was prepared for each pupil at the beginning of the year. The four cards in each envelope were pre-punched with a code number that differentiated that set from the sets used by other pupils. The schools were instructed to have each pupil place his name on an envelope containing a set of ballot cards, and to instruct him to use only cards from that envelope in responding to all the polls of the year. In this way, a pupil's ballot card could not be associated with him once it was removed from the envelope, and yet his ballot cards for the year could be reassembled to compare his responses on the various polls.

Unfortunately, not all schools found it possible to have each pupil use only his envelope of ballot cards during the year. Also, lost cards, absences, graduations and other causes interfered with the possibility of tracing the entire panel through all the polls of the year. As a means of identifying those cases which could not be traced, a question was included in each of the last three polls of the year which asked if the pupil was still using his personal supply of ballot cards and if he had been absent or otherwise missed any of the polls.

Of the 7,472 pupils enrolled in the panel during 1952–53, only 3,868 could be traced through Polls 33, 34, and 35. Each of the

3,868 cases was then checked for completeness of data on 15 variables selected for inclusion in the analyses to follow. Following this step, 1,823 cases remained.

As expected, the large loss of cases produced some possibly important biases in the characteristics of the sample. Table 31 compares the sample used in this study with the total enrollment in the panel and with the stratified random sample used to prepare the national report for Poll 33. The following groups are found to be over-represented: girls, upper grade pupils, Republicans, and "middle class" pupils. However, while the sample in this study is not sufficiently representative of the national population of high school students to justify incautious generalizations about them, it is adequate for the purpose of detecting relationships among variables. In fact, since some of the sample biases may

TABLE 31

SAMPLE COMPOSITION AS COMPARED WITH TOTAL ENROLLMENT
IN PANEL AND WITH STRATIFIED NATIONAL SAMPLE

Group	Per Cent in Study Sample	Per Cent in Total Panel	Per Cent in Stratified National Sample
Boys	44	50	51
Girls	56	50	49
Grade 9	14	18	29
Grade 10	17	21	27
Grade 11	26	26	23
Grade 12	43	35	21
Rural	42	35	40
Urban	58	65	60
Democrats	38	41	40
Republicans	51	46	45
No preference	10	12	14
Other preference	1	1	1
Socio-Economic Group			
High	8	10	12
Middle	81	61	70
Low	11	29	18
Mother's Education			
Grade School	49	52	50
High School	35	36	37
College	16	12	13

have caused restrictions of range in the variables, relationships among these variables probably will be underestimated in this study.

For each of the 1,823 cases, data to be used in later analyses were transferred from each poll's ballot cards into a single deck of IBM cards. Once this was done, the various scales and tests were scored by means of IBM equipment, and resulting scores were punched into the card deck.

Scoring the D Scale. To score each item in the D Scale, a weight of 3 was assigned to the unqualified anti-discrimination response alternative, a weight of 2 to the "undecided" but anti-discrimination alternative, and so on. The first item of the D Scale, for example, was scored as follows:

Pupils of all races and nationalities should attend school together everywhere in this country.

Agree	(Scored 3)
Undecided; probably agree	(Scored 2)
Undecided; probably disagree	(Scored 1)
Disagree	(Scored 0)

Because the scoring procedure was very time consuming even with the use of IBM equipment, the last item of the D Scale was not scored in view of its low discriminatory power (See Table 29).

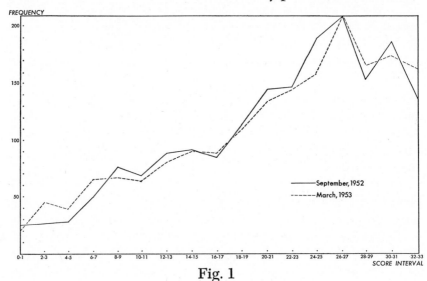

Fig. 1

The remaining 11 items produced a range of scores from zero to 33. Figure 1 presents the frequency distributions of scores obtained from Poll 33, administered in September, 1952, and Poll 34, administered the following March.

For the sample of 1,823 cases used in this study, the correlation between the October and March administrations was .827. The descriptive statistics for the two administrations of the D Scale showed virtually no change in these statistics between October and March. Means were 21.33 and 21.12 and standard deviations 8.21 and 8.55 respectively.

The D Scale's reliability was .873 based on a split test estimate.

The D Scale Change Score. While little change in response to the D Scale was apparent for the sample as a whole over the five-month period of the study, a scatter diagram of September scores versus March scores revealed that there were many individual shifts of attitude.

For each pupil, the difference between his actual March score and his predicted March score was determined. Knowing the reliability of the original D Scale and knowing the correlation between the two administrations of the scale, it is possible to estimate the reliability of the change scores. In view of the large sample of 1,823 cases used in obtaining the correlation coefficients, the resulting estimate of the reliability of the change scores is very significantly different from zero at much better than the one per cent level of significance. The March administration of the A Scale was not scored for this study.

Response set in the D and A Scales. Earlier it was mentioned that the meaning of half the items in both the D and the A Scales was opposite to that of the remaining items. This step was taken to avoid response sets in the scales. Thus, a person would have to use about as many "agree" as "disagree" responses in registering his opinions.

This measure apparently was more successful for the D Scale than for the A Scale.[1] In the D Scale, pupils seem to respond consistently regardless of the direction of wording in the item. Thus, in the D Scale, when the response indicating opposition to discrimination was "agree," 28 per cent of the national sample chose it; when it was "disagree," 25 per cent chose it. The change in direction of wording produced only a negligible change in per cent registering opposition. When the undesirable responses (i.e., those favoring discrimination) are considered, the change in wording of the D Scale items produced somewhat larger differences.

For the A Scale, however, pupils tend to agree with the items regardless of the direction of meaning. When the non-authoritarian response is "agree," 40 per cent select it; when it is "disagree," only 17 per cent select it. Similarly, when the authoritarian response is "agree," 56 per cent use it; when it is "disagree," only 25 per cent select it.

A possible explanation for the greater evidence of response set in the A Scale is the fact that the concepts in the items of the A Scale are more abstract than are the items of the D Scale. It is usually found in attitude measurement that respondents have a set to agree with items, and such a response set is particularly operative where the saliency of the measured attitude is low.[2] By contrast, the D Scale deals with concepts that are concrete and within the direct experience of teenagers.

Omission of the E Scale from the study. A factor analysis performed by Corder (See *Supra*) on selected items from Poll 33 revealed that only two factors account for the inter-relationships among items from the D, A, and E Scales. The first of these factors is identified with the attitude area tapped by the D Scale items, and the second with the area tapped by the A Scale items. Ethnocentrism, as measured by items from the E Scale, did not appear as a separate factor.

These findings, together with the fact that the items in the E Scale did not match the performance of those in the other two scales in terms of discriminating ability, obviated the use of the E Scale in this study.

Scoring other variables in the study. The vocabulary test, peer orientation scale, and the brief parental authoritarianism scale were very simply scored. For these, a weight of one was assigned to the "correct" or "good" response, while no weight was given to other alternatives. Total scores were obtained by summing the number of correct or good responses.

In the case of the list of insecurity problems (items 20 through 39 of Poll 34), only items 21, 24, 25, 26, 29, 31, 32, 33, 34, 36, 37, and 39 were scored. For these items, a weight of two was given the "often true" response, and a weight of one was given the "sometimes true" answer; "not true" was given a weight of zero.

Personal data for each respondent (sex, grade, rural or urban residence, religion, intensity of religious feeling, mother's education, number of siblings, age position among siblings and geographical region of home) were obtained from appropriate items in Polls 33 and 34.

The final variable included in the study was the number of feature, if any, in the school's intergroup education program. Administrators of the polls in the high schools were sent a check list of features typically found in intergroup education programs. They were asked to indicate which features were employed in their school, if any, and to mention any other features not listed that were also included. The number of features checked or mentioned was taken as an index of the breadth of the intergroup education program in the school. Since not all schools returned the check lists, this information was available for only 1,480 pupils in this study.

ANALYSIS OF THE DATA

As a first step in analyzing the data collected in the study, correlations between 15 variables and attitude toward social discrimination, and between these 15 variables and change in attitude toward discrimination, were computed. Note that the correlations involving the variable of number of features in the intergroup education program are based on an N of 1,480, while all others have an N of 1,823.

The correlations between the 15 independent variables and attitude change were all small, ranging from minus .34 to plus .28. However, six were significantly different from zero at the one per cent level of confidence, and one additional relationship was significantly different from zero at the five per cent level. When

135

the extremely low reliability of the change scores is considered, it is remarkable that a correlation as high as that between the number of features in the intergroup education program and attitude change ($r = .14$) was obtained. Correction for attenuation in the criterion would raise this correlation to .29. This correction applied to other correlations with attitude change scores would also result in correlations slightly higher than twice their present values. Thus, the seven statistically significant relationships between independent variables and attitude change have somewhat greater significance, both in a practical and a theoretical sense, than is indicated by their uncorrected magnitude.

By way of explaining the direction of the scale scores and considering only the significant correlations with the D Scale, girls are more opposed to discrimination than boys, upper grade pupils more opposed than lower-grade pupils, urban pupils more opposed than rural pupils, and non-peer oriented students more opposed than peer oriented students. The more authoritarian the pupil, the more he tends to endorse discriminatory practices. It is interesting to note that a significant positive relationship exists between the number of features in the intergroup education program and extent of change in response to the D Scale, but none exists between the number of program features and initial attitude toward discrimination.

The use of analysis of variance techniques was indicated for further study of the relationships between various independent variables and the highly unreliable criterion of attitude change. Thus, seven analysis of variance problems were designed to test the following hypotheses:

1. Intergroup education programs are effective in changing attitudes toward social discrimination.

2. The success of intergroup education programs depends upon the effect of such other interacting variables as:
    a. The geographic region in which the school is located.
    b. Other influences acting upon the pupil, such as his home environment and his religion.
    c. The pupil's age and grade in school.
    d. The pupil's intelligence and verbal ability.
    e. Certain personality traits in the pupil as reflected in his conformity and tendencies toward authoritarianism.

After each analysis of variance problem was completed, the sample was returned to the original group of 1,823 cases. Therefore, there is a considerable amount of overlap among the samples used in the seven analysis of variance designs. For this reason, compound probability statements cannot be used for the significance of the effect of any independent variable included in several different analysis of variance problems, even though that variable shows a significant effect within each problem in which it is used.

Analysis of Variance Problem I. The dependent variable, as in all the analysis of variance problems to be reported here, was change in attitude as measured by the D Scale. The following independent variables were included:

1. Intergroup education; pupils exposed to a program versus those not exposed.
2. Socio-economic status; "high" pupils with five or more items checked on the House-Home Scale versus "low" pupils with less than five items checked.
3. Religion; Protestants versus Catholics.

In this first problem, only exposure to an intergroup education program shows a strong relationship to the criterion of change in attitude toward discrimination. The interaction between intergroup education and religion approaches, but does not reach, significance at the five per cent level of confidence.

Pupils in schools with intergroup education programs tended to obtain their predicted March scores ($M = 50.67$). Pupils in schools without such programs tended to change toward greater endorsement of discrimination ($M = 48.98$). An interaction between religion and intergroup education, while not statistically significant, can be seen in the fact that Protestants and Catholics achieved practically the same mean change scores in schools with intergroup education programs; in schools without such programs, Protestant attitudes showed little change over the five months of the study while Catholic pupils tended to give greater endorsement to discrimination.

Analysis of Variance Problem II. The second problem used a design which included the following independent variables:

1. Intergroup education; pupils exposed to intergroup programs versus those not exposed.

137

2. Region; Eastern pupils versus Southern pupils.
3. Grade; twelfth graders versus all other grades combined.

Four significant effects were found. Again, intergroup education showed a strong effect upon change in attitude toward discrimination. Grade revealed a significant influence on attitude change, and entered into a significant interaction with region in affecting attitude change. An interaction between region and intergroup education also achieved significance.

The intergroup education programs sampled in this problem had a more noticeable effect upon attitudes than in Problem I. The significant interaction between region and intergroup education is shown by the fact that Southern pupils respond more to intergroup education than Easterners, but become more in favor of discrimination in the absence of such a program.

Intergroup education programs apparently have a greater effect upon high school seniors ($M = 52.74$) than upon pupils from other grades ($M = 50.69$), and seniors in general become more opposed to discrimination than do younger pupils. No interaction between grade and intergroup education exists, however, as shown by the fact that approximately the same differential in change scores exists between the twelfth graders and younger pupils in schools with, and in those without, intergroup programs.

An interaction effect, significant at better than the one-half of one per cent level of confidence, exists between region and grade. In the East, no difference of importance exists between the two grade levels. In the South, however, senior pupils show a change toward greater disapproval of discrimination ($M = 52.72$), while the younger pupils show a trend toward greater endorsement over the five-month period of the study ($M = 47.84$). It appears, then, that the Southern sample provided the bulk of the grade effect in this problem.

Analysis of Variance Problem III. The third analysis of variance problem employed four independent variables to learn if there existed more complex interactions than had been discovered. The Eastern portion of the sample used in Problem II was retained for this problem, and, in place of region, two additional variables were included:

138

1. Socio-economic status; "high" pupils with five or more items checked on the House-Home Scale versus "low" pupils with less than five items checked.
2. Religion; Protestants versus Catholics.

Problem III proved to be relatively barren in so far as statistically significant main effects and interactions are concerned. Intergroup education again was significantly related to change in attitude. The effect of religion on attitude change approached significance, with Catholics showing a slight tendency toward greater approval of discrimination over the period of the study.

Analysis of Variance Problem IV. A fourth problem was designed to include the same variables as Problem III, but with different points of dichotomization in the variables of grade and of socio-economic status. It was hoped that shifting the points at which these variables were dichotomized to points which seemed to mark sharper breaks in the distribution of attitude change scores might uncover relationships not found in Problem III.

The variables in Problem IV and their new dichotomies were as follows:

1. Intergroup education; pupils exposed to intergroup programs versus those not exposed.
2. Grade; eleventh and twelfth graders versus ninth and tenth graders.
3. Socio-economic status; pupils who checked four or more features on the House-Home Scale versus those who checked less than four.
4. Religion; Protestants versus Catholics.

It appears from the evidence that neither grade nor socio-economic status are related to attitude change, even after the change in points of dichotomization. Intergroup education produced a highly significant effect on attitude change, and religion proved to have a significant interaction effect with intergroup education. Catholics became considerably more opposed to discrimination after exposure to five months of intergroup education (M = 55.83), but became much more in favor of discrimination in schools without intergroup programs (M = 46.37). Protestants, on the other hand, maintained their attitudes at about the same level over the five-month study whether in schools with intergroup programs or not.

The one and only relatively substantial higher order interaction in the series of seven problems was found in Problem IV among the variables of socio-economic status, religion and grade. However, an examination of cell means revealed no clear-cut trends to account for this interaction. Whatever the nature of this interaction, it apparently is too subtle to be seen in abstracted cell means.

Analysis of Variance Problem V. This was designed to investigate the effect of the following variables on attitude change:

1. Intergroup education; pupils exposed to intergroup programs versus those not exposed.
2. Region; Eastern pupils versus Southerners.
3. Authoritarianism; "low" pupils who scored below 12 on the A Scale, "medium" pupils who scored between 13 and 17, and "high" pupils who scored 18 or above on the A Scale.

Once again, intergroup education shows a significant effect on attitude change. Region, which was not a significant variable in Problem II, is related to attitude change in this problem at better than the five per cent level of confidence. Region also produces a significant interaction with intergroup education—a finding corroborated in Problem II.

Intergroup education produced little change in attitude among Eastern pupils ($M = 50.24$) and only a slight change in the direction of increased opposition to discrimination among Southern pupils ($M = 51.43$). In schools without intergroup programs, Eastern students show almost no change in attitude ($M = 50.30$), but Southern pupils change fairly strongly in the direction of approving discrimination ($M = 45.15$).

Problem V also uncovered an interaction between intergroup education and authoritarianism that approached significance at five per cent level. This interaction shows that for schools with intergroup education programs, the more authoritarian the pupil, the more opposed to discrimination he became over the five-month study; in schools without intergroup programs, the more authoritarian the pupil, the more his attitude shifted toward approval of discrimination during this interval.

140

Analysis of Variance Problem VI. The sixth analysis of variance problem was designed to investigate the effect of vocabulary level on change in attitude as measured by the D Scale. It included the following variables:

1. Intergroup education; pupils exposed to intergroup programs versus those not exposed.
2. Region; Eastern versus Southern pupils.
3. Vocabulary level; "low" vocabulary level includes all pupils who scored six or less on the test, "middle" vocabulary level includes those who scored between seven and nine, and "high" vocabulary level includes those who scored ten or above on the 16-item test.

All three variables in Problem VI were related to attitude change, and two variables, intergroup education and vocabulary level, produced effects significant at better than the 0.1 per cent level. Attitude shifts increasingly occur in the direction of greater opposition to discrimination with increases in vocabulary level. This result is not related to the omission of items by pupils with reading difficulties; only pupils with complete data on all tests and scales were included in the study.

The results show an interaction effect between intergroup education and region; a similar effect was found in Problems II and V. In this problem, this effect is revealed by the greater difference in mean change scores in the South between pupils exposed to intergroup education and those not exposed. In this sample, the attitude shifts of Southern pupils exposed to intergroup programs is sufficiently great to cause the overall effect of region to be in the opposite direction to that found in Problem V. In Problem VI, Southern pupils tend to maintain their attitudes over the five-month period ($M = 50.79$), while Eastern pupils show a slight trend toward endorsement of discrimination over the same period ($M = 48.68$). Lastly, the effect of intergroup education is revealed in the mean of 52.06 for students exposed to an intergroup program as against a mean of 47.43 for students not exposed to such a program.

Analysis of Variance Problem VII. A small portion of the sample used by Wexler (1953) in working with his *Multiple Choice Sentence Completion Test* was found to be included in the

1,823 cases used in this study. One of the personality variables that Wexler attempted to measure with his test was that of conformity. Even though the small number of overlapping cases provided little hope of discovering relationships with the very unreliable criterion of attitude change, the possibility of such relationships was sufficiently interesting to encourage the design and computation of an analysis of variance test. Thus, 120 cases, entirely unselected in terms of grade, region or other variables, were used in a design which included the following variables:

1. Intergroup education; pupils exposed to intergroup education programs versus those not exposed.
2. Conformity; "low" conformists included all those who scored less than 70 on Wexler's test, "middle" conformists included those who scored between 71 and 83, and "high" conformists included all those who scored 84 or above.

Neither the variables of intergroup education nor conformity produced significant main effects. The interaction between these two variables also fails to reach significance, but nevertheless it is interesting to note the direction of trends among the cell means from Problem VII. In Table 29, the near-perfect reversal in direction of trends with increasing conformity, between schools with intergroup programs and schools without such programs, is striking, even if statistically insignificant. This interaction is very similar to that observed between intergroup education and authoritarianism in Problem V.

Summary and conclusions. Table 32 provides a summary of the more noteworthy relationships found in the series of seven analysis of variance problems.

Whatever conclusions are drawn from this study should be accepted only with reservations until further research can confirm or refute them. Some findings repeatedly are borne out in the analysis of variance problems with very significant F ratios, but even in these cases the differences between groups seldom amount to more than a few points on the continuum of change scores. It is difficult to say whether such differences have any practical importance. In all fairness, such a judgment should be deferred until more evidence is available.

TABLE 32

A Summary of the Seven Analysis of Variance Problems
in the Study of Attitude Change

Source	Problem Number						
	I	II	III	IV	V	VI	VII
Intergroup Education (IE)	**	****	**	****	****	****	—
House-Home (HH)	—	x	—	—	x	x	x
Religion (Rlg)	—	x	*	—	x	x	x
Grade (G)	x	****	—	—	x	x	x
Region (Reg)	x	—	x	x	**	*	x
Vocabulary (V)	x	x	x	x	x	****	x
Authoritarianism (A)	x	x	x	x	—	x	x
Conformity (C)	x	x	x	x	x	x	—
IE x HH	—	x	—	—	x	x	x
IE x Rlg.	*	x	—	**	x	x	x
IE x G	x	—	—	—	x	x	x
IE x Reg.	x	**	x	x	****	**	x
IE x V	x	x	x	x	x	—	x
IE x A	x	x	x	x	*	x	x
IE x C	x	x	x	x	x	x	—
R x G	x	****	x	x	x	x	x

Note—The symbols in the above table have the following meanings:
* indicates F was significant at better than the 10% level.
** indicates F was significant at better than the 5% level.
*** indicates F was significant at better than the 2½% level.
**** indicates F was significant at better than the 1% level.
— indicates F was not significant.
x indicates the variable was not included in the problem.

With all limitations of the study in mind, the following conclusions are now offered:

1. The D Scale appears to provide a reliable measure of attitude toward social discrimination.

2. Changes in attitude as measured by repeated administration of the D Scale after a five-month interval, while very unreliable in this study, nonetheless are related to other sociopsychological variables. Specifically:

a. Upper-grade pupils maintain their attitudes or change in the direction of greater opposition to discrimination, while pupils from lower high-school grades change in the direction of greater endorsement of discrimination.

b. Students with higher vocabulary levels change more in the direction of opposition to discrimination than do pupils with lower vocabulary levels.

c. Geographic region and religion both are related to attitude change, but their interactions with other variables have more clear-cut effects upon attitude change. These are discussed below.

3. Intergroup education programs are successful in producing greater opposition to social discrimination.

4. Certain socio-psychological variables interact with intergroup education programs to produce attitude changes, as follows:

a. In schools with intergroup programs, Catholic pupils shift more in the direction of opposition to discrimination than do Protestants. However, in schools without intergroup programs, Protestant pupils tend either to maintain their attitudes or to shift toward opposition to discrimination, while Catholic pupils tend to change toward greater endorsement of discrimination.

b. Differences in attitude change between pupils exposed to intergroup programs and those not exposed are much greater among Southern pupils than among Easterners.

c. An interaction may exist between intergroup education and authoritarianism. If confirmed in future investigations, it may be concluded that highly authoritarian pupils become more opposed to discrimination in schools with intergroup programs, but become more in favor of discrimination in schools without such programs.

DISCUSSION, INTERPRETATION AND SUGGESTIONS FOR FURTHER RESEARCH

ATTITUDE CHANGE AND RELATED VARIABLES

Limitations in this study. At several points in this report, various inadequacies in procedures or in resulting data have been noted. These inadequacies have made it necessary to add many qualifications to the findings of the study. Before attempting a discussion of these findings on the pages to follow, a brief examination of some bases of the shortcomings of this study follows.

The problems raised by the unreliability of the change scores used as criterion measures in the various analyses have already been noted in earlier sections. As Thorndike (1951) points out, change measures frequently suffer from unreliability and are therefore unsatisfactory as criterion measures. In this study, the lack of reliability in the change scores stems from the relatively high correlation between administrations of the D Scale—a result of the lack of much real change in performance on the scale. This had the effect of decreasing the total variance in the change scores, and thereby making the ratio of true variance to total variance relatively small.

Several possible hypotheses can be offered for the lack of change in performance on the D Scale over the five-month period. First of all, it is very possible that the pupils in this study maintained their attitudes at about the same level throughout the five-month period despite discussion of poll results and the impact of intergroup programs. Although no empirical evidence is available from this study to pass judgment on this possibility, it seems improbable to the investigator that this explanation is valid.

A more reasonable explanation is that real shifts in attitude did occur in the sample after the administration of Poll 33, but at the end of the five-month period these shifts had largely disappeared. This explanation suggests that if level of attitude were regularly plotted over the five-month interval of the study, a curve resembling the forgetting curve of learning experiments would be obtained. Some experimental evidence for the gradual loss of opinion change has been reported in the psychological literature (Cf. Hovland, Janis and Kelly [1953], pp. 241–68, and Hall [1938]). This is *not* to suggest, however, that the return of an attitude to its original level is a function of forgetting; it is more probable that the loss of change is due to factors involved in the etiology of the original attitudes and in the motivations of the individuals as related to maintenance of change or return to previous attitudes.

Coupled with the unreliability of the criterion scores, the low reliability of certain other measures in the study made the discovery of substantial relationships unlikely. The A Scale, in particular, is inadequate in its present form for use with high school samples similar to that used here. It appears from the evidence of response set reported earlier that the items in the A Scale may deal with concepts too abstract for most high school pupils. The scale undoubtedly could be improved by personalizing the items and by bringing the content of the scale down to areas more commonly within the range of experience and knowledge of teenagers.

Who changed, and why? Perhaps the most convincing finding in this study is the demonstrated effectiveness of intergroup education programs in producing changes in attitude toward discrimination with this sample of pupils. Precisely what was included in the intergroup education programs reported by the schools is not adequately known, although typical reports from schools frequently mentioned such things as showing movies on other groups, cultures and religions, having guest speakers, producing student convocations on intergroup relations, and so on.

Numerous studies in the literature give evidence of the effectiveness of various means of achieving attitude change (Bogardus, 1950; Christie, 1952; Cooper and Jahoda, 1947; Flowerman, 1949; Haimowitz & Haimowitz; 1950, Hall, 1938; Hovland *et al.*, 1953; Hovland *et al.*, 1949; Kagan, 1952; Mackenzie, 1948; Miller & Begelski, 1948; Mussen, 1950; Rose, 1948; Rosen, 1948; Weltman and Remmers, 1946; Williams, 1947), but none has been found which specifically evaluates what has come to be called "intergroup education in the public schools." The fact that educational measures have a demonstrated effectiveness in developing attitudes should be reassuring to those who have proposed intergroup programs in the face of pessimistic criticism.

It remains obvious, however, that new investigations into the effectiveness of specific programs under various conditions of administration should be conducted to give much needed information to the planners of intergroup programs.

In addition to discovering that intergroup education programs do affect pupils' attitudes, the data of this study also disclose that much greater changes and different directions of change are found in certain groups of pupils. For example, independent of exposure to intergroup programs, older pupils—i.e., twelfth graders—became more opposed to social discrimination over the five months of the study than did other pupils. At first thought, this finding is not completely consistent with the suggestions of intergroup educators who urge that intergroup programs should be administered in the lower grades to catch undesirable atti-

146

tudes while they are young. While such reasoning probably is valid, this study suggests that intergroup education is not wasted effort when administered to pupils in their later teens.

A possible explanation for this fact—and an area for further investigation—is that properly timed intergroup programs capitalize upon the dramatic changes in attitudes that occur in the youth of our society in late adolescence and early adulthood. A program which attacks undesired attitudes and offers new ones to replace them appears to be most effective when traditional ideologies are under evaluation and change. In agreement with this hypothesis are the findings of Weltman and Remmers (1946) who found that the attitudes and opinions of high school students became less similar to those of their parents as they progress through high school.

The data of the present study also reveal that pupils with higher vocabulary levels change more in the direction of disapproval of social discrimination than pupils with less verbal ability. The vocabulary test was included in the study to provide some control of intelligence as manifested in verbal ability. It should be remembered, however, that the sample of pupils in this study was drawn from all four grades of high school, and a high relationship between grade and vocabulary undoubtedly exists. Thus, if one wishes to generalize the meaning of vocabulary scores to any extent in this study, they should be considered as an index of "mental age" rather than of relative intelligence.

Several other factors should be considered in interpreting the relationship of vocabulary level (or, if you will, mental age) to attitude change. First of all, we have already noted that older pupils show greater changes than do their younger schoolmates and discussed the possible reasons for this fact. Perhaps, then, the age at which the re-evaluation of attitudes and beliefs is undertaken (if at all) and the intensity of this phase is related to the adolescent's mental ability.

Secondly, it is possible that students with higher vocabulary levels are more capable of dealing with the abstractions and concepts involved in the re-evaluation of feelings toward other groups. Also, pupils with higher vocabulary levels may be able to profit more from the discussions of results from the first administra-

147

tion of the D Scale, and to retain their conclusions from these discussions longer than other pupils.

Interesting interaction effects also were uncovered in this study. Most of the significant interactions pointed to the differential effectiveness of intergroup programs with various groups of pupils. For example, in schools with intergroup programs, Catholics shifted more in the direction of opposition to discrimination during the study than did Protestants; but, in schools without intergroup programs, the very opposite was true: Protestants either maintained their attitudes or shifted in the direction of greater opposition while Catholics became more approving of discrimination.

At this point, it is only possible to speculate about the basis of this interaction. Possibly, Catholic pupils as a group are more conforming than Protestants. If so, the difference between the two groups in their response to intergroup programs may be due to the greater conformity of Catholic pupils to the norms advocated by intergroup education in schools with such programs, and to their greater conformity to relatively intolerant attitudes which surround them in schools without intergroup programs.

The role of conformity in determining the effectiveness of intergroup education programs is suggested in the results of Problem VII. Although the F ratio for the effect of the interaction between conformity and intergroup education could have been obtained by chance ten to twenty times in a hundred, the trends observable in the cell means lend support to the conformity hypothesis.

The role of conformity may also underlie the interaction between authoritarianism and intergroup education, found to be significant at between the five and ten per cent level of confidence. The tenability of this explanation is supported by the relatively great emphasis given by many writers, especially Adorno *et al.* (1950), to the role of conformity in the authoritarian personality.

Still another interaction affecting attitude change was discovered in the combined relationship of intergroup education and geographical region. Differences in attitude change between pupils exposed to intergroup programs and those not exposed were greater in the South than in the East. Among Southern pupils, exposure to intergroup education programs was accompanied by general shifts toward greater opposition to discrimination, while non-exposure was accompanied by shifts toward greater approval of social discrimination. While it would be tempting to conclude that Southern students show larger shifts because they initially, as a group, are less opposed to discrimination (which is true), the change scores were found to have no relationship to initial scores.

Of the alternative hypotheses which could be advanced to explain the greater response to intergroup education among Southern pupils, two in particular seem plausible and deserve further investigation. The first of these centers around the hypothesis that Southern schools with intergroup education programs are not typical of Southern schools in general, and their pupils are an atypical sample of Southern pupils. If true, it is then possible that such schools are found in communities that are fairly liberal in their attitudes toward minorities, and large shifts in attitudes toward discrimination are thus to be expected.

A second hypothesis is that attitudes differ in their etiology, even though they produce similar scores on a scale which measures them. In this case, for example, it is possible that the basis for condoning social discrimination in the South is different from the basis for the same attitude in the East. It is possible, for example, that social discrimination has more cultural determinants, as opposed to "personal" reasons, in the South. If true, then a second hypotheses is suggested to the effect that intergroup programs are more effective with attitudes that are more directly culturally determined.

In support of this pair of hypotheses are the results of Problem II which show that the larger attitude shifts among senior pupils in the South appear to account for most of the highly significant interaction effect between grade and region. Recalling the observations and hypotheses included in an earlier paragraph which discussed the relation of grade (or age) to attitude change, it is possible that this grade-region interaction is a reflection of the process of re-evaluation of culturally determined attitudes by the maturing Southern adolescent. Again, experimental investigations of the hypotheses implicit in this explanation are needed.

149

ATTITUDE ETIOLOGY AND ATTITUDE CHANGE

At several points in this chapter, mention has been made of the possibility that differing etiologies for attitudes toward social discrimination among various groups of pupils may account for differences in the effectiveness of intergroup education programs. It also has been proposed that this possibility should be stated as a hypothesis for experimental investigation.[3] Actually, several writers already have suggested some etiological considerations for programs of attitude change; for one example, see Chein (1946).

During the planning stage of this study, a fairly exhaustive search of the literature was made. One result of this search was a compilation of some of the etiological factors underlying attitudes in general, and attitudes toward minority groups in particular. Usually, these factors were implied by writers rather than explicitly identified and discussed. To this compilation, a few of the observations and hypotheses which grew out of the present study have been added, and the net result has been drawn up into a brief and somewhat sketchy outline which is presented below. Perhaps this outline will serve to pull together some of the varied thinking on the topic. In this outline, every attitude is considered to be the product of a *number* of etiological factors.

I. *Experience Factors*

A. *Direct Experience.* At least two aspects of attitude development may be noted here. One of these is a matter of sampling. Our experience with a particular attitude object, whether it be with a group of persons or a type of food, necessarily is limited to a sample from the "population" of such objects. Occasionally, the attitude we wish to change stems from experience with an atypical sample of the attitude object; for example, some people reject all of a particular kind of food because of an experience with a sample that was not fresh, that was improperly prepared, or was otherwise atypical in quality.

On the other hand, it is possible to find undesirable attitudes that are at least partially determined by experience, and the experience has not been atypical. Particularly vexing to psychologists are cases of this general type in which the attitude determining qualities of the attitude object are partially produced by the attitude—that is, they are the result of a regenerative and circular phenomenon. Myrdal's (1944) "self-fulfilling prophecy" is an example of this phenomenon in which hostile attitudes toward a group prevent that group from achieving living and educational standards considered acceptable to society at large, and this fact in turn provides further justification for disapproval directed toward this group. Years of frustration and deprivation may actually have caused Jews, as a group, to be more aggressive, or Negroes to be "shiftless." Under such conditions, it is doubtful if information programs alone can substantially change attitudes. Allport (1950) notes that research based on the "stimulus approach" to the study of intergroup attitudes is greatly needed.

B. *Vicarious Experience.* The real or imagined experiences of others are as important as determiners of attitudes as are our own. Observations concerning the implications of representativeness of experience under A above apply equally well to vicarious experience.

C. Lack of Direct or Vicarious Experience. With no opportunity for reality testing, a person is susceptible to almost any attitude. Studies have demonstrated that persons develop hostile attitudes toward groups even when they never have had experience with members of these groups. In such cases, there is an absence of experience factors to counteract undesired attitudes or to reaffirm desired ones.

II. *Socialization Factors*

A. *The Socialization Process.* The process of socialization impresses upon each person the accumulated beliefs, norms and values of his family and culture. Religious beliefs, beliefs about the physical world, behavioral norms, and attitudes of all kinds are but a few examples of this inheritance. Sometimes, the soundness of the beliefs or attitudes remains beyond the possibility of objective evaluation, in other cases, it would be possible but heretical to test their truth.

151

However, in instances of social upheaval, enlightenment, or progress, traditional beliefs and attitudes are abandoned. Similarly, in our American culture, attitudes seem to be evaluated and changed as part of a phase of adolescence. On earlier pages, it has been hypothesized that the process of attitude modification is facilitated by such periods of social and individual re-evaluation and change.

B. *Group Memberships.* In a heterogeneous society, not all beliefs, values, norms and attitudes are common to all members. Some attitudes are specific to certain groups, and the sharing of such attitudes often functions as a criterion of membership in that group. Much attention in the literature of social psychology has been given to the role of group membership and aspiration to membership in attitude development and change.

C. *Inconsistencies.* An individual's specific attitudes may not always be consistent with the more general and abstract belief and value system of his culture or group. In some cases, this results from the person's failure to recognize the relation between his specific attitude and the value system he professes to endorse. Thus, one can find "Christians" with very un-Christian attitudes. Also, the role of socialization factors in attitude change is further complicated by the effect of multiple roles stemming from membership in different groups, of which some may advocate attitudes in conflict with those of others.

III. *Personality Factors*

A. *General Considerations.* Under the topic of personality factors, two aspects of attitude modification can be considered: kind and intensity. By kind, it is meant that personality factors may be hypothesized as limiting the range of possible attitudes that a person can adopt. An aggressive individual normally would not be expected to adopt a passive attitude toward an attitude object. Also, one could go on to discuss frustration tolerances, security feelings, and other similar concepts in so far as they are related to the kinds of attitudes an individual is likely to adopt. For the purpose at hand, it is sufficient to point out that such variables do have a bearing on the acquisition of attitudes.

The second aspect of attitudes is that of intensity. An individual may have a very extreme attitude toward some object, but that attitude may have so little intensity that it is readily changed. One of the determinants of an attitude's intensity is the function of the attitude for the individual. Some attitudes play central roles in personality structure by rationalizing aggressions, enhancing self evaluations by degrading others, and so on. To the extent that the individual thus needs his attitudes, he is resistant to change.

B. *Interaction Effects.* Up to this point, many complicating factors have been omitted in the interest of brevity. For example, the ways in which experience, socialization and personality factors interact in determining attitudes probably are at least as important as their independent effects. Specifically, a discussion of the effect of experience would be incomplete without a consideration of personality factors in perception. Experimental studies have shown that the perceptions of ego threatening things are less accurate, less efficient and less well recalled than are the perceptions of non-threatening materials.

The role of personality factors in the socialization process also represents an interaction. Some individuals differ from others in their conformity to norms; there are differentials in the perception of punishment and reward as used in the socialization process, and so on. And, to increase the complexity of the subject, the socialization process undeniably has a major role in molding the personality.

IV. *Ability Factors.* Some attitudes make more demands upon the individual's intellectual abilities than do others. For example, it requires less mental ability to hold something concrete and identifiable, such as a particular group, as the attitude object responsible for the frustrations in life than it is to wrestle with the abstractions and dynamisms used by social scientists. How much easier, for example, to blame the Republicans for the depression or to blame the Democrats for the war than to deal with such abstract concepts as supply, demand, markets, futures, nationalism and the like! Besides, blaming something tangible makes it less difficult to act appropriately; e.g., one can vote against a political party or bar Negroes from jobs.

Interaction effects involving ability factors also can be identified, just as in the case of the other factors. For example, a person's intellectual ability determines the extent to which he can evaluate experience, recall experience, interiorize norms, challenge beliefs and so on.

ATTITUDE ETIOLOGY AND THE RESULTS OF THIS STUDY

A hasty overview of the etiological factors in attitude development has been outlined to suggest why no one method of changing attitudes will be equally effective with all attitudes.

This study has not shed much light on the diagnosis or "treatment" of attitudes in terms of their etiologies. One can speculate, however, that some of the findings do suggest a variety of determinants in the attitudes of the high school sample toward social discrimination. For example, the role of the socialization component is suggested by the greater response of Southern pupils to intergroup education programs. A similar implication might be drawn from the differences between the attitude shifts of Catholics and Protestants in schools with, and in schools without, intergroup education programs.

Again, experience and ability components are suggested by the fact that pupils with higher vocabularies show greater attitude shifts than do other pupils. Lastly, and much less convincingly, is the possibility that personality factors may be reflected in the interactions between intergroup education and conformity, and between intergroup education and authoritarianism.

Admittedly, such speculations go far beyond the data of this study, but if they serve at all to provide ideas for further research in the area of attitude modification, then they are well worth the small effort represented by their inclusion here.

NOTES

1. The writer is indebted to Robert Phelan for these data.
2. Studies by others have also shown that the authoritarian personality has more of this response set than the non-authoritarian. (H. H. R.)
3. An article by Sarnoff and Katz (1954) indicates that some work in this direction already is in progress.

154

PART II

ATTITUDE STUDIES IN HIGHER EDUCATION

VIII A FACTOR ANALYTIC STUDY OF THE DIMENSIONS OF ANTI-DEMOCRATIC ATTITUDES

Dorothy Gates Rodgers

INTRODUCTION

GENERAL STATEMENT OF PROBLEM

One of the continuing tasks of social psychology is the need to account for the direction, strength, and origins of social attitudes. This responsibility is of special importance with respect to questions of social intolerance, where hostile and antipathetic attitudes may have consequences ranging all the way from personal ill will to personality disturbance and group conflict. If higher education is to be a representative of democratic principles, it must be acutely aware of the degree to which such attitudes exist among its student body.

These were some of several objectives of the *Public Opinion Panel Survey of Democratic-Authoritarian Attitudes of Students in Higher Education* conducted among students in 23 Indiana colleges and universities. The poll was conducted by the Division of Educational Reference in the fall of 1954. The opinion statements included were of an authoritarian, ethnocentric and prejudiced nature. A course of action program was also included. A copy of the poll questionnaire is in the Appendix.

The research reported here is limited to those statements broadly defined as authoritarian or anti-democratic. The definition of attitude suggests the initial step which should be taken in any attitude study. Gordon Allport's (1935, p. 810), definition derived from an examination of the many possible definitions which have from time to time been suggested, is probably the most definite for a concept which, although central to social psychology, has been elusive to precise conceptualization. His definition is:

An attitude is a mental and neural state of readiness organized through experience, exerting a directive or dynamic influence upon the individual's response to all objects and situations with which it is related.

A phrase by phrase analysis of this definition suggests several implications concerning the focus of attitude research. First, the phrase "mental and neural states of readiness" implies that they are constructs or variables which are inferred to mediate between stimulus and response. In the context of a poll questionnaire this means that they are inferred from the item stimulus and response categories provided. The phrase need not divest the concept of attitude of its affective qualities which bear upon the second phrase "organized through experience." There is abundant evidence that attitudes are learned by the individual through reinforcement and association as he interacts in the social-cultural environment which makes these attitudes accessible. We would therefore expect that the emotions concomitant to the learning of the attitude would be associated with it and contribute to its dynamic influence upon the individual's response. Further, it would be expected that a learned attitude toward one object may be generalized to a whole class of objects so that one attitude may be organized to elicit a variety of responses.

The concept of organization also suggests that there is consistency of response to a specified class of stimulus objects. This is also implied in the phrase "exerting a directive or dynamic influence upon the individual's response *to all* objects and situations with which it is related." Consistency of response to a class of stimulus objects is a fundamental assumption for establishing a model by which to study attitudes. Reasoning backward from what has already been stated, consistency of response to a given set of stimuli is the basis upon which attitudes may be inferred. Thus, if the responses to a given set of item statements covary to a significant degree, i.e., are consistent, one attitude as the underlying variable is inferred. The meaning or content of the attitude is inferred from the common quality of the item statements. The common quality is then the inferred construct which mediates between stimulus and response and accounts for the significant covariation.

Therefore, the first question which must be answered about any group of item statements from which attitudes are to be inferred is "how many dimensions are needed to describe the attitudes of individuals?" In other words, is there one underlying variable or dimension which will account for consistency of response to item statements or are the covariations of response such that more than one dimension is necessary for descriptive and analytical purposes? This procedure comes from the scientific method of describing a large number of heterogeneous objects by means of some kind of dimensional system in which the dimensions are chosen in such a way that each of them corresponds to one of the principles of heterogeneity present (Eysenck, 1949).

The item statements to be analyzed in this study have been placed in the broad category of anti-democratic or authoritarian attitudes. Authoritarian attitudes may be broadly defined as generalized attitudes toward human relations and values which are characterized by rigidity, concreteness, conformity, and dogmatism. These characterizations have been empirically substantiated as behavioral correlates. Primary attitudinal correlates are prejudice toward minority groups and ethnocentrism which are commonly judged to be contrary to democratic principles. This is one reason for the label "anti-democratic" or "authoritarian." The theoretical and methodological purposes of this study will be to determine if there is one or more attitude dimension which will account for the response patterns to the item stimuli.

Theoretical Implications of the Dimensions of Anti-democratic Attitudes

The determinants of the organization, structure, and dimensions of anti-democratic attitudes may be analyzed at four interrelated levels: the historical, socio-cultural, cognitive, and psychodynamic, or personality.[1] The current theory and research in the area of anti-democratic attitudes will be discussed at each of these levels. It should be emphasized that all of these are mutually dependent. This breakdown seems the most adequate manner of handling a highly complex problem. Complete understanding of the etiology of authoritarian attitudes will probably only ensue when their expression can be traced from the individual to his family setting to its social stratum to the broader cultural context with its historical background. Then, knowing the character of one, something of the character of the other can be inferred or predicted, and this is the most important thing from the standpoint of the behavioral and social sciences.

These levels of interpretation will be discussed with the purpose of suggesting what the specific determinants and correlates of anti-democratic attitudes are. Such a discussion should elaborate what type of dimensions might underlie responses to anti-democratic item statements.

Historical Level

In *Escape from Freedom,* Fromm (1941), developing previously expressed ideas by Weber (1930) in *The Protestant Ethic* and Tawney (1948) in *Religion and the Rise of Capitalism,* suggests that the roots of the authoritarian character structure and anti-democratic attitudes were in the collapse of the medieval social structure and the concomitant rise of a capitalist economy and Protestantism. These two interrelated historical and cultural factors gave modern man a freedom from an external authority he had not known previously. However, Fromm proposes that this freedom brought into existence a society where a man feels isolated from his fellows, where relationships in an industrial age are impersonal, and where insecurity replaces a sense of belonging. According to Fromm this sense of isolation may drive an individual to one of various forms of escape. It may drive a people to seek escape in blind devotion to a leader, in utter submission to an all-powerful State, or into a barbarous and sadistic program of aggression against minority groups or neighbor nations. The specific traits and characteristics of this authoritarian character structure will be dealt with specifically in reference to the work done by the California group (Adorno *et al.,* 1950) since their research was influenced by Fromm's hypotheses and theory.

Socio-Cultural Level

In Fromm's (1955) *The Sane Society,* he more explicitly outlines the current American social scene and the effects it has

160

upon personality and attitudes. He notes as the most important elements in twentieth-century capitalism "the disappearance of feudal traits, the revolutionary increase in industrial production, the increasing concentration of capital and bigness of business and government, the increasing number of people who manipulate figures and people, the separation of ownership from management, the rise of the working class economically and politically, and new methods of work in factory and office" (Fromm [1955], p. 108). He sees these changes reflected in certain characterological changes, such as an almost exclusive reference to the abstract qualities of things and people rather than their concreteness and uniqueness.

The central concept for understanding the social character of man in the twentieth century is alienation. Alienation is defined as the process by which "man does not experience himself as the active bearer of his own powers and richness, but as an impoverished thing, dependent on powers outside of himself, unto whom he has projected his living substance" (Fromm, 1955, p. 124). Fromm observes this process in a number of modern contexts. He believes it is the dynamic underlying idolatrous subjection to church, state, family, or clan. Security for the alienated man comes from identification with a group. This desire for security may be generalized to the extent that modern man conforms to even an anonymous authority. Much of this conformity to anonymous authority is due to the magnitude of present social and political institutions. They seem too large and extensive to be capable of management by the ordinary person.

Bureaucratization, in which relationships to people are characterized by manipulation, is seen as another reflection of alienation. Human relationships are further characterized by subtle distrust, distance, and indifference. When this distrust is carried to the extreme of sadistic interest in competitive sports and crimes as reflected in mass media, it is interpreted by Fromm as modern man's attempt to break through the surface of a life predominated by bureaucratization and routinization.

Fromm observes that work and leisure involve feverish activity in modern society. He interprets this as an escape from boredom and isolation. Closely related to boredom and isolation is the prevalence of a feeling of guilt in people. The main difference between this guilt and that of a Calvinist community, Fromm states, is that modern man's feeling of guilt is neither very conscious nor does it refer to a religiously patterned concept of sin.

Some verification for this analysis is provided in Stouffer's (1955) *Communism, Conformity and Civil Liberties* in which he reports a national attitude survey of the degree of willingness to tolerate nonconformists, such as socialists, atheists, or communists, or suspected nonconformists and the degree to which the internal communist threat is regarded as a serious danger. Among the findings pertinent here is that on the whole the majority of Americans are more preoccupied with personal problems which consume most of their conversation and interest. Very few expressed an interest or concern in the issues which were being surveyed. They evidently seemed remote from personal involvement.

This brief overview of the historical background and present analysis of the current social character has been given because it is the writer's belief that any understanding of the nature of the attitudes under consideration, their cognitive organization, and the personality characteristics which they reflect can meaningfully be understood in the final analysis only by reference to the social environment from which they were learned and in which they continue to be reinforced. As will be more explicitly pointed out with reference to the specific attitude statements, many of them are prevalent in general public opinion.

Socio-cultural agents such as class, occupation, and organized groups may be one of the organizing principles of social attitudes at this level. We find that patterns of sentiments are expressed in the programs of almost every group. Three prominent examples of this are social class, occupation and religion. Studies by such sociologists and psychologists as Davis (1953, Davis and Havighurst 1954), Havighurst and Davis (1953), Hollingshead (1949) and Centers (1948a, 1948b, 1949) have emphasized the importance of socio-economic status and related class position in both personality development and the formation of social attitudes. Centers ([1949], pp. 210–211) writes that integral to the structuring of social classes "are tendencies toward common conceptions by their members of the qualifications for membership in them, tendencies toward common conceptions of the occupational characteristics of their membership, tendencies toward common attitudes, beliefs, and behavior in economic and political matters, and perhaps tendencies toward common attitudes, beliefs, and behavior in many other ways as yet undiscovered and undefined." By means of a stratification score composed of the three indices of occupation, dominance-subordination relationships in work relations, and economic status, Centers found that socio-economic stratification as measured by this index was quite clearly the major condition related to class identification and conservatism-radicalism in political and economic attitudes.

Most studies of authoritarianism have been made on homogeneous samples of predominantly middle-class groups. Although there appears to be a negative correlation between authoritarian attitudes and education or intelligence, (Adorno et al., 1950, Gough, 1951a) no explicit research concerning the differences between classes has been conducted. It can be suggested, however, that related variables of social class such as marginality and mobility may be of importance in determining the organization and acceptance of such attitudes. Bettelheim and Janowitz (1950) found that for related attitudes such as anti-Negro and anti-Semitic attitudes, aggressive attitudes both spontaneous and elicited were most highly concentrated in the downwardly mobile group of war veterans, while the pattern was significantly reversed for those who had advanced in social status since the period of their previous civilian employment. For the few cases in which upward mobility was accompanied by overt intolerance, the individuals tended to be considerably more mobile than the others. Frenkel-Brunswik (1948) also found that a subjective feeling of marginality on the part of individuals considered mobile within the social structure was accompanied by an expression of ethnocentric attitudes by their children.

In the United States where a man's occupation is the primary means of achieving increased social status, it seems legitimate to hypothesize that his satisfactions, desires, aspirations, goals and attitudes are reflected in his selection of an occupation and that

163

these in turn are conditioned by his roles, status, and level of achievement as these are manifested in his placement in the occupational strata. In the original California study (Adorno *et al.*, 1950) the parents and grandparents of subjects low in ethnocentrism were significantly more frequently from such professional fields as medicine, law, teaching and the ministry than those of subjects high in ethnocentrism. In Frenkel-Brunswik's study of children (1948) there was a relatively high percentage of ethnocentric families among the workers, especially among those aspiring to higher status. Salesmen, policemen, firemen and their families were more frequently among the prejudiced while bus drivers, accountants, government workers and their families were more frequently among the unprejudiced. In her study she found the occupation itself to be a more differentiating factor than economic status per se.

Another group variable which might constitute a major organizing principle of authoritarian attitudes is religious affiliation. Although the humanistic element of Christianity should foster the very opposite of intolerance, the authoritarian element of religion which stresses that man is controlled by a power outside of himself and demands his submission to this power, aligns its teachings to authoritarian attitudes. The tendency for religions to stress the authoritarian element as they become institutionalized has been emphasized by Fromm ([1950], p. 85):

It is the tragedy of all great religions that they violate and pervert the very principle of freedom as soon as they become mass organizations governed by a religious bureaucracy. The religious organization and the men who represent it take over then to some extent the place of family, tribe, and state.

Adorno (1952) concluded on the basis of clinical interviews that religion does not play such a decisive role for most people as it once did and that when it is accepted it is not because of its objective truth, but on account of its value in realizing goals that might also be achieved by other means. When Sanford (1948) administered the E Scale (ethnocentrism scale) and prejudice scales to 1,200 subjects, he concluded that subjects who profess to some religious affiliation express more prejudice than those who do not. However, the crucial point seemed to be the psychological trends reflected in the way the subject accepted or rejected religion rather than the content of his religious ideology.

In a study of university faculty members Struening (1951) found that there was a coefficient of correlation of −.454 between F Scale (authoritarianism scale) and "orthodoxy" scores, as measured by Thurstone's Attitude toward the Church Scale. This correlation indicates that the individuals with more favorable attitudes toward the church tend to be more authoritarian. An analysis of variance indicated that authoritarian social attitudes differed significantly among university faculty in relation to their church affiliation. The rank order was Congregational, Christian, Methodist, Catholic, Baptist, Lutheran, and Episcopal. He also found that active church members possess the most undemocratic ideologies while nominal members and non-members were more democratic in their ideologies.

A study by Remmers and Steinberg (1954) of elementary and secondary school teachers substantiated Struening's findings with regard to the correlation of church attendance with both attitude toward the church and F Scale scores. They found that the most heavily weighted factor for predicting F Scale scores for the Catholic sample was frequency of church attendance and the most heavily weighted factor for the Protestant sample was "race."

Cognitive Level

At the cognitive level anti-democratic attitudes are viewed as constructs, expectancies, or working hypotheses which the individual has concerning his social environment. A body of research has been conducted to discern the degree to which these constructs are organized along a continuum which is a reflection of deeper personality variables. Such research has suggested that "intolerance of ambiguity" for example in social relationships and attitudes also characterizes the individual's simpler perceptual processes and approach to relatively unemotional problem-solving situations. When this is interpreted in terms of personality variables, intolerance of ambiguity presumably reflects a lack of integration among the "various levels of personality" and is a manifestation of the individual's characteristic means of handling both his internal need tensions and the demands imposed upon him by the external world.

Frenkel-Brunswik (1949), using school children in laboratory studies, found that the tendency to resort to black-white solutions, to arrive at premature closure—often at the neglect of reality—and to seek for unqualified and unambiguous solutions which had been found so characteristic of the social and emotional outlook of ethnocentric [2] subjects could also be ascertained in their perceptual responses.

Block and Block (1951) studied the relationship of "intolerance of ambiguity" and ethnocentrism using the auto-kinetic effect first used by Sherif. They found that prejudiced persons, as measured by the E Scale, established a norm for themselves in significantly fewer trials than the less prejudiced individuals.

O'Connor (1952) investigated the relationships among abstract reasoning ability, ethnocentrism and "intolerance of ambiguity" by administering a test of syllogistic reasoning problems together with the E Scale and Walker's scale of "intolerance of ambiguity" to 57 students in a classroom setting. Her results indicated that ethnocentrism is positively associated with "intolerance of ambiguity" and to poor ability to reason abstractly. However, "intolerance of ambiguity" and poor ability to reason abstractly were only significantly correlated when associated with ethnocentrism.

This restricted characteristic of the perceptual and cognitive processes of the authoritarian individual was studied by Scodel and Mussen (1953). They administered the F Scale and items from the Minnesota Multiphasic Personality Inventory (MMPI) to 276 students and selected the 27 highest scoring and the 27 lowest scoring individuals for a role-playing experiment. Each high scorer was paired with a low scorer and the two were required to spend twenty minutes together in a discussion in which they were free to discuss any aspect of radio, television, or the movies. After the twenty-minute period each subject was given

166

the F Scale and MMPI items and requested to respond on each as he believed his former partner would answer. They found that the high scorers' item mean score when taking the F Scale in the role-playing simulation of actual low scorers was only .18 lower than their own actual score. The difference was not significant. The low scorers apparently compromised when they simulated high scorers, although they were able to break from their own scores to a significant extent. The simulated item mean for low scorers was 3.56, which in actuality was slightly over halfway between their own item mean score of 2.38 and the high scorers' one of 4.62. The authors concluded that these results may be attributed to the authoritarian's reduction of ambiguity and thus anxiety by a rigid dichotomization which minimizes individual differences and evaluates people only in terms of their in-group or out-group membership.

Scodel and Freedman (1956) repeated this experiment except that high scorers were paired with other high scorers while low scorers were paired with low scorers. Under these experimental conditions the high scorers correctly estimated their partner's high score, while the low scorers tended to make inaccurate estimates of other lows in the direction of attributing middle scores to others whether these others were high or low. This suggests that low scorers are also governed by a less extreme and less frequent, but still discernible "other-stereotype."

Sarbin and Stephenson (1954) found results similar to Scodel's first experiment when they had a group of 62 undergraduates fill out E, PEC, and F Scales first as prejudiced individuals and then as tolerant individuals. It seemed that persons who score high on these scales were less able to adopt a role incongruent with their ego structure than were low scorers.

The direct relationship of anxiety created in a stress situation and "intolerance of ambiguity" has been studied by Snock (1955). He used series of five pictures in which the design became increasingly more clear on each presentation as stimulus objects. In the experimental group he created stress by requiring the subjects in one group to guess as each picture was presented to them what the object being presented was. He con-

167

cluded that the finding that psychological stress increases the striving for cognitive certainty supports the assumption that a lack of personality integration may underlie various maladaptive response patterns characteristic of the ethnocentric individual.

These various studies suggest some of the correlates of anti-democratic attitudes. Also, although there is not a one-to-one relationship between these attitudes and overt behavior, they do afford some means of predicting behavior in actual social situations.

A concept very closely related to "intolerance of ambiguity" is rigidity, which is also a reflection of cognitive processes. It has also been suggested that this characteristic is a reflection of the organization of an individual's social attitudes and ideology as well as his approach to strictly cognitive tasks. However, it has not yet been established that there is one trait of rigidity. There has not yet been a study to show that all the various tests used to measure this trait are so related as to show them all to be measures of one and the same underlying psychological factor.

Rokeach (1948) was the first to investigate the relationship of rigidity to ethnocentric and anti-democratic attitudes. He defined rigidity as "the inability to change one's [response] set when the objective conditions demand it or the inability to restructure a field in which there are alternative solutions to a problem in order to solve the problem more efficiently." He measured the degree of rigidity in his subjects by use of the *Einstellung* arithmetic problems. A mental set was first established by exposing the subjects to a series of problems which could be solved only by relatively long and complex manipulation. The subjects were then presented with further problems which could be solved either by maintaining the original set or by using a more direct and simple method. Children scoring extremely high on ethnic prejudice were found to cling more rigidly to the original set than those extremely low in expression of prejudice. Rokeach also reports a significant negative relationship between ethnocentrism and intelligence, but he points out that the differences found cannot be accounted for by differences in intelligence between ethnocentric and non-ethnocentric individuals. From these results Rokeach (1948, p. 278) concluded that:

168

The rigidity inherent in an ethnocentric person's solution of social problems is not an isolated phenomenon within the personality, but it is rather an aspect of a general rigidity factor which will also manifest itself in the solution of any problem, be it social or nonsocial.

Luchins (1949) has offered the following criticisms of Rokeach's work:

(1) The arithmetic problems do not measure deep-seated personality rigidity.

(2) No general factor of intellectual rigidity was unequivocally demonstrated.

(3) The method of combining all persons who made high or low scores on attitude scales and defining the resulting groups as prejudiced or non-prejudiced made the results unclear.

(4) The test situation could not be defined as a non-social situation.

His overall criticism of Rokeach's work is that in drawing his conclusions he did not take into consideration the field conditions which create both problem solving rigidity and ethnocentric attitudes. Further investigations of the relationship of rigidity to social attitudes cited below to some extent verify Luchin's criticisms.

Using 150 undergraduate subjects, Goodstein (1953) measured rigidity by the *Einstellung* water-jar problems, the Shipley-Hartford Retreat Scale and Anagram problems. No significant relationships could be demonstrated among the three tests of rigidity. Social attitudes were measured by the Thurstone attitude scales toward the Bible, censorship, patriotism, and law. No significant intercorrelations could be demonstrated between intellectual rigidity independently defined by each of the three tests of rigidity, and extremity of social attitudes. The author concluded that intellectual rigidity, as it had previously been conceived, is not a necessary concomitant of extreme or stable social attitudes.

Applezweig (1954) also employed other measures of rigidity including the group Rorschach, the E Scale, the Angyal Perceptual Test, the *Einstellung* problems, the Luchins Hidden Words test and a hidden objects test in a study of three groups of candi-

169

dates for a submarine school. He found no significant relationships among the tests of rigidity. After comparing the groups on these tests he concluded that at least three major components contribute to variations in the manifest behavior labeled "rigid:" the individual, the nature of the task, and the general conditions under which the tasks are administered.

Two of these conditions, the individual and the field conditions during administration of the task, have been investigated by Brown (1953). To two groups of subjects he administered the F Scale, *Einstellung* arithmetic problems, and McClelland's projective measure of need for achievement, to provide an index of achievement anxiety. The testing conditions for one group were relaxed and informal, while for the other group instructions were given calculated to ego-involve the subjects in the task. He found more correlation between F Scale scores and rigidity of problem solving behavior on the *Einstellung* problem scores in the ego-involved group than in the relaxed group. For the group that received an ego-involved orientation, both authoritarianism and rigidity were associated with achievement anxiety. For the more relaxed group, achievement anxiety was associated with high F Scale scores but not with more rigid problem solving performance.

Although these studies indicate that Rokeach's original proposition is an overgeneralization, this latter study seems to yield information which still makes the concept of rigidity as a correlate of ethnocentrism a useful one, inasmuch as it substantiates previous findings that the authoritarian personality tends to be achievement minded and easily threatened. Further research by Rokeach has however, led to the development of a broader theoretical orientation for the explanation of the relationship between cognitive organization and social attitudes such as ethnocentrism and authoritarianism. This theory developed from research on narrow-mindedness, reification and concreteness of thinking. First Rokeach (1951a) had subjects define the ten concepts of Buddhism, Capitalism, Catholicism, Christianity, Communism, Democracy, Fascism, Judaism, Protestantism, and Socialism. He categorized these definitions as abstract, reified, concrete or miscellaneous.

In concrete definitions the concept was explained in terms of a person or group holding a belief, a person being a member of a church or religion, etc., or the subject himself or another person. He found this type of definition significantly more frequently among ethnocentric subjects. Using these same concepts, he asked his subjects to write a paragraph describing in what way all of these terms might be interrelated. Content analysis of the paragraphs indicated that they could be grouped into three categories of organization: (1) comprehensive or broad and integrated; (2) isolated cognitive organization, in which the ten concepts were integrated but broken down into two or more sub-groups relatively isolated from each other; and (3) narrow cognitive organization, in which one or more of the objectively present parts was clearly missing from the subject's organization. When these categories of organization were correlated with ethnocentrism scores, he found that narrow organization increases directly with increase in ethnocentrism. This study provides the background for Rokeach's (1954) more comprehensive theory of dogmatism which is of particular interest in view of the problem of this research because it places emphasis upon the manner in which attitudes and ideology, particularly of an authoritarian and anti-democratic nature, are organized and structured.

Dogmatism is broadly defined as a hypothetical cognitive state which mediates objective reality within the individual. The construct is relatively independent of ideological content and may be applied to various types of political, religious, academic or racial ideologies. This wide application assumes that despite differences in ideological content, analysis would reveal certain uniformities in the structure, function and, to some extent, the content of dogmatism. It also assumes that objective reality is perceived by the individual on the basis of the beliefs or expectations which he has accepted as true or false. It is hypothesized then that certain characteristics of the organization and structure of these expectations are inherent in all types of dogmatic ideology. The organization and character of dogmatic expectations have the following characteristics:

(1) A relatively closed cognitive organization of beliefs and disbeliefs about reality,

(2) organized around a central set of beliefs about absolute authority which in turn,

(3) provides a framework for patterns of intolerance and qualified tolerance toward others. (Rokeach [1954] p. 197.)

Authoritarianism is related to this construct as the central organizing principle of the belief system. Thus, one postulate is that "with an increase in dogmatism there will be not only increasing admiration or glorification of those perceived in positions of positive authority but also increasing fear, hatred and vilification of those perceived in positions of authority opposed to positive authority" (Rokeach [1954], p. 201). Coordinate with this is an organization of people in general according to the authorities they line up with and an increasing polarization of cognitive distinctions between the faithful and unfaithful with increasing dogmatism. Intolerance and rejection of people or ideas are manifested when they are perceived to threaten the closed system.

This conceptualization of authoritarianism and intolerance makes the total range of phenomena, observable as manifestations of authoritarianism and intolerance, considerably broader. Thus, although dogmatism involves both authoritarianism and intolerance it need not take the form of fascist authoritarianism or ethnic intolerance. Likewise, an authoritarian orientation might take other forms than ethnic intolerance. Rokeach (1952) has demonstrated that scores on the F Scale are related substantially to measures of dogmatism independent of liberalism-conservatism, or kinds of attitudes held toward such groups as Jews and Negroes. The correlation between the two scales was .60 when ethnocentrism and politico-economic conservatism were held constant. He has also theoretically derived (1954) and empirically substantiated (1955) a distinction between dogmatism and rigidity.

If authoritarianism is thus related to dogmatism, and may be considered as one form of dogmatic ideology, we would predict that it would be characteristically organized and structured. In other words, given a set of attitudes, which express possible constructs concerning authority, human relations, and values, the interrelationships of the responses may be expected to be organized into dimensions which form a structure reflecting the basic organization of these attitudes. From these dimensions, inferences may be made concerning the dynamics underlying the organization.

Psychodynamic Level

The following represents to a certain extent the approach taken in *The Authoritarian Personality* (Adorno *et al.*, 1950). Using Maslow's (1943) and Fromm's (1941) characterizations of the authoritarian character structure and psychoanalytic theory, they postulated a characteristic personality organization reflected in attitudes toward minority groups, group relations generally, and people and life in general. They developed opinion attitude scales to obtain quantitative estimates of these surface attitudes. Attitude scales measuring anti-Semitism and ethnocentrism were found to be highly related. Ethnocentrism was defined and elaborated as:

Ethnocentrism is based on a pervasive and rigid in-group–out-group distinction; it involves stereotyped negative imagery and hostile attitudes regarding outgroups, stereotyped positive imagery and submissive attitudes regarding ingroups, and a hierarchial, authoritarian view of group interaction in which ingroups are rightly dominant, outgroups subordinate (Adorno *et al.*, [1950], p. 150).

On the basis of clinical interviews and projective techniques, this ethnocentric ideology was then conceived of as one part of a more general anti-democratic ideology which is a reflection of various needs and dispositions of individuals with authoritarian character structures. They hypothesized nine variables in different combinations and degrees which represent these needs and dispositions:

(1) Conventionalism: Rigid adherence to conventional, middle-class values.

(2) Authoritarian submission: Submissive, uncritical attitude toward idealized moral authorities of the in-group.

(3) Authoritarian aggression: Tendency to be on the lookout for, and to condemn, reject, and punish people who violate conventional values.

(4) Anti-intraception: Opposition to the subjective, the imaginative.

(5) Superstition and stereotypy: The belief in mystical determi-

173

nants of the individual's fate; the disposition to think in rigid categories.

(6) Power and toughness: Preoccupation with the dominance-submission, strong-weak, leadership-follower dimension; identification with power figures; overemphasis upon the conventionalized attributes of the ego; exaggerated assertion of strength and toughness.

(7) Destructiveness and cynicism: Generalized hostility, vilification of the human.

(8) Projectivity: The disposition to believe that wild and dangerous things go on in the world; the projection outwards of unconscious emotional impulses.

(9) Sex: Exaggerated concern with sexual "goings on" (Adorno *et al.* [1950], p. 254).

In our discussion of the organization and structure of anti-democratic attitudes these nine variables may be considered as the original hypothetical dimensions which in various combinations represent the characteristic personality organization. The California Study assumed that personality may be reflected and hence inferred from acceptance of attitudes representing these ideological trends. The original authors used these nine variables as hypotheses in collecting and writing a final thirty items to form the F Scale, designed to tap anti-democratic social attitudes at a personality level. This scale had an average reliability on groups tested of .91 and correlated with the Ethnocentrism Scale .75.

Since the publication of *The Authoritarian Personality* a preponderance of empirical correlates of the personality characteristics of those scoring high or low on this scale and the E Scale have been accumulated in the literature. Some of the correlates such as "intolerance of ambiguity" and rigidity have already been cited in connection with the characteristic cognitive organization of authoritarian ideology and attitudes. Other studies have been concerned with a further validation of these findings or observations of more general personality characteristics which substantiate the originally hypothesized ones.

Adelson (1953) found in an investigation similar to the original California Study, but on a smaller scale, that the same ideology-personality connections exist among Jewish minority groups. In exploratory interviews he found that the authoritarian

174

image of the out-group among the Jews incorporated the same essential elements of the anti-Semitic stereotype; even the contradictions were retained, as in the attribution of both seclusive and intrusive motives to the Jewish out-group. The Jewish authoritarian's image of the Gentile was also dichotomous. He characterized the "bad" Gentile as one bearing lower-class characteristics and the "good" Gentile as a middle-class figure with whom he felt joined in the solidarity of decorum. On the basis of the findings from the interviews Adelson constructed questionnaires similar to the E and F Scales but especially designed for Jews. His results indicated that the particular attitudes involved in Jewish authoritarian ideology are genotypically similar to non-Jewish authoritarian attitudes; both can be understood with references to such features of personality organization as authoritarian aggression and submission, and the need for dichotomous and invidious distinctions.

Using direct and indirect questionnaires and interviews in a study of children, Frenkel-Brunswik (1948) found that, at least after the age of ten, children's personalities also tend to fall into patterns similar to those observed in the adults described in *The Authoritarian Personality*. Thus, ethnocentric youngsters tended to display authoritarian aggression, rigidity, cruelty, superstition, externalization and projectivity, denial of weakness, power orientation and dichotomous conceptions of sex roles, of kinds of people, and of values.

In an extensive series of studies of the correlates of anti-Semitism, Gough (1951a, 1951b, 1951c, 1951d) administered the E and F Scales, the MMPI, the Allport-Vernon Study of Values, and the Rosensweig Frustration Study to a sample of high school students. His study was essentially a demonstration of the importance of personality factors in the determination of ethnocentric and authoritarian attitudes. From the test information and personal history data he characterized the intolerant individual as being of a lower intellectual level and disadvantaged economic background. In addition, the bigot was revealed to be less sociable, to have a great tendency to complain of personal dissatisfactions, to have a narrow outlook on national and interna-

175

tional affairs, to be antagonistic toward many out-groups, to place emphasis on nationalism, chauvinism, and conservatism, and to possess feelings of victimization and exploitation.

He then carried out an item analysis of the MMPI items in which he compared the reactions to each of the items by the ethnocentric and non-ethnocentric students. From this analysis he grouped the personality items into the following nine categories: (1) anti-intellectuality; (2) pessimism and lack of hope and confidence in the future; (3) cynicism, distrust, doubt, suspicion, even misanthropy and querulousness; (4) hostile and bitter outlook which ramifies into destructiveness; (5) lack of self-regard and trust in self-integrity; (6) discontented evaluation of current status; (7) rigid, dogmatic thinking; (8) lack of poise and self-assurance; and (9) a feeling of perplexity and ominous fearfulness. The parallelism of these categories with previously hypothesized dimensions and empirical correlates are evident.

Allport and Kramer (1946) using different instruments of measurement on students from three Eastern colleges report a roughly similar picture of the type of personality who shows propensities toward prejudice. The more highly prejudiced students were also inclined to cling to parental patterns, to have a jungle philosophy of life, an authoritarian or disciplinarian outlook on life, to fear fraud or trickery, and to disapprove of legislation designed to improve the status of minority groups. The prejudiced individual was found to be unaware of the influences affecting him, inaccurate in his self-knowledge, incapable of feelings of shame, and quite inclined to regard his hostilities as natural and fully justified by virtue of the misbehavior of the minority groups he happens to dislike.

The possibility that the ethnocentric person despite his willingness to adduce specific reasons for rejecting designated groups may be oriented toward a generalized misanthropy towards others was studied by Sullivan and Adelson (1954). They developed a scale using revised E Scale items with people substituted as referents for minority or foreign groups. This scale and the original E Scale administered to a group of students yielded a significant correlation. However, the correlation was not large enough to demonstrate that prejudice is the same as an underlying misanthropy or that the designation of particular minorities as objects of hate is free from social press. The generality of reference of these attitudes does, however, present the possibility that for many anti-democratic individuals there may be no in-group other than the self.

A study by Pearl (1954) illustrates the self-concept of individuals who score high on the E and F Scales. Among the major findings in *The Authoritarian Personality* (Adorno *et al.*, 1950) was that one of the most distinguishing characteristics of those high on these scales was a general lack of self-insight and self-criticism. Pearl's study more explicitly illustrates this. Before entering therapy he asked 12 individuals to sort, according to what they thought was their real self and their ideal self, 180 positive and negative self-evaluations of ninety traits related to values, self-characteristics, and relations to people. They also took the E and F Scales. A factor analysis of the self-evaluations produced two distinguishable factors; one related to self-esteem and self-reliance and another to lack of awareness of anxiety concerning problems of impulse and hostility control. He found two distinct clusters of subjects with respect to pre-psychotherapy self-concept factor loadings which clearly differentiated between high and low scorers on the E and F Scales. The first cluster, representing the highest E and F Scale scorers, were subjects with high self-esteem and feelings of adequacy. They denied having anxiety concerning their interpersonal relationships and tended to disdain knowledge of inner weakness and contradictory self-trends. They also saw themselves as possessing many of those qualities which they would ideally like to have.

The low scorers saw themselves as unworthy and inadequate with respect to many aspects of interpersonal relationships. They admitted to anxieties and were concerned about control of their impulses and hostilities. When these tests were readministered after psychotherapy there were indications that although there were changes in the self-concept of some of the patients, this was not accompanied by significant changes in E Scale scores and particularly F Scale scores. This seems to indicate that although the individual's self-evaluation and attitudes may be functionally related to his interpersonal relations, ethnocentric and prejudiced attitudes toward minority groups may be so heavily buttressed and reinforced within the broader social environment that a change in self-concept alone is not sufficient to counteract these other social forces. This is further substantiated by Gordon and Cartwright (1954) in a study of these attitudes before and after therapy. However, Tougas (1954) has found that ethnocentric attitudes may be a limiting factor in psychotherapy.

The etiology of anti-democratic attitudes and the personality structure of those accepting of such attitudes is placed in the early home setting by the California group in their original work and in further work with children by Frenkel-Brunswik. In her later work Frenkel-Brunswik (1954) has placed more emphasis upon the sociological correlates of child rearing practices, such as mobility and marginality.

Thus, it is generally supposed that the person for whom prejudice and authoritarian submission and aggression are functionally important has had childhood experiences with parents who were punitive, strict, coercive, and dominantly overprotective. The child's aggressive responses to such frustrating parental stimuli whether directed toward the parents or displaced are punished in such a way as to produce anxiety and feelings of guilt. To avoid these unpleasant guilt feelings the child represses his hostility. The individual develops modes of behavior and attitude constellations designed to bolster repression and thus allay the threat of painful guilt feelings. The authoritarian person also characteristically tends to make more use of the mechanism of projection and displacement, devices which function quite effectively in keeping repressed impulses from conscious awareness while at the same time allowing them disguised and acceptable outlets in the form of ethnocentric hostility.

Gough, Harris, and Martin (1950) gave parents and children a number of questionnaires to ascertain the degree of the prejudice of the children, and also the favorite methods of child control adopted by the parents. Their results showed a marked difference between the attitudes towards child upbringing of the mothers of prejudiced children as compared with the mothers of non-prejudiced children. Parents of prejudiced children advocated child rearing practices characterized as being strict and firm, less permissive, lacking in a close, affective emotional relationship between parent and child, and rigid.

A study by Stagner (1954) of college men's acceptance or rejection of authority and their attitudes toward their father also provides some substantiating data for emphasis upon family background and child rearing practices in the etiology of authoritarian attitudes. He constructed a ten-item opinion scale which gave an internally consistent measure of a generalized attitude toward acceptance of authority when administered to 575 students. Item counts of responses to opinion statements of the upper versus the lower fourths revealed that persons accepting authority as defined by the scale showed a conservative orientation, were hostile to labor unions, endorsed war as a policy, were nationalistic, intolerant of minority groups and leaned toward forceful solutions of social problems. Although no gross differences in attitude toward parents or family were shown by the data, item counts suggested a trend for pro-authority subjects to have a conscious idealization of parents accompanied by some latent feeling of distance from them. They also tended to perceive discipline in the home as strict but fair.

The second part of the study involved showing a series of 14 projective pictures designed to evoke authority-related responses. Only six of the pictures effectively discriminated between the two groups. On these pictures the projective responses suggested that pro-authority men were more concerned about power, more in need of a definite relationship to parents, more ethnocentric and less sympathetic. Anti-authority men perceived authority figures as inhibiting and threatening. Stagner concludes that these data very strongly support the data of the California group.

When considering the family and early child experiences as the important factors in the development of ethnocentric and authoritarian attitudes, two important factors must be considered. First, those parents who rear their children as described in these studies might also be expected to be the kind who would overtly express such attitudes in the home where the child would presumably learn them. Secondly, the family as the primary carrier of social and cultural ideology and modes of behavior reflects broader social and cultural group behavior patterns, ideology and

179

attitudes. This brings into focus one of the major criticisms of the study done by the California group; namely, that they did not take concrete cognizance of group membership, situational factors, and the greater social structure in accounting for the genesis and reflection of these character qualities and concomitant attitudes (Asch, 1952, p. 69). However, their orientation that personality is an agency through which sociological influences upon ideology are mediated has contributed much to explain consistency of behavior in widely varying situations, to explain the persistence of ideological trends in the face of contradicting facts and radically altered social conditions, to explain why people in the same sociological situation have different or even conflicting views on social issues, and why it is that people whose behavior has been changed through psychological manipulation lapse into their old ways as soon as the agencies of manipulation are removed.

This discussion indicates some of the theoretical and empirical correlates and determinants of anti-democratic attitudes. Current research, although specifying in some instances that anti-democratic attitudes represent a constellation of multidimensional attributes, has proceeded methodologically on the assumption that they are unidimensional. Thus, the scales used necessarily imply that from elicited responses to item statements one underlying continuous variable of authoritarianism may be inferred. The complexity of determinants alone in terms of the interaction of historical, socio-cultural, cognitive and psychodynamic factors would appear to indicate that this may not be a correct assumption. This assumption brings to the fore the methodological criticisms [3] of the work which has been done in this area of social attitudes.

METHOD AND PROCEDURE

THE SAMPLE OF RESPONDENTS

In the original survey 23 colleges and universities in Indiana were sampled. Each college which agreed to participate in the poll was given written instructions concerning correct sampling procedures. By the procedure adopted the population is necessarily limited to those schools which agreed to participate in a poll of this type. Instructions for sampling were made according to school size. For schools under 500 it was suggested that the questionnaire should be administered to the complete student body at the same time. For schools between 500 and 3,000, it was asked that at least half the student body be sampled by some random method such as every nth case. For schools larger than this a request was made for a random but representative sample on the variables of level of study, major field of study, wealth, religion, race, course grade, marital status, and veteran status. The original letter sent to all participating schools is included in the Appendix.

The 23 colleges and universities were classified into four categories: (1) the big three, which included Indiana University, Purdue University, and Notre Dame; (2) extension centers, which included five centers of Purdue University and Indiana University located throughout the state; (3) ten small accredited colleges, which were in most instances small denominational liberal arts colleges; and (4) five small unaccredited liberal arts colleges, four of which were Roman Catholic and the fifth Lutheran.

In view of the fact that the factor analysis results were to be used eventually as scaling criteria, three objectives were considered in selecting the sample. First, it was desired to include as many of these types of institutions as possible in order not to limit the population to which the results could be generalized and the scale used. Second, we did not want the group to be so heterogeneous that it would be difficult, if not impossible, to characterize the parent population. It seemed reasonable to assume, for instance, that the students at a large state university might differ appreciably on both stratification variables and attitudes from the students at a small denominational college. These two points suggest a balance between breadth and homogeneity in terms of the sample, which had to be further considered in light of the third practical factor—how adequate the actual samples were from each of these categories of institutions.

This factor could be considered by a comparison of the actual sample with the population figures on the variables of sex and

181

class in school. These population figures were obtained from the registrar of each college or university included in the poll. They were asked to submit the enrollment figures for the academic year 1953–1954, the year preceding that of the collection of the data. When these figures were studied, it was seen that the largest and most representative samples were from the small unaccredited and accredited colleges. These appeared to approximate most nearly the desirable compromise between breadth and homogeneity. In addition, this seemed a good group to study inasmuch as small institutions of this type are not frequently included in polls or other social-psychological research, because of inadequate funds and small staffs.

Table 33 indicates population figures and the actual sample

TABLE 33
THE POPULATION AND ORIGINAL PURIFIED SAMPLE

	Population		Sample	
School	*N*	*%*	*N*	*%*
1. Anderson Theological				
Seminary	890	8.58	298	7.43
2. De Pauw	1717	16.56	306	7.63
3. Earlham	631	6.08	429	10.69
4. Evansville	958	9.24	343	8.55
5. Franklin	431	4.15	249	6.21
6. Hanover	588	5.67	488	12.17
7. Indiana Central	349	3.36	237	5.91
8. Indiana State				
Teachers College	1665	16.06	405	10.09
9. Taylor	406	3.91	302	7.53
10. Valparaiso	1662	16.03	317	7.91
11. Marion	178	1.71	90	2.24
12. St. Francis	71	0.68	47	1.17
13. Ancilla Domini	29	0.27	18	0.45
14. Concordia	188	1.81	141	3.51
15. St. Joseph's	603	5.81	340	8.47
	10,366	100	4,010	100

obtained from each of the 15 colleges included in this study. All of the colleges are coeducational except Marian, St. Francis, and Ancilla Domini, which are Roman Catholic womens colleges, and St. Joseph's which is a Roman Catholic mens college. Out of this group Ancilla Domini is the only two-year college. Concordia, a coeducational Lutheran college, is also a two-year college. The rest of the colleges in the sample are all four-year coeducational colleges. With the exception of Taylor University, a private interdenominational college, and Indiana State Teachers College in Terre Haute, all of the other ten small accredited colleges are at least nominally sponsored by a Protestant church. Anderson College and Theological Seminary is sponsored by the Church of God; De Pauw and Evansville, Methodist; Earlham, Quaker; Franklin, Baptist; Hanover, Presbyterian; Indiana Central College, Evangelical and United Brethren; and Valparaiso, Lutheran. There is thus a good representation of the major Protestant denominations in the sample.

The number in the total population as indicated in Table 33 was 10,366. The final sample was drawn so that each school would be proportionately represented with respect to the population. To insure representative samples from within each of these schools, the 15 individual school samples were each stratified on sex and class-in-school variables. Table 34 was compiled to de-

TABLE 34

COMPARISON OF ACTUAL SCHOOL SAMPLES
AND NECESSARY REPRESENTATION

School	% of Population	Necessary No. of 4,010	Actual No. Sample	No. drawn (⅓ 4,010)
1. Anderson Theological Seminary	8.59	344	298	115
2. De Pauw	16.56	644	306	221
3. Earlham	6.09	244	429	81
4. Evansville	9.24	371	343	124
5. Franklin	4.16	167	249	56
6. Hanover	3.67	227	488	76
7. Indiana Central	3.37	135	237	45
8. Indiana State Teachers College	16.06	644	405	215
9. Taylor	3.92	157	302	52
10. Valparaiso	16.03	643	317	214
11. Marion	1.72	69	90	23
12. St. Francis	0.69	27	47	9
13. Ancilla Domini	0.28	11	18	4
14. Concordia	1.81	73	141	24
15. St. Joseph's	5.82	233	240	78

termine proportional representation from each school. If each school had been proportionately represented in the obtained sample of 4,010, it would have had the number designated in Table 34 under the column "necessary number of 4,010." A comparison of these figures with the actual number obtained from each school indicated that there was both under and over-representation from the various schools. These figures indicated, however, that if about one-third of the actual total sample of 4,010 was taken for a working sample, this sample would be large enough to minimize sampling error and yet allow proportionate representation from each school. Accordingly, one-third of the number necessary to be representative of the sample of 4,010 was taken as each school's quota. This made a total working sample of 1,338.

Within each school the population and drawn sample were both broken down on the basis of sex and class in school. These stratification variables defined the sampling cells, and the percentage by which each cell was represented in the school population was computed. This percentage times the quota which the school was being allowed in the total sample gave the number to be drawn from each cell.

Once these figures had been computed the actual procedure involved sorting the cards for each school on the IBM machines on the basis of sex and class in school. From these sorted groups, representing the cells on the stratification variables, a randon sample was drawn. Table 35 indicates the actual number from the original sample drawn for each school with respect to these two variables. For all but five cells, there was a sufficient number in the actual sample to fill the per cent quotas. In these few cases the difference did not seem significant.

In summary, the population to which this study may be generalized may be characterized as undergraduate students in small denominational liberal arts colleges in Indiana which agreed to participate in a poll of this type. This study could probably be generalized to colleges of this type in the Middle West. Further, the total sample used in this study is representative of this population in terms of each college population and sex and class in school.

TABLE 35

TOTAL SAMPLE BREAKDOWNS ON THE VARIABLES
OF COLLEGE, CLASS IN SCHOOL, AND SEX

School	Total	Fresh-men		Soph.		Junior		Senior	
		M	F	M	F	M	F	M	F
Anderson Theological Seminary	114	31	21	16	13	12	6	9	6
De Pauw	220	38	43	28	31	18	18	24	20
Earlham	80	14	16	10	12	7	6	9	6
Evansville	124	37	16	26	7	16	4	14	4
Franklin	57	16	10	9	6	4	4	5	3
Hanover	77	18	17	9	10	7	4	7	5
Indiana Central	44	13	7	7	5	4	2	4	2
Indiana State Teachers College	216	44	39	27	28	17	25	16	20
Taylor	52	10	8	6	6	7	5	6	4
Valparaiso	213	45	37	31	26	25	15	23	11
Marion	23		9		7		3		4
St. Francis	10		3		3		2		2
Ancilla Domini	4		3		1				
Concordia	25	10	3	9	3				
St. Joseph's	79	45		15		13		6	
Total	1338								

SAMPLE OF ITEMS

Items 20 through 55 of the poll were written to tap anti-democratic ideology. These items included those generally classified as authoritarian and ethnocentric. They were submitted to five judges, familiar with the research done in this area, who were asked to state whether they thought each item was sufficiently related to what is believed to be a part of authoritarian ideology to be included in a scale. The 20 items used are presented in Table 36, numbered as in the survey questionnaire. (See appendix A.).

The necessity of limiting the item number to 20 probably limits the representativeness of the sample of authoritarian statements, though a sufficient representation was given to each of the theoretical variables to allow a first approximation and delinea-

TABLE 36

F Scale Items Used for Factor Analysis

Item No.	Item
21	The true American way of life is disappearing so fast that force may be necessary to preserve it.
23	People without a deep and unquestionable faith in Almighty God should not be trusted in public office.
24	There is hardly anything lower than a person who does not feel a great love, gratitude and respect for our flag.
25	Americans are getting soft; most people need stricter discipline and the will to defend their interests.
27	Most people don't realize how much our lives are controlled by plots hatched in secret by others.
29	Obedience and a proper respect for authority should be the very first requirements of a good citizen.
35	It's a mistake to trust any nation until we are completely sure of them.
40	An insult to our honor should always be punished.
44	If people would talk less and work more, everybody would be better off.
45	Every person should have complete faith in some supernatural power whose decisions he obeys without question.
46	When a person has a problem or worry, it is best for him not to think about it, but to keep busy with more cheerful things.
47	A person who has bad manners, habits, and breeding can hardly expect to get along with decent people.
48	What youth needs most is strict discipline, rugged determination, and the will to fight for family and nation.
49	There is hardly anything lower than a person who does not feel a great love, gratitude, and respect for his parents.
50	Wars and social troubles may someday be ended by an earthquake or flood that will destroy the whole world.
51	The wild sex life of the old Greeks and Romans was tame compared to some of the goings on in this country, even in places where people might least suspect it.
52	No sane, normal, decent person could ever think of hurting a close relative or friend.
53	Books and movies ought not to deal so much with the unpleasant and seamy side of life; they ought to concentrate on themes that are entertaining or uplifting.
54	When you come right down to it, it's human nature never to do anything without an eye to one's profit.
55	Some leisure is necessary, but it is good hard work that makes life interesting and worthwhile.

TABLE 37

RANK ORDER OF PERCENTAGE RESPONSE
ON 20 DICHOTOMIZED ITEMS

Item No.	% Agree	% Disagree	Stem
55	89	11	Some leisure is necessary but it is good hard work......
29	80	20	Obedience and proper respect for authority......
49	74	26	There is hardly anything lower than a person...... respect for parents.
44	74	26	If people would talk less and work more......
27	61	39	Most people don't realize how much our lives are controlled......
52	58	42	No sane, normal, decent person could ever think of hurting......
45	56	44	Every person should have complete faith in some supernatural......
54	56	44	When you come right down to it, it's human nature......
48	55	45	What youth needs most is strict discipline, rugged determination......
47	55	45	A person who has bad manners, habits, and breeding......
25	53	47	Americans are getting soft; most people need stricter discipline......
24	52	48	There is hardly anything lower than a person...... respect for flag.
35	51	49	It's a mistake to trust any nation..until we are completely sure......
53	51	49	Books and movies ought not to deal so much with the unpleasant and......
51	49	51	The wild sex life of the old Greeks and Romans was tame......
46	46	54	When a person has a problem or worry, it is best......
23	43	57	People without a deep and unquestionable faith in Almighty God......
40	30	70	An insult to our honor should always be punished......
50	19	81	Wars and social troubles may someday be ended by an earthquake......
21	18	82	The true American way of life is disappearing so fast that force......

tion of the empirical dimensions of these anti-democratic attitudes.

Table 37 shows the rank order of the items in terms of percentage of the responses "agree" and "undecided; probably agree" versus "disagree" and "undecided; probably disagree." It indicates that the items covered the continuum of intensity between agreement and disagreement for the total sample rather well.

Correlation Matrix

The intercorrelations of all items were computed giving a 20 × 20 correlation matrix which is shown in Table 38. The correlation coefficients in the diagonal are the highest correlation of that item with any of the other 19 items and were used as the communality estimates in the factor analysis.

The range of correlations was .00 to .60. The absence of any negative correlation coefficients deserves mention because it indicates considerable homogeneity of relationship among items for this sample.

Those items having the highest correlation of .60 were Item 24, "there is hardly anything lower than a person who does not feel a great love, gratitude, and respect for our flag," and Item 49, "there is hardly anything lower than a person who does not feel a great love, gratitude and respect for his parents." Their similarity in verbal format and concept of submission to authority makes this relationship psychologically plausible. The next set of high correlations, .50, .49 and .47, are between Item 48 and Item 49, Item 49 and Item 52, and Item 23 and Item 24, respectively. These items also pertain to authoritarian submission and discipline. Item 50 has the lowest intercorrelations with the other items. In general, it is the poorest item of the group. It is probably a too overt expression of suspiciousness to be generally accepted at the educational level of this sample. Table 37 indicates that it was agreed with by only 19% of the total sample of 1,338.

Factor Analysis

Extraction of the factors was accomplished on the electronic digital computer by an eigenvector solution.

TABLE 38

Tetrachoric Intercorrelations of 20 Anti-Democratic Items

Item → / No. →	21	23	24	25	27	29	35	40	44	45	46	47	48	49	50	51	52	53	54	55
21	(.42)	.25	.22	.42	.30	.22	.25	.28	.21	.10	.10	.10	.20	.34	.11	.35	.25	.28	.19	.22
23	.25	(.47)	.47	.33	.18	.24	.26	.23	.30	.38	.16	.15	.28	.40	.00	.27	.32	.32	.19	.24
24	.22	.47	(.60)	.33	.20	.30	.40	.39	.28	.12	.34	.28	.33	.60	.20	.22	.43	.16	.24	.09
25	.42	.33	.33	(.42)	.18	.23	.19	.12	.32	.18	.10	.11	.37	.25	.18	.26	.21	.30	.14	.24
27	.30	.18	.20	.18	(.30)	.20	.19	.21	.22	.11	.10	.10	.29	.18	.13	.27	.18	.12	.25	.04
29	.22	.24	.30	.23	.20	(.45)	.30	.21	.30	.20	.20	.30	.45	.45	.10	.16	.30	.20	.30	.14
35	.25	.26	.40	.19	.19	.30	(.40)	.33	.17	.03	.10	.25	.28	.32	.12	.12	.28	.12	.28	.08
40	.28	.23	.39	.12	.21	.21	.33	(.39)	.17	.09	.16	.19	.26	.34	.13	.23	.27	.20	.23	.04
44	.21	.30	.28	.32	.22	.30	.17	.17	(.32)	.24	.16	.18	.25	.31	.00	.30	.12	.32	.12	.18
45	.10	.38	.12	.18	.11	.20	.03	.09	.24	(.38)	.13	.08	.20	.31	.12	.32	.28	.10	.10	.15
46	.10	.16	.34	.10	.10	.20	.10	.16	.16	.13	(.36)	.17	.17	.36	.06	.28	.22	.20	.20	.14
47	.10	.15	.28	.11	.10	.30	.25	.19	.18	.08	.17	(.30)	.28	.29	.05	.13	.27	.20	.13	.13
48	.20	.28	.33	.37	.29	.45	.28	.26	.25	.20	.17	.28	(.50)	.50	.19	.27	.33	.25	.20	.28
49	.34	.40	.60	.25	.18	.45	.32	.34	.31	.31	.36	.29	.50	(.60)	.21	.26	.49	.27	.32	.20
50	.11	.00	.20	.18	.13	.10	.12	.13	.00	.17	.06	.05	.19	.21	(.20)	.15	.20	.08	.12	.01
51	.35	.27	.22	.26	.27	.16	.12	.23	.30	.32	.28	.13	.27	.26	.15	(.35)	.25	.20	.23	.05
52	.25	.32	.43	.21	.18	.30	.28	.27	.12	.28	.22	.27	.33	.49	.20	.25	(.49)	.35	.23	.19
53	.28	.32	.16	.30	.12	.20	.12	.20	.32	.10	.20	.20	.25	.27	.08	.20	.35	(.35)	.22	.22
54	.19	.19	.24	.14	.25	.30	.28	.23	.12	.10	.20	.13	.20	.32	.12	.23	.23	.22	(.32)	.02
55	.22	.24	.09	.24	.04	.14	.08	.04	.18	.15	.14	.13	.28	.20	.01	.05	.19	.22	.02	(.28)

It was decided to compute factor loadings for the first three factors only, since they accounted for 81% of the total estimated common variance.

Upon this decision the variances accounted for by the first three factors were translated into standard deviation units, and the factor loadings for each item variable were computed. Table 39 shows each item with its factor loading on each factor and the communality of that variable as estimated from this first iteration. Also shown are the original estimates of the communalities. Comparison of these figures indicates that the estimates of the communalities after the first iteration are underestimates of the original estimates. Further iterations would have probably pro-

TABLE 39

FACTOR LOADINGS OF EACH ITEM VARIABLE ON FACTORS I, II, III

Item No.	I	Factor II	III	Communality Estimate $_h2$	Original Estimate
21	.4920	−.2099	.3279	.3936	.42
23	.5761	−.1839	−.1407	.3855	.47
24	.6642	.3062	−.0487	.5373	.60
25	.5026	−.3217	.1525	.3794	.42
27	.3808	−.0382	.3084	.2416	.30
29	.5528	.1104	−.0426	.3196	.45
35	.4722	.2829	.1773	.3344	.40
40	.4687	.2193	.1750	.2984	.39
44	.4643	−.2362	.0033	.2714	.32
45	.3812	−.2770	−.2901	.3062	.38
46	.3740	.1478	−.2743	.2370	.36
47	.3900	.1682	−.1071	.1919	.30
48	.6134	−.0090	.0075	.3764	.50
49	.7426	.1769	−.1653	.6101	.60
50	.2414	.0760	.1271	.0802	.21
51	.4438	−.1773	.2704	.3015	.35
52	.6024	.0930	−.1901	.4076	.49
53	.4731	−.2698	−.1185	.3107	.35
54	.4185	.1564	.1409	.2195	.32
55	.3033	−.2647	−.1704	.1911	.28
Σai^2_j	4.8506	.844	.6985		7.91
% of total variance	61	11	9		

190

duced larger communalities. However, they were believed close enough to serve for the practical purposes of psychological interpretation and scaling criteria. Table 39 also indicates that Factor I accounts for 61% of the total common variance, Factor II, 11% and Factor III, 9%.

In this form the first factor, Factor I, may be interpreted as that which is most heavily weighted with what is most liberally included in the items. Geometrically, the structure may be considered as a tube shape; Factor I represents the long continuum and the other two factors define the factor.

Three arithmetical rotations were made to positive manifold. These three rotations give a structure in which the variables are

TABLE 40

FACTOR LOADINGS OF 20 ITEM VARIABLES
ON ROTATED FACTORS, I, II, III

Item No.	I''	II'''	III'	$_h2$
21	.0701	.6119	.1190	.3935
23	.2105	.3333	.4794	.3852
24	.6392	.2880	.2134	.5371
25	.0136	.5353	.3043	.3793
27	.1451	.4695	.0086	.2416
29	.4171	.2870	.2513	.3195
35	.4743	.3292	.0308	.3343
40	.4219	.3469	.0009	.2983
44	.0821	.3789	.3479	.2713
45	.0454	.1369	.5342	.3062
46	.3777	.0001	.3070	.2369
47	.3779	.1188	.1866	.1917
48	.3497	.4005	.3058	.3762
49	.5995	.3013	.3997	.6099
50	.1821	.2170	.0071	.0803
51	.0766	.5304	.1194	.3014
52	.4545	.2228	.3891	.4076
53	.0789	.3117	.4552	.3106
54	.3476	.3124	.0314	.2194
55	.0083	.1655	.4045	.1911
Σai_j^2	2.2046	2.4143	1.77	
% of total variance	28	31	22	

in a positive manifold. All of the requirements of simple structure are not completely met, but no further rotation could be done without distorting the positive manifold structure. The factor loadings on the rotated factors are shown in Table 40.

In summary, the rotation of the original factors has established a reference system with all variables in the positive quadrant. The factors are uncorrelated, although the items may be related to more than one of these factors. By interpretation of these factors, this reference system may be used to increase understanding of the organization of anti-democratic attitudes.

DISCUSSION OF FACTORS

NAMING THE FACTORS

The factors are subject to interpretation at three levels. The first is a purely descriptive level at which the factor "is a condensed statement of relationships obtaining between a set of variables which can be used mathematically to stand for these variables" (Eysenck [1953], p. 106). In the context of this study, the interpretation would rest at conceptualizing the item as the stimulus, and the agreement or disagreement with it as the response. The factors then describe those items so related that they elicit the same type of verbal behavior from the respondents. This is the only level which does not involve an inferential step.

The second level of interpretation regards the factor as a principle of classification. The extraction of factors has separated clusters of items, which have more in common with each other than they have with the other measures. The commonness is inferred from the consistency of response. The factor is named in accordance with the features that these clusters have in common and that are unique to them.

The third level of interpretation is to infer on the basis of this classification the underlying dynamics of the observed relationships. At this stage of inference there is a close link between the functions of confirming and generating hypotheses through factor analysis.

To classify the items in accordance with their factor structure, they were separated according to the factor on which they had their highest factor loading. Tables 41, 42, and 43 are provided for this purpose. Table 41 presents Factor I″ with the items in rank order which had their highest factor loadings on this factor. The factor loadings on the other factors are also presented for the purposes of comparison. Tables 42 and 43 present Factors II‴ and III′, respectively, in a similar manner. Examination of these tables to discern that which was common to each factor but unique in semantic content was the procedure followed in deriving the classification discussed here.

TABLE 41

RANK ORDER OF ITEM VARIABLES WITH HIGHEST
FACTOR LOADINGS ON FACTOR I″

Item No.	I″	Loadings II‴	III′	Stem
24	.64	.29	.21	There is hardly anything lower than a person who does not feel a great love, gratitude and respect for our flag.
49	.60	.30	.40	There is hardly anything lower than a person who does not feel a great love, gratitude, and respect for his parents.
35	.47	.33	.03	It's a mistake to trust any nation until we are completely sure of them.
52	.46	.22	.39	No sane, normal, decent person could ever think of hurting a close relative or friend.
40	.42	.35	.00	An insult to our honor should always be punished.
29	.42	.29	.25	Obedience and proper respect for authority should be the very first requirements of a good citizen.
47	.38	.12	.19	A person who has bad manners, habits, and breeding can hardly expect to get along with decent people.
46	.38	.00	.31	When a person has a problem or worry, it is best for him not to think about it, but to keep busy with more cheerful things.
54	.35	.31	.03	When you come right down to it, it's human nature never to do anything without an eye to one's profit.

TABLE 42

RANK ORDER OF ITEM VARIABLES WITH HIGHEST FACTOR LOADINGS
ON FACTOR II'''

Item No.	Loadings II'''	I''	III'	Stem
21	.61	.07	.12	The true American way of life is disappearing so fast that force may be necessary to preserve it.
51	.53	.08	.12	The wild sex life of the old Greeks and Romans was tame compared to some of the goings on in this country, even in places where people might least suspect it.
25	.54	.01	.30	Americans are getting soft; most people need stricter discipline and the will to defend their interests.
27	.47	.15	.01	Most people don't realize how much our lives are controlled by plots hatched in secret by others.
48	.40	.35	.31	What youth needs most is strict discipline, rugged determination, and the will to fight for family and nation.
44	.38	.08	.35	If people would talk less and work more, everybody would be better off.
50	.22	.18	.01	Wars and social troubles may someday be ended by an earthquake or flood that will destroy the whole world.

Factor I

No items are pure measures of Factor I, i.e., have zero or close to zero factor loadings on the other two factors. Items 24 and 49, though, have distinctly high loadings on this factor and may be used as referents. They both refer to submission to authority figures or symbols of the in-group, e.g., the flag or parents. Item 29 also connotes submission to authority while 52 and 40 suggest a close identification with an in-group. Item 52 expresses over-idealization of the in-group whereas Item 40 emphasizes honor and protection of this honor. These items all concern attitudes toward the in-group and authority symbols of that group. Item 35, on the other hand, expresses an attitude toward an out-group. It is one of suspiciousness which would be expected in light of

TABLE 43

RANK ORDER OF ITEM VARIABLES WITH HIGHEST FACTOR LOADINGS
ON FACTOR III'

Item No.	III'	Loadings I''	II'''	Stem
45	.53	.05	.14	Every person should have complete faith in some supernatural power whose decisions he obeys without question.
23	.48	.21	.33	People without a deep and unquestionable faith in Almighty God should not be trusted in public office.
53	.46	.08	.31	Books and movies ought not to deal so much with the unpleasant and seamy side of life; they ought to concentrate on themes that are entertaining or uplifting.
55	.40	.01	.17	Some leisure is necessary, but it is good hard work that makes life interesting and worthwhile.

current theories of ethnocentrism and authoritarianism. Since these items all display different aspects of submission to authority, this appears to be the common factor. The factor was named "submission to authority symbols," since all of the attitudes were in reference to some particular symbol of authority. Corollaries of this submission to authority then are identification with an in-group and overidealization and protection of the authorities of this group. The group identifications may extend from the family through to the national level.

Factor II

Items 21 and 51 are relatively pure measures of Factor II. The first emphasizes force and aggression in preserving the clichéd "American way of life," while the second contains a reference to suspicion of others, particularly in the area of sex. Item 27, also a relatively pure measure of this factor, connotes a suspiciousness or fear of being controlled and plotted against from those outside. Item 50 may be classified as having a suspicious element; the referent here is the supernatural. Items 25 and 48, in support of Item 21, are again related to the aggressive defense of family and nation. Two common but related factors are contained in the semantic content of these items; suspiciousness and aggression. It could be inferred that the suspicious orientation toward the outside world necessitates aggressive control and defense. The factor was labelled "suspiciousness and aggression."

Factor III

Items 45 and 23 are similar in their reference to religious values. The factor has been labeled "conventional religious morality" to distinguish it from the religious morality which has been more interiorized. "Conventional" has also been included because the statements are clichéd and designed to tap conventionality. Item 53 with its statement of avoiding "the unpleasant and seamy side of life" and concentrating "on themes that are entertaining or uplifting" can also be viewed as reflecting one element of "conventional" religiosity, the element of "God's in his heaven all's right with the world" (Robert Browning—*Pippa Passes*). Item 55 represents an orientation at the other end of the continuum by expounding hard work which makes life "interesting and worthwhile." This is almost a direct statement of one of the economic virtues that waste of time is the "first and in principle the deadliest of sins" (Weber [1930], p. 157). These economic virtues were concomitant to the rise of Protestant groups. Item 45, used as the main referent in this classification, was considered by its authors (Adorno *et al.*, 1950) to be a measure of "authoritarian submission." However, Christie and Garcia (1951) report that when a cluster analysis was done on their more conservative Southern sample, a cluster denoting "religious morality" was found and Item 58 was located in this cluster. This factor analysis likewise indicates that these attitude statements, generally labelled authoritarian, have one component which measures a religious orientation. Validation of this factor should be done by further factor analyses of these few items with others which are written specifically to measure "conventional religious morality."

Since each factor has been named according to the major semantic referent of the items with the highest loading on it, it is instructive to analyze those items classified under each factor but having loadings on the other factors to determine how well this

196

classification holds up. In other words, the item's lower loadings on the other factors indicate that it additionally measures something common to these. The question is whether there is a reference in the item which is consistent with the classification of the factors. Only those items with a loading of .30 or higher on another factor will be considered since this is regarded as a moderate loading.

Items 24, 35, 40, and 54, classified under the factor of "submission to authority symbols," also have large enough loadings on the factor of "suspicion and aggression" to deserve mention (Table 41). Item 24 also has a loading of .29 on this second factor. For both this item and Item 49, the element common to the suspicion and aggression factor would seem to be the disdain or hostility denoted by the introductory statement: "There is hardly anything lower. . . ." The relationship of the other three items to the second factor is more clear-cut than this. Both 35 and 54 convey a strong element of distrust and suspiciousness of others. Item 35 states: "It's a mistake to trust any nation" and Item 54 questions the motives of human beings. In fact, Item 54 has nearly as high loadings on Factor II as it has on Factor I, .31 and .35, respectively. Item 40, on the other hand, reflects the aggressive component common to Factor II. This is inferred from the idea expressed of punishing any insult to honor. Items 29, 52 and 46 have additional moderate loadings on Factor III, "conventional religious morality," although their highest loading is on Factor I. Both items 29 and 52 are expressions of respect, love, etc. of parents or relatives. This would explain their additional relationship to Factor III since these attitudes toward parents are found in most religious teachings. Item 46 mentions both aspects of the "conventional religious morality" mentioned previously—keeping busy and the cheerful pleasant side of life.

Four items, classified by their highest loadings on the "suspiciousness and aggression" factor, have moderate loadings on the other factors. Item 48 has loadings of .35 and .31 respectively on Factor I and Factor III. This is a complex item which contains elements of all the factors isolated. The protection of the family and nation seems to relate it to the "submission to authority symbols" factor while the strict discipline element relates it to the "conventional religious morality" factor. Item 25 has a similar connotation of strict discipline and is also related to the "conventional religious morality" factor with a loading of .30. Although Item 44 has been classified under Factor II, it has almost an equally high loading on the third factor. Again, the component of hard work may be inferred to account for the observed relationship.

Items 23 and 53 have been classified under the "conventional religious morality" factor, but they have loadings of moderate size on Factor II. Item 23 has an element of the distrust previously commented on. In this case there is distrust of anyone in control who is not subjected to the same authority. The relationship of Item 53 to the "suspiciousness and aggression" is not as clear-cut, although the content "unpleasant and seamy side of life" may be interpreted as being related to suspiciousness.

The discussion has been devoted to the interpretation of the factors as classification systems. The purpose has been to analyze the verbal content and the actual factor loadings to ascertain the common element running through each factor. The separate attitude elements discerned were "submission to authority symbols," "suspiciousness and aggression," and "conventional religious morality." In addition, items with complex loadings have been analyzed to determine if their verbal content is explainable by the factor classifications set up. This procedure, it should be pointed out, is not intended as a validation of either the factor or the classification system but as a means of further understanding the factor and the item variables or, in other words, to make psychological sense.

Comparisons with Previous Research

Most comparisons of the findings of this study with previous studies of the organization of attitudes of similar ideological content must be primarily suggestive since items, techniques, and samples have differed markedly.

In comparison with the original work in *The Authoritarian Personality* the nine variables that they hypothesized are not isolated. However, conclusions should be cautious as not as many items were used as were in their final scale. It is possible that factor analysis with additional items might unfold other dimensions. The factor that is here labeled "submission to authority symbols," however, seems closely related to their hypothesized "authoritarian submission" dimension as indicated by their definition:

Authoritarian submission was conceived as a very general attitude that would be evoked in relation to a variety of authority figures—parents, older people, leaders, supernatural power, and so forth (Adorno *et al.* [1950], p. 231).

This dimension they interpret (p. 232) as "a way of handling ambivalent feelings toward authority figures: Underlying hostile and rebellious impulses, held in check by fear, lead the subject to overdo in the direction of respect, obedience, gratitude and the like."

Factor II labeled here as "suspiciousness and aggression" seems most closely related in content to the "authoritarian aggression," "destructiveness and cynicism," "projectivity," and "power and toughness" dimensions. Even in their descriptions these dimensions appear to be highly related with many of the same items written to tap two or more dimensions, e.g., "an insult to our honor should always be punished" is listed under both authoritarian aggression and power and toughness. Again with more items a factor analysis might isolate other dimensions. It seems more probable that although there might be some distinct traits which distinguish among these hypothesized dimensions, they are so functionally related that they appear together as one empirical factor. This explanation has some verification from their own definitions of these dimensions. For example, authoritarian aggression is elaborated as follows:

The individual forced to give up basic pleasures and to live under a system of rigid restraints is likely not only to seek an object upon which he can "take it out" but also to be particularly annoyed at the idea that another person is "getting away with something" . . . the present variable represents the sadistic component of authoritarianism (Adorno *et al.* [1950], p. 232).

They (p. 239) also write with respect to items written to tap destructiveness and cynicism:

Thus, some items offered justifications for aggression and were formulated in such a way that strong agreement would indicate that the subject needed only slight justification in order to be ready for all out aggression. Other items dealt with contempt for mankind, the theory being that here the hostility is so generalized, so free of direction against any particular object that the individual need not feel accountable for it.

As mentioned previously the factor which we have labeled "conventional religious morality" was not hypothesized as a separate dimension. The components which have been here suggested as a part of this dimension suggest that it is most closely related to the dimensions of conventionalism, authoritarian submission, and superstition which were originally suggested by the California group.

As previously mentioned, Stagner's (1942) factor analytic study of fascist attitudes also isolated three factors. These, however, do not seem closely related to the patterns here except for the "aggressively nationalistic pattern." This may be due to the different types of items used. However, these results do substantiate his conclusion that "fascist attitudes are an integration of three or more separable uncorrelated factors which could exist apart from their combination in this form."

Eysenck (1954) equates "authoritarianism" as measured by the F Scale with a conservative ideology and a "tough-minded" or extraverted personality type. Although he has demonstrated that tough-mindedness and authoritarianism are highly related, perusal of the items which he uses to define this quadrant indicate that this ideological-personality combination is more related to the factor that has been isolated in this study as "suspiciousness and aggression." Following are his items to measure the tough-minded conservative quadrant (pp. 277–79):

9. The so-called underdog deserves little sympathy or help from successful people.
10. Crimes of violence should be punished by flogging.
28. Compulsory military training in peacetime is essential for the survival of this country.
38. European refugees should be left to fend for themselves.
41. It is just as well that the struggle of life tends to weed out those who cannot stand the pace.

43. Nowadays, more and more people are prying into matters which do not concern them.
58. The maintenance of internal order within the nation is more important than ensuring that there is complete freedom for all.

THEORETICAL AND METHODOLOGICAL IMPLICATIONS
FOR FURTHER RESEARCH

It has been suggested that the third level of factor interpretation is to infer the underlying dynamics of the observed consistency of response. In other words the psychological or sociological processes which might account for the constellations of attitude items are inferred. However, the assumption that one can deduce the content of psychological processes from the content of attitude items is hardly justified. Naming the factors has necessitated attaching labels on the basis of the similarity of content of the items. Whether the "submission to authority" factor is a reflection of psychological mechanisms of the individual responding is a question which can only be answered by continued experimentation.

Validation of the factor as evidence of a unity which represents the attitudes and psychological mechanisms of the individual responding necessitates several steps. The problem of this research was to isolate the dimensions of anti-democratic attitudes. We found that the responses to the items which represented these attitudes are so related that the anti-democratic attitudes under observation can be described in three dimensions. Before inferences can be made concerning the psychological processes which determine these dimensions it is necessary to establish that they represent functional unities and are not just an artifact of the particular sample, items, sampling, or measurement errors. This represents the basic question of factor invariance and there are several methods by which it can be answered.

The first is to repeat this experiment on a different sample, preferably one from a different population. If the same factor analysis was done on the large universities in the original sample of this opinion poll and the same dimensions could be isolated, it would serve as confirmation that three dimensions of "submission to authority symbols," "suspiciousness and aggression," and "conventional religious morality" do represent the structure of anti-democratic attitudes.

Even more confirmation of this fact could be derived by repeating this experiment on a sample from a population which differed markedly from this one on such variables as age, education, and geographical location.

Another method of validating the dimensions would be to add new items to any subsequent factor analyses. These items would be written explicitly to measure one of the dimensions. For example, if items were written to measure specifically a factor of "conventional religious morality," they should have high loadings on this factor when subjected to future analysis. Such items might be derived from conventional religious clichés. Also, personality measures might be included in the analysis with the item variables. If the dimension of "submission to authority symbols" and "suspiciousness and aggression" are reflections of personality on social attitudes, objective measures of submissiveness or aggressiveness and paranoia should have high loadings on these respective factors.

Cattell ([1952], p. 337) writes that the process of encountering similar factors in successive researches is essential to the denotative defining of a given factor. When the factor can be discovered in several contexts and in matrices with diverse variables, the meaning of the factor becomes fixed "because one knows definitely where to find it and in what company." On the other hand, one may seek to define connotatively the factor or assign attributes to its essential nature. This process of definition and validation must proceed on the bases of hypotheses based either on empirical or logical constructs. He (Cattell [1952], p. 337–38) cites the following example of this procedure:

One might observe that all the variables highly loaded in a certain factor in sociological data involve aggressive social responses, and call it a factor of social aggressiveness. On the other hand, a person might harbor a theory that one of the most powerful factors in this region is economic deprivation, and he may choose to interpret all these loaded variables as consequences of economic deprivation although he cannot see a single sign of economic deprivation in the empirically given variables.

This, it may be noted, is the same process as inferring the reasons for the observed relationships. Examples of defining the factors as logical constructs would be as follows. An historical analysis such as Fromm's would interpret the "submission to authority symbols" and "suspiciousness and aggression" factors as contrasting consequences of a reaction to a freedom from external authority with which modern man was unable to cope. The "conventional religious morality" factor would be a further reflection of characterological changes which resulted from economic and social changes and were intensified by religious doctrines. The product of these three forces in terms of character qualities were "compulsion to work, passion for thrift, the readiness to make one's life a tool for the purposes of an extra-personal power, asceticism, and a compulsive sense of duty" (Fromm, [1941], p. 102). With subsequent social and economic changes in the twentieth century, these same qualities would be reinforced by the process of alienation. "Submission to authority symbols" would be a reflection of modern man's need to identify with an external power of group, while "suspiciousness and agression" would be a reflection of the characteristic human relationships of modern man. "Conventional religious morality" would be a reflection of man's inability to cope with the problems of existence. Because of this inability he accepts a clichéd answer and further resolves it through feverish activity.

At the individual cognitive level, the constellations of responses would be reflections of the organization of constructs by which the individual interprets his social environment in authority relationships, relations with other human beings, and problems of existence. There is now a considerable body of theory and research which indicates that attitudes as cognitive constructs do influence what and how an individual perceives his environment (Bruner and Postman, 1949, Postman *et al.*, 1948).

Possession of these constructs could be interpreted psychodynamically as the results of a developmental process. Acceptance of items measuring the "submission to authority symbols" factor is the product of a learned response to coercive parental figures which has been generalized to all other figures or symbols of authority. Submissiveness and overidealization are constructs developed to cope with the ambivalent, hostile, repressed feelings concerning the parents. The generalization to other authority symbols is reinforced by the fact that many of these attitudes are generally rewarded in the culture.

The threat orientation of "suspiciousness and aggression" construct is accepted as a projection of the individual's own hostile and aggressive tendencies. Aggressiveness is seen as an early response to restriction by the parents. However, the individual was unable to express hostility because of the dependency upon the parents so that the hostile attitudes are displaced and projected onto others. Aggressive attitudes are conceptualized then as a reaction to fear of illicit tendencies within the self and instead projected onto conventional targets or generalized to encompass humanity.

Items of the "conventional religious morality" factor are accepted as attitudes condoned and rewarded in the culture.

The validity of the empirical or logical construct, however, depends upon its usefulness for predicting further relationships. Testing hypotheses concerning the factor is thus another means of determining whether the factor does represent a functional unity. The above theoretical levels are probably all of some validity in this regard. Working at the group level, however, any theoretical explanations and consequent hypotheses must be stated in such a manner that they are testable with the data available.

Before stating hypotheses which might be tested concerning the three isolated dimensions of this study, it would be necessary to consider the methodological problem of constructing instruments with which to measure the predicted relationships. This was one of the initial considerations of the factor analysis problem. On the basis of the factor loadings of this research, multiple regression weights of each item on each factor have been computed for the 20 items on each factor. The estimated reliabilities for the factor scales are .71, .68, and .61 for Factors I, II and III, respectively. These are sufficiently high reliabilities for group purposes. This will provide separate measures of the isolated dimensions of anti-democratic attitudes which should be more precise than one score of authoritarianism.

The problem of description, measurement, validation, and prediction of the dimensions of anti-democratic attitudes were originally conceptualized with reference to the analysis of the data for the *Purdue Opinion Poll of Democratic-Authoritarian Attitudes of Students in Higher Education.* Therefore, the previously stated problem of deriving testable theoretical explanations and hypotheses must be considered within this frame of reference.

Deriving hypotheses in terms of group membership and roles seems the best procedure. This is particularly true if one makes the assumption that the organization of attitudes among group members may be related to at least two groups of factors: (1) the selective ones affecting initial entry into and continuing membership in the group, and (2) the dynamics of group functioning which lead to ideological conformity among its members. Groups would be defined as any organization with which the individual identifies through membership. The functional relationship between group membership and social attitudes is particularly well expressed by Murphy *et al.,* (1937) as a conclusion to *Experimental Social Psychology:*

Interrelated attitudes are rarely individual affairs, but are largely borrowed from groups to which we owe strongest allegiance. Individual variations such as age, sex, and various personality characteristics have much to do with the nature of the groups with which one becomes affiliated, and with the degree of permanence of such affiliations. Individual experiences, whether of accidental or occasional nature, on the other hand, or those occasioned by family membership or residential community, on the other, are also instrumental in determining group membership. This is by no means to deny the importance of purely psychological factors. But such experimental evidence as is available has led us to the conclusion that the latter are effective largely through their power to select this rather than that group affiliation, to react to it with greater or less intensity, and, to some extent perhaps to modify it. The social psychology of attitudes is the sociology of attitudes illuminated by an understanding of the personality factors which determine individual susceptibility to group influences.

Also relevant to the relationship between group membership and anti-democratic attitudes is the concomitant relationship between prejudice and the dimensions of authoritarianism which ensues from group membership variables. First, it would be desirable to ascertain the degree of general relationship between prejudice and each dimension or factor. The items were originally written to be more subtle measures of the attitudes related to discrimination toward minority groups. Having isolated dimensions of these attitudes means that more precise relationships may be uncovered. For example, it could be hypothesized that the dimension of "suspiciousness and aggression" defined and measured by the factor score would be more closely related to advocacy of discrimination against minority groups than "submission to authority" or "conventional religious morality." Once the relationships had been analyzed on a general level further elaboration could be done in terms of observing the covariation of each factor with prejudice across different groups.

The selective and group conformity factors of group membership would appear to be logical assumptions about an individual's choice of college. If this and the stated nature of the attitude dimensions are assumed, it would be expected that there would be significant differences among colleges on the three factors of this analysis. For example, it might be predicted that Roman Catholic colleges would be more accepting of the attitude statements measuring submission to authority symbols than colleges of a more secular liberal nature, while colleges of a more secular nature would be more accepting of the attitude items measuring "suspiciousness and aggression." Colleges at which a religious orientation is stressed should be more accepting of the "conventional religious morality" factor than colleges of a predominantly secular nature. Essentially the same hypotheses could be stated concerning the relationship between church membership and this factor.

Relationships between church attendance and religious intensity and "submission to authority" symbols and "suspiciousness and aggression" factors might be more explicitly predicted using the attitude factors as the dependent variables. If it may be assumed that frequent church attendance and a feeling of intensity about religion reflects an acceptance of religious authority and this acceptance is generalized to all authority symbols, then an individual with these characteristics should score

206

higher on a scale measuring "submission to authority symbols." The "suspiciousness and aggression" factor as the dependent variable would be accepted less at either end of the continuum of religious intensity and church attendance. Prejudice would be predicted to be negatively related to "suspiciousness and aggression" at these two extreme ends.

The rationale for these hypothesized relationships is that the group who attend church infrequently and do not feel intensely about their religion will not be as threatened or suspicious of other groups and people. This was suggested in Stouffer's *Communism, Conformity and Civil Liberties* (1955). People who did not frequently attend church were more tolerant of nonconformists than those who attended quite frequently. This breakdown was only in terms of whether the people had attended church within the last month, so that we might extend this to state that those who attend as frequently as eight to ten times a month may be people who have assimilated humanistic Christian ethics to the extent that aggressive actions would be incompatible with their beliefs. This rationale would also account for the predicted relationship between prejudice and "suspiciousness and aggression" as a function of frequent church attendance.

Occupation, or for a college sample, choice of a major field of interest, may be considered as a group variable inasmuch as persons electing a specific area of study are usually found to have a characteristic pattern of interests, attitudes and values. There are numerous studies in the literature which indicate that students in major fields of interest may be differentiated according to interests and values tests (Duffy, 1940; Duffy, Crissis, 1940; Sarbin and Berdia, 1940; Todd, 1941). It might be predicted, for example, that those who are enrolled in a business curriculum in which their future success will depend on their aggressiveness and ability to manipulate people and abstract symbols will be more accepting of the "suspiciousness and aggression" factor. Physical education majors would also be predicted to be higher on this factor. On the other hand those whose training is directed toward working with and understanding people, such as social science majors, would be expected to be less accepting of the items measuring this factor. Those vocations which depend primarily on conformity to middle-class values and mores might be expected to be higher on the "submission to authority symbols" factor. Education majors, for example, might be found in this group.

If the factors of "submission to authority symbols," "suspiciousness and aggression," and "conventional religious morality" are in reality functional representations of attitude constellations, they should discriminate between men and women in light of conventional sex roles. In the American culture it is commonly assumed that women should play a submissive role. Therefore, we would predict that women would score significantly higher on the "submission to authority symbols" factor scale than men, while men who are expected to assume an aggressive role should score higher on "suspiciousness and aggression" factor. In addition, part of the females' role in American culture is to transmit religious teachings. This seems apparent in national surveys in which it is found that women particularly among Protestant groups attend church more frequently than men (Stouffer, 1955). Therefore, it would be predicted that the "conventional religious morality" factor would also discriminate between men and women.

SUMMARY AND CONCLUSIONS

A factor analysis of 20 authoritarian and anti-democratic item statements, as empirically defined by previous research, was computed to determine the number of dimensions necessary to describe the structure and organization of these attitudes. The sample of items and respondents were taken from a *Purdue Opinion Panel of Democratic-Authoritarian Attitudes of Students in Higher Education* conducted among 23 Indiana colleges and universities in the fall of 1954. The specific sample of respondents for this study was drawn from a population of 15 small accredited and unaccredited colleges. The sample was representative of this population with respect to the proportion drawn from each school and the variables of sex and age within each school.

Item intercorrelations were estimated by tetrachloric correlation coefficients. From the consequent 20 × 20 correlation matrix, three factors which accounted for 81% of the original estimated common variance were extracted by the "method of principal components." These three factors were rotated to a positive manifold and factor loadings were computed. On the basis of the factor loadings and semantic content of the item variables the dimensions were connotatively defined as "submission to authority symbols," "suspiciousness and aggression," and "conventional religious morality."

Isolation of three dimensions indicates that the assumption of unidimensionality on which the scale methodology on anti-democratic attitudes has been based to date is not warranted.

It was suggested that inferences concerning the psychological and sociological processes which determine the observed dimensions of relationships must be based on verification of the factors as functional unities. These suggestions included replication of the analysis on samples from different populations and with new item variables added. Other methods of determining the psychological processes reflected in the relationships would be based on the construction of scales in which the items would be weighted in accordance with their factor loadings. If predictions based on hypotheses concerning the nature of these dimensions and their relationship to other group variables and attitude measures of prejudice could be confirmed with these scales, this would constitute further verification for the functional unity of the observed relationships.

NOTES

1. This order was suggested to the writer by Allport in *Nature of Prejudice* (1954). However, the interpretation of the categories is somewhat different than that which he gives.

2. Since ethnocentrism was a central concept in formulating anti-democratic attitude statements, studies which have used this measure will also be included in the discussion.

3. A following section "Methodological Implications of the Organization of Anti-Democratic Attitudes," chiefly of interest to the research specialist, has been omitted here to save space. (H. H. R.)

IX ANTI-DEMOCRATIC ATTITUDES IN MIDWEST UNIVERSITY

Elmer L. Struening

PROCEDURE AND METHODOLOGY

PURPOSE

The purpose of this study is to describe, explain, and predict the behavior of certain observed phenomena. The focus is on selected social attitudes of the faculty members of a large midwestern university. In particular, we are interested in describing the various facets of authoritarianism and an important correlate, prejudice, as they are possessed by this population. We wish to explain the functional role of the acceptance of these attitudes as individuals adapt to their society. The third purpose is to predict relationships between the degree of attitude acceptance and certain demographic and social-psychological variables. Out of this process should result suggestions for additional research to further clarify the problem under consideration.

PROBLEM

The problem of this study is to isolate the dimensions of authoritarian and prejudiced attitudes and to predict, from a theoretical framework, their distribution and covariation across selected divisions of a university faculty population. The following classification variables provide the divisions of the population: age, rank in university, level of education, teaching or research area, frequency of church attendance, church denomination, and intensity of feeling about religious beliefs and practices.

The order of presentation will be as follows:

1. The refinement of an instrument suitable for measuring authoritarian attitudes of a university faculty population.

2. The development of an instrument to measure prejudiced attitudes.

3. The development of a theoretical framework based on an analysis of the theories of Fromm (1941, 1947, 1955), Horney (1945, 1937), May (1950), Merton (1949) and those studies employing the theory and scales of *The Authoritarian Personality* (Adorno *et al.*, 1950).

4. From the above theoretical frame, hypotheses will be deduced and tested.

University faculty populations are seldom studied, even though the importance of their influence on the basic values of our culture is obvious. Consequently, other empirical studies which may aid prediction in our case are rare.

THE POPULATION

The universe sampled for this research is composed of the staff members of a large Midwestern university, hereafter known as Midwest University. Staff members are defined as full-time members of the various departmental staffs; all graduate students employed by the university on a part-time basis (either in a teaching or research capacity or as assistants to instructor); and full-time employees serving in an administrative or service capacity. The latter category includes the professional members of the following staffs: Student Health Service, Residence Halls for Men and Women, Division of Technical Extension, Division of Adult Education, Student Memorial Union, and Physical Plant.

A questionnaire entitled *"The Purdue Opinion Panel,* a Survey of Public Opinion" (see Appendix) was sent to 1,862 staff members meeting the standards outlined above. A mimeographed letter, signed by the president of Midwest University, included the following paragraph:

By filling out and returning the enclosed questionnaire you will be making an important contribution. Since no signature is requested, the names of all participants will remain anonymous. Your cooperation in this matter is very much appreciated.

Of the 1,862 questionnaires sent, 965 (52%) were returned by campus mail. The percentage return is a conservative estimate because the mailing list included staff members who were on leave of absence or had left the university. However, it was the only available list of faculty members and proved more accurate than the staff directory. Of the 965 questionnaires returned, 911 (94% of the received sample) contained enough responses to be used in this study. The number of unusable questionnaires did not, on investigation, appear to be related to the departmental membership of the participant but were randomly distributed across departments.

To gain some evidence concerning the representativeness of the sample, the parent population and the final usable sample were stratified by department and rank in the university. Percentages for all cells formed by this two-way classification were computed by dividing each cell frequency by the number of people in the population from which the cell was formed. The results are presented in Table 44. For example, the upper value in the engineering-by-professor cell is the percentage of the parent population who are full professors in engineering; the second value in the same cell is the percentage of full professors in engineering in the sample. Marginal totals to the right of Table 44 contrast the percentage of engineers in the parent population with the percentage of engineers in the sample; marginal totals at the bottom of the table contrast the percentage of professors in the parent population with the percentage of professors in the sample. Inspection of the total percentages across departments reveal, in the main, slight variation between parent and sample population percentages.

Seven hundred and seventy-three respondents make up the sample included in Table 44. The other 138 were not included for the following reasons: (a) the classification variables of rank in the university and departmental membership were omitted; (b) a number of the respondents are not members of an academic department and are not classified as to rank; (c) the rank of the respondent did not fit into the classification system of Table 44. For example, several departments employ technicians. Although they have degrees in a particular area of specialization, they do not carry academic rank in the university. Questionnaires with omissions were retained in the final sample for the purpose of relating such omissions to the attitudes being studied.

TABLE 44

CHARACTERISTICS OF THE PARENT AND SAMPLE POPULATIONS

Classified by Department and Rank

	Prof.	Assoc. Prof.	Assist. Prof.	Instr.	Grad. Student	Total
Engr.	3.49	3.49	2.95	7.23	6.69	23.85
	3.88	3.75	3.10	6.08	6.99	23.80
Agri.	2.59	3.13	2.65	3.92	6.51	18.79
	2.20	2.85	3.49	4.01	5.95	18.50
Home Econ.	.48	.30	.66	.60	.72	2.77
	.39		.90	.39	.65	2.33
Chem.	.54	.18	.78	.66	11.02	13.19
	1.03	.13	1.16	.90	8.41	11.64
Physics	.54	.60	.18	.90	3.67	5.90
	.52	.52	.39	.26	3.62	5.30
Math.	.48	.42	.96	.90	2.95	5.72
	.52	.90	.78	.52	2.72	5.43
Biology	.48	.48	.18	.36	2.83	4.34
	1.29	.78	.90	.65	3.23	6.86
Pharmacy	.42	.06	.18	.12	1.99	2.77
	.39		.39	.26	1.81	2.85
Hist., Govt.	.42	.66	.30	.24		1.63
Economics	.52	.78	.52	.13	.13	2.07
English	.66	.72	.92	2.05	.12	4.52
	.39	1.03	1.16	1.29		3.88
Mod. Lang.	.18	.12	.18	.60		1.08
	.13	.13	.26	.39		.90
Speech	.24	.18	.18	.54	1.93	3.07
	.13	.39	.39	.26	1.81	2.97
Education	.54	.72	.30	.36	.36	2.29
	.39	1.03	.39	.52	.26	2.59
Psychology &	.30	.66	.42	.36	3.01	4.76
Sociology	.52	.65	.26	.39	4.66	6.47
Mili. Sci.		.48	.84	1.45		2.77
	.26	.52	.52	.26		1.55
Phy. Educ.	.12	.36	.78	1.20	.06	2.53
	.26	.26	.78	1.29	.26	2.85
Total	11.51	12.59	12.53	21.51	41.87	100.01
	12.81	13.71	15.39	17.59	40.49	99.99

213

THE REFINEMENT OF AN INSTRUMENT
FOR MEASURING AUTHORITARIAN ATTITUDES

THE ORIGINAL F SCALE

The purpose of this section is to construct a satisfactory instrument for estimating authoritarian attitudes of a university faculty population.

Two primary purposes guided the authors of *The Authoritarian Personality* in their construction of the F Scale:

1. It was to provide a covert measure of prejudice without mentioning minority groups, or current political-economic groups.
2. To validate the scale by means of later clinical studies.

The authors then proceeded, primarily on the basis of material from interviews, the Thematic Apperception Test, and other studies involving ideological determinants, to formulate hypotheses which would link overt ethnocentric ideology to underlying personality trends. They postulated that certain personality trends would predispose the individual, given the proper social climate, toward the acceptance of ethnocentric attitudes.

The authors derived and defined a number of variables, which, operationally defined by the F Scale items, would estimate the above mentioned personality trends. In their words:

Each [variable] was regarded as a more or less central trend in the person which, in accordance with some dynamic process, expressed itself on the surface in ethnocentrism as well as in diverse psychologically related opinions and attitudes. These variables are listed below together with a brief definition of each.

a. Conventionalism. Rigid adherence to conventional, middle-class values.
b. Authoritarian submission. Submissive, uncritical attitude toward idealized moral authorities of the in-group.
c. Authoritarian aggression. Tendency to be on the lookout for, and to condemn, reject, and punish people who violate conventional values.
d. Anti-intraception. Opposition to the subjective, the imaginative, the tenderminded.
e. Superstition and stereotypy. The belief in mystical determinants

214

of the individual's fate; the disposition to think in rigid categories.

f. Power and "toughness." Preoccupation with the dominance-submission, strong-weak, leader-follower dimension; identification with power figures; overemphasis upon the conventionalized attributes of the ego; exaggerated assertion of strength and toughness.

g. Destructiveness and cynicism. Generalized hostility, vilification of the human.

h. Projectivity. The disposition to believe that wild and dangerous things go on in the world; the projection outwards of unconscious emotional impulses.

i. Sex. Exaggerated concern with sexual "goings on."

These variables were thought of as going together to form a single syndrome, a more or less enduring structure in the person that renders him receptive to anti-democratic propaganda. One might say, therefore, that the F Scale attempts to measure the potentially anti-democratic personality. This does not imply that all the features of this personality pattern are touched upon in the scale, but only that the scale embraces a fair sample of the ways in which this pattern characteristically expresses itself (Adorno *et al.* [1950], p. 228).

Successive forms of the F Scale, revised on the basis of item analysis, resulted in a final 30-item form (number 40–45) with a mean reliability coefficient (based on split-half correlation) of .90. Reliability coefficients ranged from .81 to .97 over 14 groups.

To determine the inter-item relations of Form 40–45, it was administered to 517 women in an elementary Psychology class at the University of California. An item-by-item correlation matrix was computed; the average of the 435 coefficients was .13, the range $-.05$ to .44. Each item was correlated with the remainder of the scale, resulting in a mean r of .33 and a range .15 to .52. The authors concluded: "Despite the scale's relative lack of surface homogeneity, however, we are justified in speaking of an F Pattern or syndrome, for the items do 'hang together' in the sense that each is significantly correlated with the scale as a whole."

The above mentioned matrix was subjected to factor analysis by Melvin reported in Eysenck (1954). He found that a very strong general factor ran through all of the items, thus confirming the hypothesis of Adorno *et al.* that the F Scale is essentially unidimensional, although the dimension is of a complex and involved nature. The mean of correlations between the F and E (Ethnocentrism) Scales was roughly .75 over 17 groups with a total N of 1570. Correlation of the F Syndrome with political-economic conservatism was somewhat lower, the average r for forms 40–45 with the Political Economic Conservatism Scale being .57.

In summary, it appears that Adorno *et al.* have constructed a highly reliable, essentially unidimensional scale (at least on college women) which is quite highly related to acceptance of ethnocentric attitudes (measured by the E Scale) and moderately related to political-economic conservatism.

THE F' SCALE

To distinguish the scale used in this study from the various forms of the F presented in *The Authoritarian Personality*, it will be called the F' Scale. The F' Scale consists of 18 items, 13 of which were selected from the various forms (78, 60, and 40–45) of the F Scale. The remaining five items were constructed by the editors of Poll 33 of the *Purdue Opinion Panel*. Except for Item 35 (see Table 46) they are almost identical to the original F Scale items. Items were selected on the following basis: (a) They must not antagonize the respondents; for this reason some of the extremely ambiguous items were omitted, (b) They must break the responding population into two reasonably equal groups in terms of agree-disagree responses; for this reason extremely oversimplified and superstitious items were excluded.

Using the above standards, the 18 items listed by number in Table 46 were selected to form the F' Scale. One original F Scale item included in the questionnaire did not meet standard (b) above and therefore was excluded from statistical analysis.

The Factor Analyses of the F' Scale. While Melvin's (reported in Eysenck (1954) factor analysis of form 40–45 on a college women population resulted in a unidimensional scale, we could not assume that similar results would occur on a university faculty population using a somewhat different set of items. Therefore an inter-item correlation matrix was computed. In view of the large N of 911, tetrachloric correlation coefficients were accepted as accurate enough approximations of the product mo-

TABLE 45

CORRELATION MATRIX OF EIGHTEEN F′ SCALE ITEMS *

(N = 911)

Item No.	36	37	38	40	42	48	53	57	58	59	60	61	62	64	65	66	67	68
36	*55* †	60	30	37	42	33	45	34	59	40	30	47	55	24	34	41	20	31
37	60	*67*	37	33	62	40	55	37	44	21	27	61	73	30	43	37	18	43
38	30	37	*38*	40	42	30	33	40	38	20	27	50	36	30	32	35	30	40
40	37	33	40	*35*	30	33	27	30	30	19	24	40	31	40	20	24	35	27
42	42	62	42	30	*61*	40	55	47	44	25	44	70	56	35	41	38	29	42
48	33	40	30	33	40	*33*	40	37	21	14	28	38	40	28	38	20	17	21
53	45	55	33	27	55	40	*49*	38	46	34	36	55	57	27	42	40	22	28
57	34	37	40	30	47	37	38	*46*	40	40	30	40	57	33	30	27	23	46
58	59	44	38	30	44	21	46	40	*49*	28	37	25	48	11	39	42	23	32
59	40	21	20	19	25	14	34	40	28	*28*	33	30	33	20	38	31	21	21
60	30	27	27	24	44	28	36	30	37	33	*33*	37	34	41	20	30	22	30
61	47	61	50	40	70	38	55	40	25	30	37	*68*	65	40	37	36	40	43
62	55	73	36	31	56	40	57	57	48	33	34	65	*71*	36	57	43	28	50
64	24	30	30	40	35	28	27	33	11	20	41	40	36	*36*	37	26	37	15
65	34	43	32	20	41	38	42	30	39	38	20	37	57	37	*43*	31	19	30
66	41	37	35	24	38	20	40	27	42	31	30	36	43	26	31	*35*	34	36
67	20	18	30	35	29	17	22	23	23	21	22	40	28	37	19	34	*29*	19
68	31	43	40	27	42	21	28	46	32	21	30	43	50	15	30	36	19	*41*

* Decimal points omitted

† The italicized diagonal values are the multiple r² communality estimates for the respective items.

ment correlation coefficients. They are shown in Table 46. Inspection of this table indicates all correlation coefficients are positive, ranging from .11 to .73, with a mean coefficient of .36.

The first three factors accounted for 74.9% of the common variance. Factor I accounted for 63.6% of the common variance, while Factors II and III accounted for 6.4% and 4.9% respectively. Factor I in this unrotated solution, may be viewed as a general factor. That is, all items are strongly related to Factor I and the correlation matrix may be viewed as unifactorial with the items forming essentially one dimension. Table 46 presents the eighteen F' Scale items rank ordered according to their factor loadings on Factor I. A factor loading is the correlation between an item and a factor. After rotation, Factors I', II' and III' accounted for 22.4%, 20.5%, and 30.7% of the common variance respectively.

DISCUSSION OF THE FACTORS

The Unrotated General Factor: FG. As previously discussed, the meaning of a factor is determined by the meaning of those item variables most highly related to it. In a one-factor solution the magnitude of the loadings of the items on that factor indicate the correlation (degree of relationship) between the items and the factor. Table 46 gives the items in rank order of their loadings on unrotated Factor I, the general factor symbolized by FG. Thus, the items, in the order presented, are decreasingly important in defining the meaning of FG.

Items 48 and 49, with loadings of .80 on FG, fit into the "power and toughness" and "authoritarian aggression" categories hypothesized by Adorno *et al.* as important characteristics of authoritarianism. Item 48 is a prescription for the younger generation (and probably anyone agreeing with this item) to enable them to get along better in their environment. On an interpretative level, an acceptance of this item appears to be the expression of a need for support in an individual who is to some degree struggling to maintain himself in what he has unwittingly learned to perceive as a hostile environment (the jungle), part of which are his own unconscious hostile impulses. To compensate for a weak ego, he admires and identifies with such "virtues" as external dis-

218

TABLE 46

RANK ORDER OF EIGHTEEN F′ SCALE ITEMS BY UNROTATED LOADINGS ON FACTOR I

Item No.	I	Factor II	III	Item
48	.80	.11	.13	What youth needs most is strict discipline, rugged determination, and the will to fight for family and nation. (Agree = 41%; W = 9) *
49	.80	−.23	.01	There is hardly anything lower than a person who does not feel a great love, gratitude and respect for his parents. (Agree = 40%; W = 9)
24	.75	−.30	.18	There is hardly anything lower than a person who does not feel a great love, gratitude and respect for our flag. (Agree = 35%; W = 8)
29	.75	−.01	.20	Obedience and a proper respect for authority should be the very first requirement of a good citizen. (Agree = 59%; W = 8)
40	.68	−.16	.02	An insult to our honor should always be punished. (Agree = 19%; W = 6)
23	.66	−.25	−.27	People without a deep and unquestionable faith in Almighty God should not be trusted in public office. (Agree = 28%; W = 6)
45	.64	−.10	−.30	Every person should have complete faith in some supernatural power whose decisions he obeys without question. (Agree = 24%; W = 5)
44	.62	.14	.05	If people would talk less and work more, everybody would be better off. (Agree = 59%; W = 5)
52	.58	−.07	.12	No sane, normal, decent person could ever think of hurting a close relative or friend. (Agree = 44%; W = 4)
25	.57	.24	−.01	Americans are getting soft; most people need stricter discipline and the will to defend their interests. (Agree = 39%; W = 4)
55	.55	.00	.04	Some leisure is necessary, but it is good hard work that makes life interesting and worthwhile. (Agree = 79%; W = 3)
53	.55	.00	−.24	Books and movies ought not to deal so much with the unpleasant and seamy side of life; they ought to concentrate on themes that are entertaining or uplifting. (Agree = 40%; W = 3)
35	.51	.04	.22	It's a mistake to trust any nation until we are completely sure of them. (Agree = 35%; W = 2)

219

TABLE 46 (Continued)

Item No.	Factor I	Factor II	III	Item
27	.50	.31	−.07	Most people don't realize how much our lives are controlled by plots hatched in secret by others. (Agree = 43%; W = 2)
47	.50	.06	.01	A person who has bad manners, habits and breeding can hardly expect to get along with decent people. W = 2.
51	.49	.30	.04	The wild sex life of the old Greeks and Romans was tame compared to some of the goings on in this country, even in places where people might least suspect it. (Agree = 20%; W = 2)
46	.43	−.08	−.33	When a person has a problem or worry, it is best for him not to think about it, but to keep busy with more cheerful things. (Agree = 29%; W = 1)
54	.42	.36	−.14	When you come right down to it, it's human nature never to do anything without an eye to one's profit. (Agree = 30%; W = 1)

* W-weight, in scoring; explained *infra*.

cipline, determination, and the will to fight for conventionally valued institutions. The other side of the coin is the seeking out of those groups who do not meet these standards, with the idea of punishing or relegating them to an inferior social position (a form of punishment). This behavior, although unrealistic, satisfies the need to feel superior, another way to stabilize and inflate a struggling ego.

The acceptance of Items 24 and 49 represent attitudes toward those who do not have the "proper" feelings toward authority figures and the symbol of the nation, the flag. Those who deviate are held in contempt; although the authoritarian has desires to deviate, any tendency in this deviation elicits anxiety, the awareness of which deters other than his usual restrained, over-conventional behavior. Thus, he gives up freedom to maintain a feeling of safety. At the same time he resents those who are free to deviate, hence the desire to punish them, a desire often rationalized on moral grounds (punishment prevents crime, etc.). In part a person may vicariously experience pleasure in the deviates, but awareness of such pleasure results in self-punishment displaced onto the deviate.

Item 29 fits the "authoritarian submission" category—a statement of what conditions should be required of "good citizens." The acceptor of this item appears to need a rigid authority structure in which to operate, a structure he would like to impose on others since continued non-acceptance by other persons would reflect the acceptor as a deviate. This need to submit to an external authority may grow out of the individual's feeling that he is unable to govern himself due to the lack of a fully developed inner authority or conscience. It follows that such individuals would feel the need for a fairly definite set of social rules and regulations to provide a structured context in which to behave. This is opposed to individuals who behave according to broad principles interpreted within each situational context. The structure, on the other hand, seems to function as support for an ego which cannot adequately mediate between a complex environment and the impulses and inner demands of the individual.

Item 40 was classified under both the "authoritarian aggression" and "power and toughness" categories. In this item, punishment, as a reaction to "insult to honor," is recommended in a rigid, almost absolute sense, as though an alternate reaction would not be feasible. The strength of this statement, together with the emphasis on honor and punishment, suggests the acceptor would be highly sensitive to threats to his position as administrator, father, and to other "power" positions, with the threat producing an excuse for exercising rather thinly veiled hostility needs. The dynamic may be the following: feelings of inadequacy → guilt → projection → punishment of those on whom guilt was projected as temporary release of hostility (safety valve) → rationalization ("They deserved it" or "It will make a man of him," etc.).

Item 23 tends toward both "authoritarian submission" and "authoritarian aggression" as defined by Adorno *et al.* (1950). Those who do not have faith should have opportunities denied them. Obviously, it would seem, those individuals who accept this statement have faith and are not restricted; they, in turn, ask that those who do not believe should be punished. They ask the authority, which they accept, to protect them by restricting (punishing) the rejectors of the authority. Thus, having faith leads to a practical, secondary reward of greater opportunity, probably rationalized on the basis of providing better public servants. There is also the tacit assumption that only those who have faith can be trusted, setting the "moral" standards for an approved in-group.

Item 45 is a very over-generalized statement of the "authoritarian submission" variety. It implies a strong need for "divine" guidance followed without question. Furthermore it is recommended for "every person." This item suggests a lack of self-confidence, with the acceptance of the supreme authority figure (Sullivan's "cosmic papa") as a prop for a faltering and inadequate ego. It would seem that most acceptors of this item would recognize the role of their own conscience in receiving the "decision." It seems that dependency needs and feelings of inadequacy would also be in operation.

Item 44, classified into the anti-intraception and authoritarian aggression categories, equates "more work" with progress or being better off. It endorses the Protestant ethic, with its emphasis on the ascetic life of hard work and its opposition to an imaginative and value-questioning point of view. One accepting this item, according to Adorno et al., tends to avoid thinking about himself and other human phenomena for fear of having wrong (hostile and anxiety provoking) thoughts. Hard work, highly valued by our society, drains off excess energy and, if shrewdly applied in certain phases of the economic cycle, leads to material possessions and greater power, two values highly prized by the authoritarian. Opposition to the theoretical, intellectual, artistic and subjective, hypothesized as characteristic of the authoritarian, would lead to a rejection of certain occupational groups, especially those who might question ultra-conservative, traditional values and thereby threaten the authoritarian objects of identification. In summary, the sequence suggested by this item is: hard work → avoidance of anxiety provoking thoughts and rationale for criticism of others (channelized hostility) → secondary rewards of material gain.

The content of Item 52 suggests a strong need to be completely approving and uncritical of a particular in-group, close friends and relatives. It fits into the authoritarian submission category and, as in other items of this type, indicates a weak ego in need of support from, as well as in fear of, the immediate environment. The rationale for accepting this item has moral connotations: you are not sane, normal, or decent if you reject it. This item goes along with orthodox interpretations of what is "bad"; that is, thinking is almost the same or as bad as doing. Acceptance of this item is probably often related to strong orthodox religious beliefs, with criticism and disobedience of parents, relatives, and other in-group authorities regarded as sinful or "bad." Here again is the moral rationale for the acceptance of a world-view tacitly designed to support a weak and struggling ego.

Item 25 presents an existing condition and a recommended remedy. It is similar to Item 48 in its emphasis on discipline, placing it in the "power and toughness" category. There is probably some externalization involved—attributing to Americans that which is felt about the self. The reaction is the old-fashioned exercise of free will toward that which is undesirable—getting soft.

In Item 55 good hard work is emphasized as interesting and meaningful. It is of special interest that 79% of our sampled population agreed with this item, placing an unusually high premium on the value of work. This item falls into the anti-intraceptive category and is similar to Item 44. Number 54, categorized as an anti-intraceptive item, chooses to avoid the unpleasant, seamy and possibly tragic elements of life by selectively focusing on the entertaining (escape) and uplifting (supportive) aspects of the cultural scene. This world-view is opposed to the thoughtful, probing, and introspective mind which seeks a deeper meaning in life than that reflected in the mass media, popular religion, and a clichéd interpretation of traditional values. This attitude avoids the investigation of the failures of our society and therefore the assumptions on which the values of our society rest. May (1950) points out that such questioning often elicits anxiety responses, an uncomfortable condition which pushes the individual toward an acceptance of popular modal values and conforming, uncritical behavior. It seems likely that the acceptor of this item is unwilling or unable to move through the anxiety-provoking experience of facing the unpleasant

223

aspects of life around him; the reaction is one of avoidance and the reaching out for support. Happy endings are preferred to viewing the development and end of a pitiable character like Willie Loman (Miller, 1949).

The remaining items which compose the F′ Scale play a relatively minor role in defining the meaning of FG and will not be discussed in detail at this time. Three items, Numbers 35, 27, and 51, fall in a projective category; Number 47 is considered a convential item while Items 46 and 54 are classified as anti-intraceptive and cynical. These six items will be of more specific importance in the rotated solution.

What is measured in common by the above items? This variable, abstracted from what is measured in common by the 18 items, would be the appropriate label for FG.

From the nature of attitude structure it may prove fruitful to infer the operation of certain emotional, cognitive, perceptual, and need processes. From the nature of these inferred processes we may be able to make predictions regarding the group membership, political preference, occupational choice, etc. of our respondents.

Fromm (1941) describes such behavior and attitude acceptance as characteristic of the individual who finds it impossible or at best difficult to maintain the type of autonomy and individuality which can lead to harmonious human relationships. Instead he usually needs the structure of a submissive, dependent, or of a dominant, controlling relation with others. As is often the case, this type of individual selectively accepts what might seem incompatible poles of a personality continuum; that is, he is submissive to part of his human environment and dominating in another sector. This is supported in our factor structure where items representing both submissive and aggressive attitudes follow each other in defining the general factor. Fromm describes the type of behavior manifested by the sado-masochistic personality as "escape from freedom" in the sense that his need for submissive-dominant relationships prevent him from entering rewarding relationships with a wider variety of people.

In this sense his freedom is restricted, and because of such needs, he is less autonomous as a thinking, critical citizen, especially in the area where such criticism may threaten ultra-conservative, conventional values and behavior. For this type of individual needs also the support gained from modal (socially approved) behavior even though his emotional involvement in this type of behavior is shallow and not integrated into other facets of his personality. This need stems basically from the hostility which accompanies dependency in its many forms; that is, the dependent individual is constantly in different stages of rebellion, usually on an unconscious level, with the part of his environment on which he is dependent. In the authoritarian personality described by Adorno *et al.*, which seems in many characteristics similar to Fromm's (1941) sado-masochistic, the hostility is externalized on to minority groups, the culturally determined out-groups of the society, an attitude especially acceptable to the uncritical thinker with unconscious hostility needs.

Analogous to Fromm's "escape from freedom" is Horney's (1937) "drive for safety," where the individual, propelled by the discomfort of anxiety, seeks essentially the same type of human relationships described by Fromm. Her "moving toward people" is quite similar to the masochistic, dependent syndrome, while the characteristics of those "moving against people" seem very much like those with strong needs to dominate and control.

Rollo May (1950), obviously influenced by Horney (1945, 1937) and Fromm (1941, 1947), refers to a particular type of religious dependency as "the divine right to be taken care of" by God, the supreme father figure. May (1950) reached his conclusions from an astute analysis primarily influenced by the neo-Freudians and on the basis of extensive experience in the psychotherapeutic treatment of students and pre-ministers with strong religious orientations. May also describes the religiously dependent person as lacking autonomy and the necessary self-confidence (and positive self-image) to move through anxiety provoking experiences to greater maturity. The orientation described by May seems appropriately measured by Items 49, 23 and 45.

The above is intended only as a description of a blend of personality characteristics and certain inferred, underlying needs tapped by FG. No attempt at etiology is intended, although O'Neil (1954) in an interesting study of university sophomores enrolled in education courses, demonstrated the close relationship between attitudes measured by the F Scale and punitive, dominant attitudes toward child rearing.

In summary, from the interpretation of the item content and from the personality theories of those who have influenced the constructors of the items, together with the restrictions imposed upon the interpretations (relative importance of each item) by the results of the factor analysis, a label for our general factor, FG, is deduced. From a group response pattern to a set of 18 item stimuli (manifest behavior), we are attempting to infer the complex of needs (latent variables) which explains the response pattern of covariation of items variables. (The ego is defined as a complex organization of psychological processes which mediates between these needs and the external world.)

The following common needs are inferred to play varying roles in the acceptance of the F' items:

1. The need for the safety, assurance, and support of defined, structured, dominant-submissive human relationships. These relationships are structured according to ultra-conservative, traditional values (man-woman, parent-children, superior-inferior).

2. A need correlate of this type of dependency is hostility, often on an unconscious level, and manifest usually in terms of dominant ("masculine") behavior, contempt for and restriction of those who violate ultra-conservative values, and rejection and restriction of culturally determined out-groups, often stereotyped as violators of the ultra-conservative values.

3. A further correlate of dependency and hostility is the need to have a negative concept of people in general (perhaps another form of hostility), indicated by the suspicious and cynical items of the F' Scale (Nos. 27, 51 and 54). The acceptance of these items suggests the operation of selective perception as a means of supporting attitudes accepted to satisfy strong needs.

Thus, the primary need assumed to run through the F' Scale items is the need for assurance, support, and security. This is achieved by entering into structured (submissive-dominant) human relationships and by strongly adhering to modal, ultra-conservative (socially approved) behavior, with accompanying (unconscious) hostility channelized into rejection of minority groups and violators of conventional mores, rationalized in a hyper-moralistic context. How the ego mediates between these needs and the external environment will be covered in specific predictions of social psychological correlates of the needs. We turn now to the rotated solution of the factor analysis.

THE ROTATED SOLUTIONS: FACTORS I′, II′, AND III′

As previously discussed, three factors were rotated to positive manifold with maximized factor loadings to form the rotated solution. We now turn to the definition of the three factors. For the purposes of discussion, the three rotated factors are tentatively named in terms of item content as follows: Factor I′—Authoritarian Submission; Factor II′—Cynicism and Suspicion; Factor III′—Authoritarian Aggression.

Table 47 gives the eight most important items in defining Factor I′ in rank order of their factor loadings on that factor, along with the factor loadings on rotated Factors II′ and III′.

The two items, 23 and 45, with the highest loadings have a definite religious content, emphasizing complete faith as a recommended way of making decisions in Item 45 and as a criterion for public office in Item 23. As previously discussed, Item 23 fits into both the "authoritarian submission" and "authoritarian aggression" categories. Here we note the heavy loading on Factor I′ and the moderate loading on Factor III′ (labeled Authoritarian Aggression), indicating statistical support of hypothesized content. Items 46 and 53 are of the anti-intraceptive variety and suggest a way of life often suggested by popular inspirational religious literature—selective focusing on the cheerful, entertaining and uplifting; avoidance of worry, problems, and the unpleasant. Neither item is important in the definition of Factors II′ and III′.

Item 49 is similar to the fourth commandment in its punitive, i.e., contemptuous attitude toward those who do not have certain attitudes toward their parents. Relevant is the heavy loading of this item on the Authoritarian Aggression factor (number III′); this follows from the connotation of "There is hardly anything lower . . . ," which originally placed the item in the "authori-

TABLE 47

EIGHT ITEMS RANK ORDERED BY HIGHEST FACTOR
LOADINGS ON ROTATED FACTOR I′

Item No.	Factor I′	II′	III′	Items *
23	.66	.13	.36	People without a deep and unquestionable faith in Almighty God should not be trusted in public office. (W = 9) *
45	.59	.26	.27	Every person should have complete faith in some supernatural power whose decisions he obeys without question. (W = 8)
46	.51	.18	.09	When a person has a problem or worry, it is best for him not to think about it, but to keep busy with more cheerful things. (W = 6)
53	.50	.29	.22	Books and movies ought not to deal so much with the unpleasant and seamy side of life; they ought to concentrate on themes that are entertaining or uplifting. (W = 6)
49	.50	.20	.63	There is hardly anything lower than a person who does not feel a great love, gratitude and respect for his parents. (W = 6)
40	.41	.20	.52	An insult to our honor should always be punished. (W = 4)
24	.37	.11	.73	There is hardly anything lower than a person who does not feel a great love, gratitude and respect for our flag. (W = 4)
48	.28	.49	.58	What youth needs most is strict discipline, rugged determination, and the will to fight for family and nation. (W = 2)

* The eight items listed form the AS Scale, named "Authoritarian Religious Submission." W = weights in scoring.

tarian aggression" category. Item 24 is almost identical in content to Item 49, except for the substitution of a national symbol for parents, which, in terms of factor loadings, places it more strongly in the "authoritarian aggression" category. Apparently respect for parents is more closely tied to a certain type of religious faith than to respect for the flag. Item 40 is also heavily loaded on both Factors I′ and III′, suggesting that the item possesses both aggressive and submissive components.

As indicated by the unrotated, uni-factor solution, "authoritarian submission" and "authoritarian aggression" items are highly related. The rotated solution supports the hypothesis that these two categories are related, but that they can also be conceptualized as separate variable, defined by appropriate parts of the same item. These results simply tell us that some respondents emphasize submission, others aggression, while the remaining are a blend of the two. However, the pattern is such that submissive items covary more consistently with themselves than with aggressive items.

Thus, the items most important to Factor I' emphasize deep, unquestionable and complete faith in a supernatural power or Almighty God together with an emphasis on avoidance of the unpleasant aspects of life. A great love, gratitude and respect for parents is demanded to avoid classification as a "low" person. Emphasis is on the authoritarian facet of religion described by Fromm in *Psychoanalysis and Religion*. Love, respect and gratitude are "encouraged" through punishment, while faith has its pragmatic rewards (Schneider & Dornbusch, 1957). Religious belief which leads to a moral position as a basis for social criticism cannot be inferred from the content of Items 46 and 53. It is interesting to note the change in content of the items as they become less important in defining Factor I'; that is, there is a progression from submission to the supernatural, to escape and avoidance, to submission to parents, followed by a particular type of chauvinistic nationalism and the type of training which will produce strong authoritarian nationalism. The heavy loading of the last three items on Factor III' suggests the content of that factor.

An appropriate label for Factor I' in terms of manifest content is Authoritarian Religious Submission. Underlying the acceptance of these attitudes are, in varying intensities, the need for submission to and identification with a strong and powerful figure who will protect, guide, make decisions and provide an absolute structure of rules and regulations in which to behave. Punishment is the reward for deviation. Because of the close relationship of Factors I' and III' the latter will now be discussed.

Table 48 shows the eight items most important in defining Factor III', rank ordered by their loadings on that factor.

The first five items important to Factor III' have obvious con-

TABLE 48

EIGHT ITEMS RANK ORDERED BY HIGHEST FACTOR
LOADINGS ON ROTATED FACTOR III′

Item No.	Factor III′	I′	II′	Item *
24	.73	.37	.11	There is hardly anything lower than a person who does not feel a great love, gratitude and respect for our flag. (W = 7) *
29	.64	.25	.35	Obedience and a proper respect for authority should be the very first requirement of a good citizen. (W = 6)
49	.63	.50	.20	There is hardly anything lower than a person who does not feel a great love, gratitude and respect for his parents. (W = 6)
48	.58	.28	.49	What youth needs most is strict discipline, rugged determination, and the will to fight for family and nation. (W = 5)
40	.52	.41	.20	An insult to our honor should always be punished. (W = 4)
52	.49	.24	.22	No sane, normal, decent person could ever think of hurting a close relative or friend. (W = 3)
35	.48	.09	.27	It's a mistake to trust any nation until we are completely sure of them. (W = 1)
55	.39	.26	.27	Some leisure is necessary, but it is good hard work that makes life interesting and worthwhile. (W = 1)

* The eight items listed form the AN Scale, labeled "Aggressive Authoritarian Nationalism." W = weights in scoring.

notations of authoritarian chauvinistic nationalism. In addition to what "should be," there is a strong hint of how to produce the desired attitudes; punishment in the form of contempt ("there is hardly anything lower") and on a direct level as in Item 40. Most of these items would fit into the acceptance of a certain type of conservative (unquestioned) nationalism as a socially approved and rewarded form of channelized hostility. There is the familiar submission to a narrowly conceived in-group and hostility and contempt for those who deviate. In a mixture of authoritarian submission and aggression items, the latter dominates. Item 35 carries chauvinistic nationalism to its logical conclusion, while Item 40 suggests both a sensitivity to "insult" and the prescribed reaction. Item 48 recommends a way of rearing our youth which would obviously produce many who would support the type of nationalism described. Item 29 provided the requirements of a "good citizen."

The label for the manifest content of Factor III′ is "Aggressive Authoritarian Nationalism." Its underlying needs are socially approved expression of hostility and dominance and the accompanying need to identify with a strong, elite in-group. Ambivalence toward the in-group is inferred; that is, there exists the possibility of transference to another group if it more fully satisfied the hostility and dominance needs.

Table 49 gives those items most important in defining Factor II′ in rank order by factor loadings. Item 54 presents a concep-

TABLE 49

Eight Items Rank Ordered by Highest Factor
Loadings on Rotated Factor II′

Item No.	II′	Factor I′	III′	Item *
54	.53	.20	.17	When you come right down to it, it's human nature never to do anything without an eye to one's profit. (W = 7) *
27	.52	.20	.18	Most people don't realize how much our lives are controlled by plots hatched in secret by others. (W = 7)
51	.50	.12	.25	The wild sex life of the old Greeks and Romans was tame compared to some of the goings on in this country, even in places where people might least suspect it. (W = 6)
25	.50	.22	.30	Americans are getting soft; most people need stricter discipline and the will to defend their interests. (W = 6)
48	.49	.28	.58	What youth needs most is strict discipline, rugged determination, and the will to fight for family and nation. (W = 6)
44	.43	.24	.38	If people would talk less and work more, everybody would be better off. (W = 4)
29	.35	.25	.64	Obedience and a proper respect for authority should be the very first requirement of a good citizen. (W = 2)
47	.30	.23	.32	A person who has bad manners, habits, and breeding can hardly expect to get along with decent people. (W = 1)

* The eight items listed form the CS Scale, labeled "Cynical and Suspicious View of Human Environment." W = weight in scoring.

tion of human nature—not a particularly optimistic conception —but one which is practically an assumption of our economic system. From this conception of human nature one could not infer on the part of the acceptor a comfortable, secure view of the human environment. This is substantiated by Item 27, which, to say the least, has a paranoid "flavor." It is an interesting fact in itself that 43% of our sampled population agree with this item. The suspicions of Item 27 are carried over into the sexual area by Item 51. A reaction to the cynicism and suspiciousness is contained in Items 25 and 48. The following sequence of reactions seems psychologically sound: because people look out strictly for themselves (Item 54) and because they are also plotting to control others (especially me), and are not too moral in other areas (Item 51), I should be especially well disciplined and on guard to defend my interests. By thinking less of these disturbing events and working especially hard (Item 44), I can best achieve mental peace and a measure of security in this hostile world in which I live. Further, I shall be obedient and respectful and avoid trouble with authority and my own superego.

Thus, the acceptors of items important to Factor II′ perceive the characteristics and motives of their human world, and probably themselves, as somewhat cynical and suspicious. The reaction to this world view is one of determination, hard work, and readiness to fight and defend against this hostile world. The mechanism of externalization is probably in operation in most of those who accept a majority of the above items; that is, unacceptable views of the self and negative motives and desires are attributed to the surrounding society. Since many of these attitudes are the active propaganda of certain segments of our society, there is no problem of a lack of subjectively formulated justification for such attitudes.

The manifest content is tied together by a certain human world-view and selected reaction correlates. Loadings on Factors III′ and I′ are quite moderate on the first four items, while Item 48 had a heavy loading on Factor III′. Further, the content of this factor seems more descriptive of personality characteristics, while Factors I′ and III′ appear to be strongly related to religious and nationalistic ideology. Factor II′ hints strongly at the type of selective perception which operates in the acceptance of certain attitudes, and supports the familiar relation between perception and ideology. An appropriate label of the manifest content is "cynical and suspicious view of human environment." The mechanism of externalization operates to handle underlying hostility and negative motives.

Internal Consistency

The internal consistency of the scores of Factors I', II', and III' are .67, .54 and .77 respectively, determined by Hoyt's (1941) analysis of variance technique and based on a random sample of 100. These coefficients are adequate for group predictions.

Based on a random sample of 100 subjects Factor I' has a .62 correlation with Factor II' and a .69 correlation with Factor III'. Factors II' and III' have a .69 correlation. Therefore, the content of the factors is quite highly correlated, as the content of our items and the uni-factorial solution suggest.

For the items of the unrotated factor, FG, scored as already described, the internal consistency of the general factor is .79, highly adequate for group consideration.

Validity of the Scales

The validity of an instrument is usually defined as the accuracy with which an instrument measures what it purports to measure. It is commonly accepted that the F Scale measures authoritarianism, a rather complex syndrome of personality characteristics which imply a certain way of adapting to the social environment and a variety of perceptual, cognitive and motivational correlates. What, precisely, is measured by the F Scale just is not known.

Our approach was an attempt to refine this instrument through the isolation of dimensions hypothesized to exist in the F Scale syndrome of the chosen population. It was hoped that the structure of these dimensions (if obtained) would provide a firmer basis for inferring the variables being tapped by the scale. To some extent this hope was realized in the results of the rotated solution, which indicate the "tendency" at least toward three "psychologically meaningful" dimensions. It is conceivable that these dimensions could be more accurately defined by "purer" measures of the orthogonal dimensions. For example, in our case this would amount to writing "pure" submission and aggression items that would better define Factors I′ and III′ so that non-related scales could be developed. As the solution stands, the relationships between our items gave rise to a psychologically meaningful structure.

It follows that inferences made about the item content (what they measured) must consider this structure. This restriction should help to make more accurate inferences and thus enhance the validity of the four scales. In our case validity rests on our ability to infer accurately what is being measured by the items which define a factor. This inferring, in turn, is aided by the nature of the factor structure. Whether or not this inferring was accurately done will be tested by our ability to predict, since accuracy of prediction is a function of the validity of the instrument.

Correlates of the Four Scales

The four scales discussed in this section were correlated with a measure of prejudice, which will be discussed in the next section. The following product moment correlation coefficients resulted on the total sample of 911: prejudice with the general factor, FG = .28; with Factor I′, "authoritarian religious submission" = .28; with Factor II′, "cynical and suspicious view of human environment" = .31; with Factor III′, "aggressive authoritarian nationalism" = .33. Eleven of the 16 items of the prejudice scale were worded in the reverse direction of the F′ Scale items, so the above correlations should be spuriously low rather than high if "tendency to agree" is in operation.

THE DEVELOPMENT OF THE PREJUDICE SCALE

Introduction

Thirteen of the 16 items which form the prejudice scale (hereafter known as the P Scale) were selected from the questionnaire used in Poll No. 33 of the *Purdue Opinion Panel.* These items had previously met conventional item analysis standards on a high school population. The remaining three items (Numbers 71, 72, and 73, Table 51) were designed to measure discriminatory attitudes peculiar to college campuses. Some items were chosen for their broad implication: they appeared to indicate the presence of generalized prejudice, rather than prejudice having as referents specific racial or religious groups. Other items made specific references to particular types of "out-groups," such as foreigners and criminals; it was hypothesized that acceptance of the restriction of the socio-economic participation of groups because of their national origin, race, or religion would be generalized to other conventionally accepted "out-groups." Further, it was hypothesized that those favoring general discrimination would accept discriminatory clauses in fraternities and sororities. A certain conception of nature and human nature as measured by Items 37 and 69, was also hypothesized.

FACTOR ANALYSIS OF THE P SCALE ITEMS

To test the hypothesis of uni-dimensionality, it was decided to employ the method of factor analysis. The responses to the 16 items were dichotomized into agree-disagree categories and tetrachoric correlation coefficients were computed to form the 16 by 16 correlation matrix presented by number in Table 50. The highest correlation of an item with any of the other 15 items under consideration was accepted as the communality estimate; these values are presented in the diagonal of the correlation matrix. (See Table 50, p. 236.)

The 120 correlation coefficients (Table 50) vary from .17 through .82, with a mean coefficient of .45. Thus, the items tend to "hang together," and support the hypothesis of common content.

The factor analysis showed that the first three accounted for 78.3% of the common variance. Factor I accounted for 65.4%, while Factors II and III accounted for 8.2% and 4.7% respectively. Rotation of three factors into various positions did not result in a meaningful solution; therefore, the solution can best be

TABLE 50

CORRELATION MATRIX OF SIXTEEN P SCALE ITEMS *

Item No.	28	36	37	59	60	61	62	63	65	66	67	68	69	71	72	73
28	43	24	27	35	20	36	23	33	28	43	32	35	38	27	34	37
36	24	50	28	37	34	37	24	50	44	43	49	49	38	28	39	34
37	27	28	37	17	22	32	20	37	20	30	32	20	20	20	27	20
59	35	37	17	78	32	70	30	57	50	70	58	78	37	53	63	50
60	20	34	22	32	68	43	68	45	40	40	50	40	31	34	38	42
61	36	37	32	70	43	76	33	63	60	76	70	76	43	57	57	50
62	23	24	20	30	68	33	68	50	45	45	55	42	43	30	26	25
63	33	50	37	57	45	63	50	82	48	70	68	82	48	63	64	55
65	28	44	20	50	40	60	45	48	72	72	70	63	35	48	50	50
66	43	43	30	70	40	76	45	70	72	77	65	77	47	55	48	53
67	32	49	32	58	50	70	55	68	70	65	70	65	53	35	57	45
68	35	49	20	78	40	76	42	82	63	77	65	82	47	65	63	57
69	38	38	20	37	31	43	43	48	35	47	53	47	53	33	38	30
71	27	28	20	53	34	57	30	63	48	55	35	65	33	65	62	58
72	34	39	27	63	38	57	26	64	50	48	57	63	38	62	65	65
73	37	34	20	50	42	50	25	55	50	53	45	57	30	58	65	65

* Decimal points omitted

TABLE 51

RANK ORDER OF SIXTEEN P SCALE ITEMS BY
LOADINGS ON UNROTATED FACTOR I

Item No.	I	Factor II	III	Item
68	.88	−.18	−.04	All theaters should admit people of all races and nationalities, and allow them to sit anywhere they want. (W = 9) *
66	.84	.05	−.21	Public eating places should serve people of all races and nationalities, even at the same table if the customers want it that way. (W = 9)
63	.84	.00	.07	Hotels are right in refusing to admit people of certain races or nationalities. (W = 9)
61	.82	−.13	−.15	Swimming pools should admit people of all races and nationalities, to swim in the same pool. (W = 8)
67	.80	.21	−.19	Property owners or their agents should prevent people of some races or nationalities from living in the better neighborhoods. (W = 8)
59	.76	−.22	−.09	Pupils of all races and nationalities should attend school together everywhere in this country. (W = 7)
65	.74	.06	−.12	People of different races and nationalities should be allowed to live in the same neighborhood. (W = 7)
72	.73	−.22	.22	Discrimination in housing because of creed, color or national origin should be illegal and subject to fines if practiced. (W = 7)
73	.68	−.38	.31	Where racial, religious or national discrimination is a fact, an intergroup council of students, faculty and townspeople should be organized with the aim of eliminating such discrimination. (W = 6) *
71	.68	−.25	.31	Discriminatory clauses with reference to creed, color or national orgin in fraternity and sorority charters should be immediately removed. (W = 6)
60	.58	.48	.31	People of different races should not dance together. (W = 4)
69	.57	.18	−.16	There are people of some races and nationalities who are by nature less capable of advancement. (W = 4)
62	.56	.59	.12	There should be laws against marriage between persons of different races. (W = 4)
36	.55	.08	−.14	We should not limit and control immigration of foreigners into this country as much as we now do. (W = 4)

237

TABLE 51 (Continued)

Item No.	I	Factor II	III	Item
28	.46	−.03	−.10	Criminals, especially those guilty of sex crimes, should have mental and medical help rather than severe punishment. (W = 2)
37	.36	.10	−.08	Despite what people say about human nature, all of the people of the world will someday live peacefully together. (W = 1)

* W = scoring weights.

viewed as uni-factorial with one general factor running through all items. The items are presented in Table 51 according to the rank order of their loadings on Factor I.

INTERPRETATION OF THE GENERAL FACTOR

Those items with highest factor loadings on Factor I present a certain situation which "should" exist in such important areas as housing, education, travel, eating and recreation. These items may be viewed as defining a general prejudice factor. Item 71, which has a specific referent as the discriminator, also has a heavy loading on the general prejudice factor. Item 69, with a particular interpretation of the role of nature, gives some hint about the reasoning process of the prejudiced individual. Items 36 and 28, with reasonably high loadings on the general factor, support the hypothesis of prejudice as a generalized attitude, easily extended to conventionally defined "out-groups."

The content of items most important in defining the general factor fit under the label "social, cultural, and economic restriction of groups simply because of their race, religion, or national origin." Stereotypes of these groups are "in the air" as a rather definite part of the cultural ethos; the social structure, with its many restrictions for various groups provides actual examples to substantiate the stereotypes. Thus certain minority groups, restricted to low income status, substantiate for the prejudiced person the stereotype of inferior capabilities.

The acceptance of prejudiced attitudes is a complex affair, involving situational factors, selective perception, faulty cognition, and a host of other factors. However, in any intense form it usually includes a need for hostile expression and in many cases involves a general dislike for people (Sullivan and Adelson, 1954). The underlying need inferred from the item content is hostility. Prejudice, as defined above, is simply a socially approved form of channelized hostility.

SCORING THE ITEMS

The items of the P Scale were scored in proportion to their loadings on the general factor, Factor I.

The internal consistency of the resulting P Scale of .85 for random sample of 200 subjects is judged to be highly satisfactory for group predictions.

THE CULTURAL CONTEXT [1]

Societies create in their members a variety of needs and at the same time provide for satisfying these needs approved behavior patterns, which may vary throughout different strata of the society. The need hierarchies which individuals acquire are highly related to the dominant values of the society. By values we refer to those social positions, possessions, and ideals highly valued and sought after by the members of the society. Valued objects, positions, and ideals become the goals of the people. They are propelled (motivated) toward these goals by certain needs, to some extent acquired from the surrounding culture through conditioning and learning. Socially approved behavior patterns, varying in different strata of the society and limited by various forms of punishment and reward, regulate the behavior of members of the society in their pursuit of the goals. Secular and religious myths support the probability of reaching and the "goodness" of striving for the prescribed goals. Varying levels of prestige are assigned to those judged successful and unsuccessful; those who achieve success gain prestige and power and are emulated by many, while those who are on the other end of the continuum are often depreciatively stereotyped as not being intelligent, determined, or willing to work.

The achievement of these socially prescribed and valued goals is intimately related to the individual's view of himself; that is, his self-esteem and self-worth is estimated on the basis of his success in reaching these goals. In turn, the individual's self-concept is very closely related to his concept of others, a condition which has perceptual, cognitive, motivational and behavioral correlates.

This total interacting and ever-changing process produces a wide variety of personality types. As individuals engage in the process of pursuing primary goals, peripheral needs and ideological correlates are acquired. Some of these needs are satisfied through membership in established organizations and groups, while others give rise to new organizations and to the transformation of those already established.

The conclusions reached, admittedly on a thin web of evidence, are summarized in the following sequence:

1. The marked discrepancy which exists between highly valued but relatively undefined goals (Merton, 1949) leads to intensive competitive striving (May, 1950) and deviation from institutionalized means of reaching these goals (Sutherland, 1949).
2. This situation gives rise to intrasocial hostility (May, 1950) which permeates many of our human relationships (Horney, 1937).
3. The above hostility places barriers between people and leads to what Fromm (1941) calls "alienation," May (1950) a "lack of community," and Merton (1949) the "strain toward anomy."
4. These conditions, in turn, create anxiety, as a reaction to hostility impulses and loneliness; guilt, due to not having reached unclearly defined success goals; cynicism, a reaction to professed values and actual behavior (Horney, 1945), (Sutherland, 1949); inner conflict (Horney, 1945), because of many inconsistent role expectancies, and negative self-concept (May, 1950).
5. Such feelings and needs lead to various types and combinations of personality types capable of achieving only restricted interpersonal relationships. Fromm's (1941, 1947) typologies include, among others, the automaton conformist, the sado masochist, and the market-oriented personality types. The former two represent important aspects of the authoritarian personality (Adorno et al., 1950).
6. The dominant characteristic of the above types is an inadequate ego (Adorno et al., 1950), unable to mediate between the com-

plex environment perceived as hostile, and his many inner demands and needs unless he enters into structured and restricted human relationships (Fromm's "escape from freedom") and identifies with ultra-conventional mores (socially approved), prestigeful goals (validation of self), material gain (culturally defined security and power), and strong authority figures (source of support). These relationships and identifications gain support for his faltering and inadequate ego, although in the process he restricts his freedom of choice in developing human relationship, often resulting in a type of unresolved dependency. But, as Horney (1937) observes, dependency leads to hostility which the authoritarian often channels into prejudice toward minority groups (Adorno *et al.*, 1950), and into competitive striving (May, 1950). Thus, the authoritarian looks down upon some groups (Adorno, 1950), (Christie and Jahoda, 1954) while at the same time aspiring for highly valued goals (Adorno, 1950; Kaufman, 1957).

Perhaps one of the tragic and ironic characteristics of our culture is that many of its members identify so strongly with the very values and goals, which, intensely pursued, create in members of our culture feelings of discontent, anxiety, loneliness, and loss of self-identity.

This discussion forms a theoretical framework for predicting the relationships between the acceptance of authoritarian and prejudiced attitudes and certain social psychological variables. Specific predictions will be made in the following sections.

AUTHORITARIANISM, PREJUDICE AND AREA OF SPECIALIZATION

INTRODUCTION

This section is concerned with certain functional relationships between the acceptance of prejudiced and authoritarian attitudes and areas of specialization in Midwest University. Authoritarian attitudes are measured by the four scales resulting from the factor analysis of the F′ Scale previously presented. The four scales will be abbreviated as follows: the scale from the general factor as the FG Scale; the scale from the "authoritarian religious submission" factor as the AS Scale; the scale derived from the "aggressive authoritarian nationalism" factor as the AN Scale; and the scale from the "cynicism-suspiciousness" factor as the CS Scale. Prejudiced attitudes are measured by the P Scale derived from the first general factor of the factor analysis of the 16 prejudice items.

Eighteen areas of specialization were designated from responses to the questionnaire: administration, pharmacy, physical education, military science, agriculture, education, engineering, chemistry, library science, home economics, biological science, foreign language, history-government-economics, mathematics, physics, speech, English-art, and psychology-sociology.

RELEVANT LITERATURE

Strong (1943) has differentiated occupational groups with a measure of interests and attitudes. Studies with the Allport-Vernon Study of Values reveal value differences across university students classified by major area of interest. Roe (1953, 1951a, 1951b), in her studies of eminent biologists, physicists and social scientists, found that the scientists came from homes of above-average socio-economic backgrounds which stressed learning as an end in itself and had strong needs for independence and achievement. The biological and physical scientists indicated a "decided preference for a very limited social life." Terman's (Darley and Hagenah, 1955) follow-up of the upper one per cent (measured by his test) of a large group of children revealed that those who later became scientists demonstrated both an interest and ability in scientific activities at an early age. Roe in her recent book on occupations (Roe, 1956) stresses the importance of personality variables in occupational selection and adjustment.

Thus, vocational choice appears to be related to a variety of factors, among them: the occupational structure of the society, the values, interests, and personality characteristics of the individuals making the choice, their socio-economic, religious (Myers, 1951), and family backgrounds, and the economic condition of the society at the time of choice.

In our particular problem we are dealing with a highly selected population—almost 100% have had four or more years of college. Therefore, their opportunity for selecting a particular field of interest is not as limited as is that of the random member of society. It follows that individual preference, rather than economic necessity, lack of opportunity, and other restricting factors, would play an important role in selecting an area of specialization. The conclusion, then, is that personality variables, and in our case social attitudes, have an excellent chance of being related to area of specialization in a university faculty population.

A rough categorization would place the high groups in applied science close to industry and business. Education, although not fitting this classification, apparently is dependent on the value orientations of this group. The middle group may be roughly placed in a theoretical science category, while the low group is best placed in a liberal arts classification.

Struening (1955) found a somewhat similar pattern of scores when the same instrument was administered to 655 undergraduates in a large midwestern university.

In summary, differences across occupational groups have been demonstrated on a range of variables, among them values, interests, aptitudes, attitudes toward learning, socio-economic background, and intelligence. Two studies indicated marked differences across fields of interest in both an undergraduate and a faculty population with respect to social attitudes measured by a 30-item F Scale. However, the sampling procedures of both studies warrant criticism. It was noted that in a faculty population, obviously having the opportunity for a college education, the probability of free selection of field of interest would be higher than in strata of the society where such choice was probably more highly restricted. It is reasoned, then, that personality characteristics and certain attitudes may play an important role in influencing the selection of a field of interest by a university faculty member.

The samples under consideration in the following hypotheses were formed by classifying the subjects according to area of specialization. The authoritarian and prejudiced attitudes were estimated by the FG, AS, AN, CS, and P Scales previously described.

HYPOTHESES

The alternative to the null hypothesis of no differences across population means on authoritarian and prejudiced attitudes is predicted. These characteristics of the authoritarian individual relevant to predicting area of specialization are:

1. The need to identify with strong, powerful, prestigeful and socially approved groups. Within the range available to a university faculty population, those occupations which rate highest in the occupational prestige-success ladder would receive the highest authoritarian scores.

2. The overemphasis on masculinity (Allen, 1954) as a way of reacting to feelings of inadequacy, suggests that physical education majors would receive high authoritarian ratings.

3. The need for a dominance-submission structure. This would apply particularly to administrators and members of the military science group.

4. The tendency toward anti-intraception and over-acceptance of ultra-conventional values and assumptions of society. Generally speaking, English, art, and social science majors probe more deeply into accepted values and assumptions in their subject matter than do those in the applied sciences. Such probing also results in a questioning of one's own values and behavior, a practice which the authoritarian tends to avoid. Physicists and mathematicians, who constantly question basic assumptions in their work, may to some extent generalize this curiosity into the social and self areas. The facing of basic assumptions is not as omnipresent in the applied sciences of engineering, agriculture and pharmacy.

5. An authoritarian religious orientation is probably found most often among those faculty members in education and agriculture departments who come largely from lower-middle class and rural backgrounds.

The above characteristics suggest a low-high continuum of group means from social science–English–art to administrative–military–physical education on the four estimates of authoritarianism. The means of the applied sciences, as represented by engineering, pharmacy and agriculture are predicted to be higher than the means of the theoretical-biological sciences, represented by chemistry, mathematics, biology and physics. Since authoritarianism and prejudice are positively correlated, the continuum on the prejudice variable should be similar.

RESULTS AND DISCUSSIONS

To test the hypothesis outlined above, a one-way analysis of variance was applied to each of the five variables under consideration. All five F ratios were significant, well beyond the one per cent level.[2] Evidently the groups formed by area of specialization do not come from psychologically common populations on the variables under consideration.

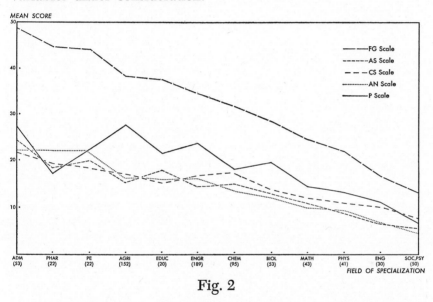

Fig. 2

The mean scores of the groups, excluding military science, library science, home economics, foreign language, history-government-economics, and speech are presented in Figure 2. The above six were omitted because of spatial problems and because they represent small samples. In addition, the means of the 18 groups on the five variables are presented in Table 52. Inspection of the graph indicates that, on the FG Scale, our directional hypotheses were roughly substantiated on the four authoritarian scales. On the authoritarian (high) end of the continuum are administration, pharmacy, physical science, and military sci-

245

TABLE 52

MEANS OF AREA OF SPECIALIZATION
GROUPS ON FIVE SCALES

	FG Scale	AS Scale	CS Scale	AN Scale	P Scale	N
Admin.	49.0	23.6	21.5	21.6	27.0	53
Pharmacy	44.9	18.4	19.2	21.5	17.8	23
Phy. Educ.	44.3	20.1	18.6	21.6	21.5	22
Mili. Sci.	43.4	18.9	21.3	19.2	15.8	15
Agri.	36.9	16.2	17.2	16.5	26.7	152
Educ.	36.7	17.6	15.4	15.8	21.3	20
Engr.	34.6	14.4	16.1	15.9	23.3	189
Chem.	32.4	14.5	16.3	13.6	17.8	95
Libr. Sci.	30.4	10.7	16.1	12.9	10.6	7
Home Econ.	29.5	13.8	10.8	13.4	18.3	20
Biology	28.8	12.9	13.5	12.6	19.5	53
Mod. Lang.	28.6	11.1	13.9	12.7	36.9	7
Hist., Govt. Economics	27.6	11.9	11.9	12.4	34.1	16
Math.	24.8	11.3	12.0	10.0	14.7	43
Physics	21.9	8.4	10.8	9.6	13.3	41
Speech	18.3	6.3	10.1	8.1	11.5	23
Engl. & Art	17.0	6.2	10.0	6.6	11.5	30
Psychology & Sociology	13.2	5.3	7.4	4.9	6.5	50

ence, while on the low end are psychology and sociology, English and art, and speech. Applied science, represented by agriculture, pharmacy, and engineering are higher in rank than chemistry, biology, mathematics and physics. The latter two are considerably lower than chemistry and biology. Education ranks high, between agriculture and engineering, indicating, as in the results of Struening and Spilka (1952), that it cannot be classified into the social science group. Home economics falls between the applied and theoretical sciences. Three groups, library science, foreign language and history-government-economics would generally, according to our rationale, fall below the theoretical-natural sciences, and closer to the social science groups. One possible explanation for this deviation is the small-

246

ness of our sample sizes, where one or two high scores would have a large effect on the mean. Another explanation may be that the high scores are characteristic of these groups at Midwest University, but possibly not of like groups in a variety of universities.

The means of the AS, AN, and CS Scales on our various groups add interesting detail to our findings. The social, physical, and theoretical sciences are more accepting of the cynicism-suspicious items, in preference to AS and AN items, than are the other groups. Within these groups the social scientists emphasize this tendency most strongly, while pharmacy, physical education and history-government-economics are more accepting of the authoritarian nationalism items measured by the AN Scale and rejecting more often the AS and CS Scale items. Members of the administration, education, and home economics groups tend to prefer the authoritarian submission items rather than the items of the CS and AN Scales. One possible explanation for the emphasis on cynicism in the science groups is an extension of the curious, questioning approach which scientists must have toward the assumptions and theories of their chosen area. It would follow that cynicism would be most prevalent in the social sciences where theoretical formulations are most questionable.

The relationship between area of specialization and prejudice is somewhat different from that between authoritarianism and area of specialization, although the social science, theoretical-natural science, and applied science rationale generally holds. The low (on acceptance of prejudice) end of the continuum is essentially the same, with the exception of library science, now among those with somewhat similar training backgrounds. The military and physical education groups tend to drop down considerably, a fact which may reflect greater acceptance of minority groups in these areas. The marked exceptions to the rank order of the groups on authoritarianism are the foreign language and history-economic-government groups. Again, this deviation from expectancy may be due to error inherent in small sampling, or the results may reflect the attitudes of these departments at Midwest University and could not be generalized to other institutions.

SUMMARY

The results of this section indicate that area of specialization is an important stratification variable in the distribution of authoritarianism and prejudice. In general, the distribution of the means of scales measuring authoritarianism follow a low-high continuum from social science to theoretical-natural science to applied science to military-physical education-administration. The prejudice continuum is quite similar, with the marked exception of the history-government-economics and foreign language groups which were higher and the physical education, pharmacy, military science, and library science groups which were somewhat lower in relative rank than they were on authoritarianism.

POLITICAL PREFERENCE, AUTHORITARIANISM, AND PREJUDICE

BASIS FOR PREDICTION: LITERATURE AND THEORY

Traditional association of the Republican party with business interests or a conservative political bent suggests a tendency for that party to favor maintenance of existing institutions or the status quo. The Democratic party on the other hand has favored, through the Wilson, Roosevelt, and Truman eras at least, increased melioration of socio-economic conditions on the part of the federal government. This generalization is definitely qualified by the position of southern Democrats on civil rights issues. Still we expect differences in party ideology to be related to authoritarianism. The Republican Party ideology is distinctly steeped in and supported by tradition, and has a more thorough and systematic rationale by virtue of its relative consistency in the social myth which calls for rationalization or modification.

In general, the Democrats are not as thoroughly convinced as the Republicans that the virtues of free enterprise, rugged individualism and little government interference, except for an occasional protective tariff, will produce the best possible society. Right Wing Republican support and defense of McCarthyism

248

seems to reflect needs on the part of these individuals to discharge anti-group (stereotyped, non-discriminate) hostilities in a context of hypermoral judgment based on the extreme authority criterion of national loyalty. These are tendencies which we have found to be frequently involved in authoritarian personality dynamics. The ideological position of this group seems best represented by the third rotated factor, aggressive authoritarian nationalism, combined with elements of Factor Two, labelled "cynical and suspicious view of the human environment." In terms of the Republican-Democrat dichotomy, the former group would appear to be more accepting of authoritarianism.

In summary, authoritarianism appears to be related to the extremes of the political continuum, but there is little to substantiate the prediction of significant differences between the two major parties, although small differences are accentuated in middle-class groups. Those who were not politically active received higher authoritarian scores than did those who voted and took an active part in political affairs. Studies from which one could infer the social attitude correlates of political preference in university faculty populations are extremely rare. Therefore, direct empirical bases for prediction are not available.

An important characteristic of the town in which Midwest University is located is its Republican tradition.[3] The town is composed largely of faculty members of Midwest University and upper-middle class business and professional families. To be a liberal Democrat borders on deviate behavior, at least in a normative sense. Thus, political lines are more acutely drawn in this town than in many.

The population under consideration in the following hypotheses were formed by classifying the 911 subjects by political preference. Authoritarian and prejudiced attitudes were estimated by the FG, AS, AN, CS, and P Scales previously discussed.

Hypotheses

The alternative to the null hypotheses of no differences across population means on authoritarian and prejudiced attitudes is predicted. Republicans, Independents and Democrats will compose a conservative-liberal continuum with authoritarian and prejudiced attitudes decreasing in the liberal direction. Those with "other" political preferences are undefined and relatively unimportant with an N of eight. If those with "no political preference" are viewed as "politically inactive," we would, according to Sanford's (1950) results, except high scores on that group.

Results and Discussion

To test the above hypotheses, one-way analysis of variance was applied to each of the five variables under consideration. All of the five resulting F ratios were significant far beyond the one per cent level of significance; hence the political preference

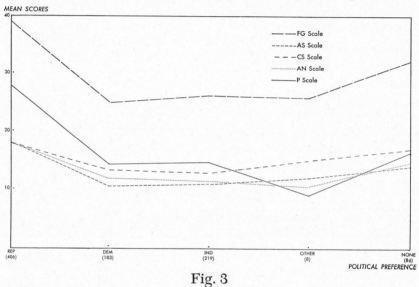

Fig. 3

groups do not come from a common population on the five considered variables.

The means of the five variables on the political preference groups are graphically presented in Figure 3. On the general factor, FG, the five groups fall into three rather distinct categories, with Republicans in the high group, Democrats, Independents and "others" in the low group, and "nones" in an intermediate group.

This pattern generally holds throughout the remaining four variables, with the exception of those in the "other" category who are lower on prejudice and more accepting of the cynical-suspicious items than the Republicans and Democrats. The latter tendency prevails with the "nones." The Democracts and Independents also tend to be more accepting of the cynical-suspicious and authoritarian nationalism items than are the Republicans.

In summary, political preference as a classification variable is highly related to the acceptance of authoritarian and prejudiced attitudes by a Midwestern university faculty. Generally, the continuum moves from Republicans to "nones" to Democrats, Independents, and "others" in the direction of acceptance-rejection of authoritarian and prejudiced attitudes. These findings, while logical enough in view of the previous discussion, are not characteristic of the general population, although there was some support of the possibility in a middle-class stratum. Faculty members as a particular segment of the middle class may accentuate these differences. In addition, in the conservative Midwest even a small segment of the political continuum may have recognizable ideological correlates. This is substantiated by the small number ($N = 8$) who prefer something other than the conventional party preferences. Perhaps our highly sophisticated and educated population is exceptionally astute in perceiving the nuances of difference which separate Republicans from Democrats, a task which seems especially difficult at election time.

Whether the above results would be identical for other Midwestern college and university faculties is a matter of conjecture. The marked differentiation obtained in this study supports the possibility of such a generalization.

AUTHORITARIANISM, PREJUDICE, AND CHURCH ATTENDANCE

INTRODUCTION

This section is concerned with the relations between frequency of church attendance and the acceptance of authoritarian and prejudiced attitudes. Authoritarian and prejudiced attitudes

RESULTS AND DISCUSSION

were estimated with the FG, AS, CS, AN, and P Scales previously discussed. Church frequency groups, based on information from Item 13 of the questionnaire, are divided into the eight categories: zero, one, two, three, four, five to seven, eight to ten, and 11 or more times per month.

HYPOTHESES

The alternative to the null hypothesis of no differences across population means on authoritarian and prejudiced means is predicted. The literature suggests some evidence of a curvilinear relationship between ethnocentrism and church attendance, but relationships between authoritarianism and church attendance, on a compressed continuum, were linear. Considering the education level of our population and the generally tolerant attitude of campus churches, it seems that increased church attendance has a deterring effect to the acceptance of prejudiced attitudes. Therefore, a curvilinear relationship is predicted.

RESULTS AND DISCUSSION

To test the above hypothesis, one-way analysis of variance was applied to each of the five variables under consideration. The five F ratios were all significant far beyond the one per cent level of significance. Therefore, we infer that the groups formed by frequency of church attendance do not come from a common population on the variables under consideration and our hypothesis is substantiated.

The means of the groups on the five scales are presented in Figure 4. It is immediately obvious that the relationship between church attendance and prejudice is curvilinear in nature; also prejudice is the only variable where those attending church receive a lower score than those who never go. This, however, places them in the "11 or more" times per month category.

In general, those who do not attend church received the lowest scores on all five variables, excluding the one example just mentioned. On the general authoritarian factor, FG, the peak score is reached at attending three times per month. Mean scores then fall off to form a tendency toward a curvilinear relationship, only to rise sharply at 11 or more times per month. Here is the unusual circumstance of having our highest FG Scale mean associated with the lowest P Scale. The decrease in FG Scale scores after three times per month is illuminated by inspecting distribution of AS, CS, and AN Scale means; that is, the CS and AN Scale means decrease while the AS Scale means remain constant

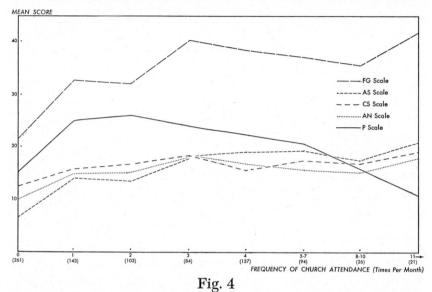

Fig. 4

or rise slightly, if we consider the 8–10 per month score a chance deviation. These results suggest that church attendance beyond three times per month is related to slightly increased "authoritarian religious submission" while "aggressive authoritarian nationalism" and "cynicism-suspiciousness" is decreased, along with a marked decrease in prejudice. The overall relationship between AS scores and frequency of church attendance is practically linear, providing post hoc construct validity for the scale.

Another interesting relation is the high FG Scale mean at three times per month while the high P Scale mean is at two times per month, decreasing rapidly at three times per month. One plausible explanation is that the authority submitted to by this group also militates against prejudice; that is, those individuals who attend church three or more times per month approach it more from

253

a humanistic point of view than do the more or less ambivalent church attenders who go only once or twice a month. The latter group may reflect the conventional participant who wants to be seen in church, but has little emotional involvement with it.

SUMMARY

Marked differences were found across groups formed by frequency of church attendance on four scales of authoritarianism and on one scale of prejudice. Those who do not attend church were found to be less prejudiced and authoritarian than all other groups, except those who attended church more than 11 times per month, who were very low on prejudice but received the highest authoritarian scores.

The relationship between prejudice and church attendance is definitely curvilinear, with the peak at two times per month and the low points at zero and 11 or more times per month. This supports our directional hypothesis suggested by the formulations of Fromm (1950) and Allport (1954).

Authoritarian religious submission was linearly related (except for one mean) to church attendance. This fact, concomitant with the curvilinear relationship with prejudice, suggests that certain types of religious experiences are not associated with prejudice.

The means of the general factor scale FG, rise sharply from zero to three times per month, then taper off to form a tendency toward a curvilinear relationship. This curve is closely paralleled by the "aggression authoritarian nationalism" means. The CS Scale differentiates sharply between zero and four times per month, but after that the curve smooths out and shows little differentiation.

General conclusions support church attendance, as an index of institutional participation, as an important variable in the understanding and prediction of authoritarianism and prejudice.

IMPLICATIONS FOR FURTHER RESEARCH

The research reported in this study is part of an incomplete project. Papers concerning the relationships between the accept-

254

ance of authoritarian and prejudiced attitudes and the following classification variables are in preparation: age, rank in the university, religious affiliation, intensity of religious belief, and education level. A number of hypotheses regarding the amount of variance accounted for by one classification variable while another classification variable is held constant are being tested.

Further investigation of attitude structure in the population studied is proposed. For example, we would hypothesize that the structure of the Republican sample would have a more constricted (individual items would have higher intercorrelation coefficients) structure on the F' Scale items than would the Democrats and Independents. This hypothesis is based on the results of *The Authoritarian Personality* (Adorno *et al.*, 1950) which indicate the high-scoring (acceptance of F' Scale items) groups to be more consistent in their response than low scorers. Such consistency would lead to higher inter-item correlations and probably a more constricted factor structure. This type of analysis could be performed on a variety of groups hypothesized to have varying factor structures. In this research project there would probably be, among others, interesting differences along the age continuum, between frequency of church attendance groups, and between members of different denominations.

Thus, the structure of attitude constellations provides information about the relationship between attitudes which form a functional unity. From the qualitative characteristics of these functional unities and from their variation across groups, it may be possible to make interesting inferences about the function of these attitudes as the acceptor makes his adjustment to society. It is interesting that the factor structure of the three rotated factors of this study were very similar to the three isolated by Gates as reported in Chapter 8 even though her population—undergraduates of small liberal arts colleges—was quite different from the sample of this study. This suggests the presence of similar response patterns across populations.

The testing of the generality of our results on other university faculty populations is in process. Data gathered from the faculties of several small Midwestern colleges and universities is being analyzed.

SUMMARY AND CONCLUSIONS

The problem of this research was to isolate the dimensions of authoritarian and prejudiced attitudes and to predict, from a theoretical framework, their distribution and covariation across selected divisions of a university faculty population.

A 93-item questionnaire, including 15 classification variables and a number of items designed to measure authoritarianism and prejudice, was mailed to the faculty members of a large midwestern university. Approximately 50 per cent of the questionnaires (N = 911) were satisfactorily completed and representative of the faculty as to rank in the university and area of specialization.

The principal components method of factor analysis was applied to the inter-item correlation matrix of 18 F' Scale items. Of the factors extracted from the first matrix, the first factor accounted for a major portion of the common variance. The 18 items which defined this unrotated factor were assigned weights in proportion to their factor loadings, resulting in a highly internally consistent instrument named the FG Scale. Three factors which accounted for the most variance were then rotated into positive manifold and simple structure, resulting in three psychologically meaningful factors. Weights assigned to the eight most highly loaded items of each factor resulted in three scales with coefficients of internal consistency satisfactory for group prediction. The factors were named as follows: Factor I'—Authoritarian Religious Submission, the basis of the AN Scale; Factor II'—Cynical and Suspicious View of the Human Environment, the basis of the CS Scale; Factor III'—Aggressive Authoritarian Nationalism, the basis of the AN Scale.

The principal components method of factor analysis was also applied to an inter-item correlation matrix of 16 prejudice items. One factor accounted for a major proportion of the variance. The 16 items were weighted according to their factor loadings on the general factor; a highly internally consistent instrument resulted and was designated the P Scale.

A theoretical framework, entitled "The Cultural Context," was developed, which, combined with results of empirical studies, provided a basis for predicting the relationships between authoritarian and prejudiced attitudes and three stratification variables: area of specialization, frequency of church attendance, and political preference. Authoritarian and prejudiced attitudes were operationally defined by the above scales.

Marked differences were found among means across the groups formed by area of specialization on the five variables under consideration. The means of these groups formed an authoritarian-less authoritarian continuum ranging roughly from administration, physical education, military science, to applied science to theoretical, biological science to English, and speech social science. This continuum was not as clearly defined on the prejudice scale, although the deviation was primarily in those samples with small N's. It is concluded that area of specialization is an important variable in predicting the distribution of authoritarian and prejudiced attitudes in a university faculty population.

Political preference was also found to be highly related to authoritarian and prejudiced attitudes. Results clearly indicated a three-point continuum. Republicans are highest on both prejudice and authoritarianism followed by those who have no political preference. Democrats, Independents, and those who prefer a party other than those named are by far the lowest on prejudice and authoritarianism. Political preference, it was concluded, is also an important stratification variable in predicting prejudiced and authoritarian attitudes in a university faculty population. This is a fact not common to other strata of the United States society, although there were tendencies in this direction in certain middle-class groups.

Frequency of church attendance was also highly related to prejudice and authoritarianism. The relation between prejudice and church attendance was curvilinear, while the relation between church attendance and "Authoritarian Religious Submission" was rectilinear. The other scales tended toward a curvilinear relation, although the curve rose much more sharply from zero to three times per month than it declined beyond three times per month. Thus another variable was found which plays an important role in the distribution of prejudice and authoritarianism.

In final summary, four scales designed to measure authoritarianism and one scale to measure prejudice were developed. Their internal consistencies were determined. A theoretical framework was formed to predict the relationship between these variables and three stratification variables: church attendance, area of specialization, and political preference. Predictions were substantiated and the three stratification variables are concluded to be important in understanding prejudiced and authoritarian attitudes in a university faculty population.

NOTES

1. Dr. Struening's extended analysis is omitted here and only summarized. (H. H. R.)

2. The summary quantitative results are given in the appendix of Dr. Struening's dissertation on file in the Purdue University Library. (H. H. R.)

3. In a recent local municipal election the vote was 60 per cent Republican and 40 per cent Democratic, closely predicted by a pre-election poll by my class in the Psychology of Attitudes. (H. H. R.)

X DEMOCRATIC-AUTHORITARIAN ATTITUDES: COMPARISON OF THE FACTOR PATTERNS FROM SEVERAL POPULATIONS

Larry Dennis Cannon

PURPOSE

This study was designed to investigate the stability of factors underlying an authoritarian attitude scale consisting of 18 items. Previous research with the instrument, called the F' Scale (Struening, 1957), led to the development of three factors:

I' Authoritarian Religious Submission
II' Cynical and Suspicious View of the Human Environment
III' Aggressive Authoritarian Nationalism

The sample used in the previous research consisted of faculty members of Midwest University.

The same instrument was administered to faculty members from 23 Indiana colleges and universities. On the basis of number of respondents, five of these institutions were selected for the present study. Item responses were intercorrelated for each of the schools, producing five 18 by 18 matrices of tetrachoric coefficients of correlation.

Each of these five matrices was factor analyzed, and three factors accounting for the most variance were selected from each of the analyses.

The three factors thus obtained from each of the five schools were compared, in terms of items loading highest on them, with the three factors from Midwest University studied in the previous research, to determine whether the factors isolated are similar to the three factors associated with "Midwest University" studied by Struening (1957). If they are similar, they will be evidence for the factorial invariance of his factors.

To accomplish this analysis, the following procedure was used.

1. For each institution, a matrix of intercorrelations was developed between the 18 items of the F' Scale.
2. Each of these matrices was factor-analyzed.
3. The factors obtained from each school were compared with the factors associated with Struening's "Midwest University."

THE RESPONDENTS

On the basis of number of respondents, five of 23 Indiana colleges and universities were selected for the present study. The five schools have been numerically coded. School 1 is a small liberal arts university; School 2 is a Catholic institution; School 3 is a teachers college; School 4 is a state university; and School 5 is a small municipal college.

There were 92 faculty respondents from School 1; 149 from School 2; 93 from School 3; 75 from School 4, and 51 from School 5. The respondents are classified according to teaching area and according to sex in Tables 28 to 32 in the appendix. The groups of respondents are admittedly small, and generalizations from the present study may suffer because of this. However, most teaching areas are represented by the respondents from each school.

As is true of all mail questionnaires, there is conjecture as to whether respondents, by the mere fact that they do respond, are

TABLE 53

MEANS, STANDARD DEVIATIONS, AND RELIABILITIES
OF THE F' SCALE FOR EACH OF THE FIVE GROUPS
OF RESPONDENTS

School Number	F' Scale Mean *	SD	r **	N ***
One	51.79	11.46	.859	77
Two	43.74	11.71	.859	114
Three	48.56	11.27	.854	82
Four	52.85	10.75	.849	68
Five	44.36	11.17	.843	41

   * a high score means low authoritarianism, and vice versa
  ** computed by analysis of variance
*** for each school the number of cases these statistics are based on is
    somewhat less than the total number of respondents from that school,
    since not all respondents answered all items

different from non-respondents, in terms of their attitudes on the scale in question. It has been suggested that authoritarians are less likely to respond than others.

Reliabilities were computed for the F' Scale for each of the five groups of respondents by means of Hoyt's analysis of variance technique (1941). These ranged from .843 to .859. Table 53 lists the reliabilities, means, standard deviations, and the number of cases they were based on for each of the five groups.

In the present study, considering the data from School 1, the first factor accounted for 60.7% of the variance, the second factor accounted for 17.3% of the variance, and the third factor for 9.2%. All three factors thus accounted for 87.2% of the variance. Arbitrarily, it was decided that this was satisfactory, so these three factors were retained for rotation. Table 54 lists the per

TABLE 54

PER CENT OF THE VARIANCE ACCOUNTED FOR BY THE FIRST
THREE FACTORS * OBTAINED FOR EACH OF SIX SCHOOLS

	Per Cent of Variance Accounted for			
School Number	Factor 1	Factor 2	Factor 3	Total
One	60.7	17.3	9.2	87.2
Two	71.4	10.9	8.7	91.0
Three	56.6	17.5	10.6	84.7
Four	56.4	16.9	11.2	84.5
Five	49.6	19.0	13.3	81.9
Six **	63.3	6.4	4.9	74.9

* unrotated factors
** data from Struening (1957)

cent of variance accounted for by unrotated factors 1, 2, and 3 for each of the schools.

For each school, the three factors which accounted for the largest part of the variance were selected for study.

Struening (1957) labelled his factors (in order, I', II', and III') "Authoritarian Religious Submission," "Cynical and Suspicious View of the Human Environment," and "Aggressive Authoritarian Nationalism." For comparison with his results see Chapter 9.

INTERPRETATION OF THE FACTORS

In this section, the eight items ranked according to highest loading on each of the three rotated factors, A, B, and C, will be presented in tables for each of the schools. Following each set of tables (one set per school), there will be a discussion of the fac-

TABLE 55

SCHOOL 1

EIGHT ITEMS RANK ORDERED BY HIGHEST FACTOR
LOADINGS ON ROTATED FACTOR A

Item No.	A	Factor B	C	Item
23.	.817	−.002	.167	People without a deep and unquestionable faith in Almighty God should not be trusted in public office
24.	.762	.280	.226	There is hardly anything lower than a person who does not feel great love, gratitude and respect for our flag.
45.	.724	.211	.120	Every person should have complete faith in some supernatural power whose decisions he obeys without question.
44.	.651	.484	−.114	If people would talk less and work more, everybody would be better off.
40.	.602	.250	−.034	An insult to our honor should always be punished.
53.	.593	−.018	.425	Books and movies ought not to deal so much with the unpleasant and seamy side of life; they ought to concentrate on themes that are entertaining or uplifting.
46.	.552	−.072	.265	When a person has a problem or worry, it is best for him not to think about it, but to keep busy with more cheerful things.
49.	.511	.583	.293	There is hardly anything lower than a person who does not feel great love, gratitude and respect for his parents.

tors for that school, comparing them, in terms of similar items, with Factors I', II', and III' of School 6 (Struening's factors).

School 1. The first rotated factor, A, shares seven of its top eight (in terms of loadings) items in common with Struening's Factor I', (School 6). It therefore seems reasonable that this factor can be called "Authoritarian Religious Submission" as Struening labeled it. On the basis of similar items having high loadings on this factor, then, it would seem that the factor is stable from School 6 to School 1.

TABLE 56

School 1

Eight Items Rank Ordered by Highest Factor
Loadings on Rotated Factor B

Item No.	B	Factor A	C	Item
54.	.786	.057	−.190	When you come right down to it, it's human nature never to do anything without an eye to one's profit.
35.	.719	.269	.057	It's a mistake to trust any nation until we are completely sure of them.
27.	.707	.015	.091	Most people don't realize how much our lives are controlled by plots hatched in secret by others.
25.	.703	.088	.466	Americans are getting soft; most people need stricter discipline and the will to defend their interests.
48.	.689	.239	.431	What youth needs most is strict discipline, rugged determination, and the will to fight for family and nation.
49.	.583	.511	.293	There is hardly anything lower than a person who does not feel great love, gratitude and respect for his parents.
47.	.572	.179	.169	A person who has bad manners, habits, and breeding can hardly expect to get along with decent people.
44.	.484	.651	−.114	If people would talk less and work more, everybody would be better off.

Six of the eight items with the highest loadings on Factor B are the same as six of the eight items with highest loadings on Factor II′ of School 6, so here, Factor B and Factor II′ seem to be similar in the two schools. Factor B might then tentatively be called a cynicism factor, similar to Struening's "Cynical and Suspicious View of Human Environment" label for his Factor II′.

On Factor C, however, only five of the eight highest-loaded items are common with those on Factor III′ of School 6. The

263

TABLE 57

School 1

Eight Items Rank Ordered by Highest Factor
Loadings on Rotated Factor C

Item No.	C	Factor A	B	Item
51.	.788	.185	.124	The wild sex life of the old Greeks and Romans was tame compared to some of the goings on in this country, even in places where people might least suspect it.
25.	.466	.088	.703	Americans are getting soft; most people need stricter discipline and the will to defend their interests.
29.	.464	.496	.547	Obedience and a proper respect for authority should be the very first requirements of a good citizen.
48.	.431	.239	.689	What youth needs most is strict discipline, rugged determination, and the will to fight for family and nation.
53.	.425	.593	−.018	Books and movies ought not to deal so much with the seamy side of life; they ought to concentrate on themes that are entertaining or uplifting.
52.	.390	.414	.232	No sane, normal, decent person could ever think of hurting a close friend or relative.
55.	.343	.237	.426	Some leisure is necessary, but it is good hard work that makes life interesting and worthwhile.
49.	.293	.511	.583	There is hardly anything lower than a person who does not feel great love, gratitude and respect for his parents.

content of the eight items with the highest loadings on Factor C is partly "suspiciousness" and partly "aggressive nationalism." On the whole it appears as if the factors identified with School 1 are similar in content to those of School 6, notwithstanding the lack of close agreement between Factors C and III′.

School 2. In comparing factors identified with this school and those identified with School 6, it becomes apparent that the relationship between Factors A, B, and C, and respectively, I′, II′, and III′ breaks down. Six of the eight top-loaded items of Factor C are the same as six of the eight top-loaded items of Factor III′, indicating that these two factors are reasonably similar.

TABLE 58

School 1

NUMBER OF ITEMS COMMON TO THREE FACTORS (A, B, C)
FROM SCHOOL 1 AND THREE FACTORS (I', II', III')
FROM SCHOOL 6

School 1 Factor	No. of Items Common	School 6 Factor
A	7	I'
B	2	I'
C	3	I'
A	1	II'
B	6	II'
C	4	II'
A	3	III'
B	3	III'
C	5	III'

However, five of the eight top-loaded items of Factor C also are the same as five of the eight top-loaded items for Factor I'. Thus Factor C of this school appears to be related to both Factors III' and I'. The items with highest loadings are suggestive of a combination label for Factor C—submission and aggression.

Items dealing with cynicism and suspicion are most heavily loaded on Factor B, which thus seems most similar to Factor II' of School 6.

Factor A is difficult to label for this school. It contains elements of all three Factors I', II', and III' in about equal amounts. School 2 is a Catholic institution, and this fact may be responsible for the appearance of religious items in both Factors A and C.

School 3. The three factors for School 3 might on the basis of their content be labeled the same as Struening's Factors I', II', and III'. Items with religious-superstitious content, and with submission content load on Factor A. However, only four of these items are the same as those of Factor I'. This Factor A taps other items than Factor I', but these other items have the religious submission content of Factor I'.

TABLE 59

School 2

Eight Items Rank Ordered by Highest Factor
Loadings on Rotated Factor A

Item No.	Factor A	B	C	Item
46.	.756	.051	.230	When a person has a problem or worry, it is best for him not to think about it, but to keep busy with more cheerful things.
47.	.675	.132	.202	A person who has bad manners, habits, and breeding can hardly expect to get along with decent people.
29.	.685	.486	.301	Obedience and a proper respect for authority should be the very first requirements of a good citizen.
49.	.523	.348	.512	There is hardly anything lower than a person who does not feel a great love, gratitude and respect for his parents.
24.	.407	.365	.619	There is hardly anything lower than a person who does not feel a great love, gratitude and respect for our flag.
44.	.386	.488	.368	If people would talk less and work more, everybody would be better off.
48.	.372	.346	.608	What youth needs most is strict discipline, rugged determination, and the will to fight for family and nation.
40.	.316	.328	.715	An insult to our honor should always be punished.

Factor B comes through with five of the same items as Factor II'. These are items of cynical and suspicious content; therefore this factor can be called a "cynicism and suspiciousness" factor, similar to the label for Factor II'.

Factor C shares five of eight items with Factor III'. "Aggressive Nationalism" would seem to be an appropriate label for this factor, although several items with a submissive content also load on this factor, and these must be taken into account in interpretation. In addition to these items with submission content, four items which load highly on Factor C also load highly on Factor II', thus making C a difficult factor to interpret in regard to Factors I' and II'.

TABLE 60

School 2

Eight Items Rank Ordered by Highest Factor
Loadings on Rotated Factor B

Item No.	B	Factor A	C	Item
51.	.668	.164	.177	The wild sex life of the old Greeks and Romans was tame compared to some of the goings on in this country, even in places where people might least suspect it.
45.	.618	.165	.126	Every person should have complete faith in some supernatural power whose decisions he obeys without question.
25.	.586	.011	.152	Americans are getting soft; most people need stricter discipline and the will to defend their interests.
53.	.506	.074	.223	Books and movies ought not to deal so much with the unpleasant and seamy side of life; they ought to concentrate on themes that are entertaining or uplifting.
44.	.488	.386	.368	If people would talk less and work more, everybody would be better off.
29.	.486	.685	.301	Obedience and a proper respect for authority should be the very first requirements of a good citizen.
27.	.438	−.002	.488	Most people don't realize how much our lives are controlled by plots hatched in secret by others.
23.	.406	.271	.438	People without a deep and unquestionable faith in Almighty God should not be trusted in public office.

School 4. In comparing the factors for Schools 4 and 6, the general relationship between Factors A and I′, B and II′, and C and III′ prevails fairly well. A, B, and C each share five top-loaded items with their corresponding Factors I′, II′, and III′. On closer inspection, it can be seen that Factor B is also related to Factor I′, as indicated by the fact that four of eight top-loaded items in the two factors are common.

From this school, Factor B appears to be a combination of cynicism and superstition, which would account for its relationship with both Factors I′ and II′.

Factor C shares four top-loaded items with Factor II′. This

267

TABLE 61

School 2

Eight Items Rank Ordered by Highest Factor
Loadings on Rotated Factor C

Item No.	C	Factor A	B	Item
52.	.865	.102	.234	No sane, normal, decent person could ever think of hurting a close friend or relative.
40.	.715	.316	.328	An insult to our honor should always be punished.
35.	.623	.246	.113	It's a mistake to trust any nation until we are completely sure of them.
24.	.619	.407	.365	There is hardly anything lower than a person who does not feel great love, gratitude and respect for our flag.
48.	.608	.372	.346	What youth needs most is strict discipline, rugged determination, and the will to fight for family and nation.
49.	.512	.523	.348	There is hardly anything lower than a person who does not feel a great love, gratitude and respect for his parents.
27.	.488	.438	−.002	Most people don't realize how much our lives are controlled by plots hatched in secret by others.
23.	.438	.271	.234	People without a deep and unquestionable faith in Almighty God should not be trusted in public office.

relationship was found between Factor II′ and Factor C in Schools 1 and 3, as well as here in the 4th School.

School 5. In this school, Factor A appears to be a religious submission factor, as does Factor C, although the latter seems to have more of a "pure" submission content, rather than a "religious" submission content.

Factor B is clearly a "cynical and suspicious" factor, as a glance at the items with highest loadings indicates. Six of these are common with those items loading high on Factor II′.

One fact tends to cloud the picture in this school—each of the three factors, A, B, and C, have four items in common with the eight items loading highest on Factor III′. The actual numeric values of the loadings are not similar in all cases, but the fact

TABLE 62

SCHOOL 2

NUMBER OF ITEMS COMMON TO THREE FACTORS (A, B, C)
FROM SCHOOL 2 AND THREE FACTORS (I′, II′, III′)
FROM SCHOOL 6

School 1 Factor	No. of Items Common	School 6 Factor
A	4	I′
B	3	I′
C	5	I′
A	4	II′
B	5	II′
C	2	II′
A	5	III′
B	1	III′
C	6	III′

remains that all three factors associated with School 5 are related to Factor III′ from School 6.

GENERAL DISCUSSION OF THE FACTORS

In spite of individual dissimilarities, there is a general picture of agreement between Factors I′ and A, II′ and B, and III′ and C, in the content of the items which load highest on the factors.

However, in several of the five schools, Factor A shows about as much relationship to Factor III′ as to Factor I′, and the same holds true for Factor C compared with Factors I′ and III′. This suggests that Factors I′ and III′ are probably not invariant over several samples.

Factor B appears to be the most invariant over all schools. For each school, it shares at least five of the eight top-loaded items of Factor II′. In Schools 3 and 4, Factor B, as in the other schools, shares more of its top-loaded items (5 in each school) with Factor II′ than with either of the other two factors isolated by Struening. However, four of the items of Factor B, School 3, are common with the items of Factor III′; and in School 4, four of the items of Factor B are common with the items of Factor I′.

269

TABLE 63

SCHOOL 3

EIGHT ITEMS RANK ORDERED BY HIGHEST FACTOR
LOADINGS ON ROTATED FACTOR A

Item No.	Factor A	B	C	Item
52.	.715	.106	.157	No sane, normal, decent person would ever think of hurting a close friend or relative.
44.	.706	.378	.014	If people would talk less and work more, everybody would be better off.
49.	.675	.337	.452	There is hardly anything lower than a person who does not feel great love, gratitude and respect for his parents.
46.	.647	.014	.098	When a person has a problem or worry, it is best for him not to think about it, but to keep busy with more cheerful things.
29.	.551	.232	.533	Obedience and a proper respect for authority should be the very first requirements of a good citizen.
53.	.493	.098	.066	Books and movies ought not to deal so much with the seamy side of life; they ought to concentrate on themes that are entertaining or uplifting.
35.	.441	.487	.205	It's a mistake to trust any nation until we are completely sure of them.
45.	.393	.034	.061	Every person should have complete faith in some supernatural power whose decisions he obeys without question.

We might say that, for these two schools at least, Factor B "can't make up its mind" whether to be "cynicism" or "submission" or "aggression." It is not that Factor B lacks similarity with Factor II', it is, rather, that it is also similar to Factors I' and III'. If the sample is adequate, this similarity may be due to the characteristics of the schools—School 3 is a teachers college, and School 4 is a liberal state university. If the sample is not adequate, then characteristics of the sample may be responsible.

It may also be the method of rotation used, although this method was the same for all schools. Struening (1957) originally rotated his factors graphically; for the present study his unro-

TABLE 64

SCHOOL 3

EIGHT ITEMS RANK ORDERED BY HIGHEST FACTOR
LOADINGS ON ROTATED FACTOR B

Item No.	Factor B	A	C	Item
51.	.765	.163	.061	The wild sex life of the old Greeks and Romans was tame compared to some of the goings on in this country, even where people might least suspect it.
40.	.746	.119	.145	An insult to our honor should always be punished.
27.	.722	−.094	.259	Most people don't realize how much our lives are controlled by plots hatched in secret by others.
48.	.667	.057	.476	What youth needs most is strict discipline, rugged determination, and the will to fight for family and nation.
47.	.664	.365	.125	A person who has bad manners, habits, and breeding can hardly expect to get along with decent people.
35.	.487	.441	.205	It's a mistake to trust any nation until we are completely sure of them.
54.	.428	.095	.077	When you come right down to it, it's human nature never to do anything without an eye to one's profit.
44.	.378	.706	.014	If people would talk less and work more, everybody would be better off.

tated factors, as well as those for Schools 1 to 5, were rotated analytically. The largest discrepancy between Struening's factor loadings rotated graphically and rotated analytically was only .03, however. For example, graphic rotation might have given a factor loading of .47, where analytic rotation would give the same item a loading of .50. In regard to the method of rotation, Dr. James Norton, of the Statistical Laboratory at Purdue University, has suggested that for future research the analytically rotated factors for Schools 1 to 5 might be subjected to further rotation, graphically, to determine whether they could be made more similar in terms of the actual numerical values of the factor loadings.

Struening's Factor II′ seems the most invariant of the three

271

TABLE 65

SCHOOL 3

EIGHT ITEMS RANK ORDERED BY HIGHEST FACTOR
LOADINGS ON ROTATED FACTOR C

Item No.	Factor C	A	B	Item
25.	.730	−.091	.359	Americans are getting soft; most people need stricter discipline and the will to defend their interests.
24.	.656	.200	.159	There is hardly anything lower than a person who does not feel a great love, gratitude and respect for our flag.
23.	.538	.189	.040	People without a deep and unquestionable faith in Almighty God should not be trusted in public office.
29.	.533	.551	.232	Obedience and a proper respect for authority should be the very first requirements for a good citizen.
48.	.476	.057	.667	What youth needs most is strict discipline, rugged determination, and the will to fight for family and nation.
49.	.452	.675	.337	There is hardly anything lower than a person who does not feel a great love, gratitude and respect for his parents.
55.	.324	.273	.134	Some leisure is necessary, but it is good hard work that makes life worthwhile.
27.	.259	−.094	.722	Most people don't realize how much our lives are controlled by plots hatched in secret by others.

TABLE 66

SCHOOL 3

NUMBER OF ITEMS COMMON TO THREE FACTORS (A, B, C)
FROM SCHOOL 3 AND THREE FACTORS (I′, II′, III′)
FROM SCHOOL 6

School 1 Factor	No. of Items Common	School 6 Factor
A	4	I′
B	2	I′
C	4	I′
A	2	II′
B	5	II′
C	4	II′
A	5	III′
B	4	III′
C	3	III′

TABLE 67

School 4

Eight Items Rank Ordered by Highest Factor
Loadings on Rotated Factor A

Item No.	A	Factor B	C	Item
40.	.919	.006	−.116	An insult to our honor should always be punished.
24.	.718	.226	.268	There is hardly anything lower than a person who does not feel a great love, gratitude and respect for our flag.
23.	.714	.143	.423	People without a deep and unquestionable faith in Almighty God should not be trusted in public office.
52.	.645	−.148	.132	No sane, normal, decent person could ever think of hurting a close friend or relative.
44.	.591	.531	.403	If people would talk less and work more, everybody would be better off.
51.	.570	.228	−.012	The wild sex life of the old Greeks and Romans was tame compared to some of the goings on in this country, even in places where people might least suspect it.
53.	.569	.382	.222	Books and movies ought not to deal so much with the unpleasant and seamy side of life; they ought to concentrate on themes that are entertaining or uplifting.
45.	.567	.116	.227	Every person should have complete faith in some supernatural power whose decisions he obeys without question.

factors he isolated from the F′ Scale. This is the factor labeled "Cynical and Suspicious View of Human Environment." For each of the five schools in the present study, Struening's Factor II′ was more similar to Factor B of the present study than to Factors A or C of the present study.

Struening's Factor I′, "Authoritarian Religious Submission," was most often, for the five schools, similar to Factor A. However, in several of the schools Factor I′ was as similar to Factor C as to Factor A.

His Factor III′, "Aggressive Authoritarian Nationalism," while generally similar to our Factor C, was also similar, for several of the schools, to Factor A.

273

TABLE 68

SCHOOL 4

EIGHT ITEMS RANK ORDERED BY HIGHEST FACTOR
LOADINGS ON ROTATED FACTOR B

Item No.	B	Factor A	C	Item
46.	.802	.111	.040	When a person has a problem or worry, it is best for him not to think about it, but, to keep busy with more cheerful things.
25.	.616	.314	.121	Americans are getting soft; most people need stricter discipline and the will to defend their interests.
44.	.531	.591	.403	If people would talk less and work more, everybody would be better off.
47.	.492	.034	.183	A person who has bad manners, habits, and breeding, can hardly expect to get along with decent people.
48.	.478	.159	.771	What youth needs most is strict discipline, rugged determination, and the will to fight for family and nation.
49.	.415	.491	.453	There is hardly anything lower than a person who does not feel a great love, gratitude and respect for his parents.
53.	.382	.569	.222	Books and movies ought not to deal so much with the unpleasant and seamy side of life; they ought to concentrate on themes that are entertaining or uplifting.
27.	.328	−.172	.494	Most people don't realize how much our lives are controlled by plots hatched in secret by others.

It appears then, that the factors labeled "Authoritarian Religious Submission" and "Aggressive Authoritarian Nationalism" are not invariant over several groups of respondents, at least not as invariant as in the factor labeled "Cynical and Suspicious View of the Human Environment."

It must be remembered that the authors of *The Authoritarian Personality* attempted to construct individual items for the F Scale which would be capable of measuring more than one facet of authoritarianism, and that 13 of the items in the present study are from this F Scale. Perhaps their success in constructing this

TABLE 69

SCHOOL 4

EIGHT ITEMS RANK ORDERED BY HIGHEST FACTOR
LOADINGS ON ROTATED FACTOR C

Item No.	Factor C	A	B	Item
48.	.771	.159	.478	What youth needs most is strict discipline, rugged determination, and the will to fight for family and nation.
29.	.690	.223	.163	Obedience and a proper respect for authority should be the very first requirements of a good citizen.
55.	.566	.257	.274	Some leisure is necessary, but it is good hard work that makes life interesting and worthwhile.
35.	.532	.144	.047	It's a mistake to trust any nation until we are completely sure of them.
54.	.515	.088	−.307	When you come right down to it, it's human nature never to do anything without an eye to one's profit.
27.	.494	−.172	.328	Most people don't realize how much our lives are controlled by plots hatched in secret by others.
49.	.453	.491	.415	There is hardly anything lower than a person who does not feel a great love, gratitude and respect for his parents.
23.	.423	.714	.143	People without a deep and unquestionable faith in Almighty God should not be trusted in public office.

type of item is related to our lack of success in finding perfectly invariant factors over several populations. As is true of any work, the results are dependent on the kind of materials worked with.

SUMMARY AND CONCLUSIONS

This study was designed to investigate the stability of factors underlying an authoritarian attitude scale consisting of 18 items. Previous research with the instrument, called the F′ Scale (Struening, 1957) led to the development of three factors:

I′ Authoritarian Religious Submission
II′ Cynical and Suspicious View of Human Environment
III′ Aggressive Authoritarian Nationalism

TABLE 70

School 4

NUMBER OF ITEMS COMMON TO THREE FACTORS
(A, B, C) FROM SCHOOL 4 AND THREE FACTORS
(I', II', III) FROM SCHOOL 6

School 4 Factor	No. of Items Common	School 6 Factor
A	5	I'
B	4	I'
C	3	I'
A	2	II'
B	5	II'
C	4	II'
A	3	III'
B	2	III'
C	5	III'

TABLE 71

School 5

EIGHT ITEMS RANK ORDERED BY HIGHEST FACTOR
LOADINGS ON ROTATED FACTOR A

Item No.	Factor A	B	C	Item
40.	.777	.101	.217	An insult to our honor should always be punished.
24.	.772	.121	.355	There is hardly anything lower than a person who does not feel a great love, gratitude and respect for our flag.
48.	.695	.399	.311	What youth needs most is strict discipline, rugged determination, and the will to fight for family and nation.
49.	.567	.251	.600	There is hardly anything lower than a person who does not feel a great love, gratitude and respect for his parents.
45.	.517	−.161	.606	Every person should have complete faith in some supernatural power whose decisions he obeys without question.
23.	.480	−.556	.106	People without a deep and unquestionable faith in Almighty God should not be trusted in public office.
44.	.477	.202	−.068	If people would talk less and work more, everybody would be better off.
25.	.386	.724	−.118	Americans are getting soft; most people need stricter discipline and the will to defend their interests.

276

TABLE 72

SCHOOL 5

EIGHT ITEMS RANK ORDERED BY HIGHEST FACTOR
LOADINGS ON ROTATED FACTOR B

Item No.	Factor B	A	C	Item
54.	.836	.151	.140	When you come right town to it, it's human nature never to do anything without an eye to one's profit.
25.	.724	.386	−.118	Americans are getting soft; most people need stricter discipline and the will to defend their interests.
35.	.697	.202	.200	It's a mistake to trust any nation until we are completely sure of them.
55.	.548	.076	.190	Some leisure is necessary, but it is good hard work that makes life interesting and worthwhile.
29.	.434	.228	.494	Obedience and a proper respect for authority should be the first requirements of a good citizen.
48.	.399	.695	.311	What youth needs most is strict discipline, rugged determination, and the will to fight for family and nation.
27.	.386	.213	.200	Most people don't realize how much our lives are controlled by plots hatched in secret by others.
51.	.341	−.293	.664	The wild sex life of the old Greeks and Romans was tame compared to some of the goings on in this country, even in places where people might least suspect it.

The sample used in the previous research consisted of faculty members of a large Midwestern University.

The same instrument was administered to faculty members from 23 Indiana colleges and universities. On the basis of number of respondents, five of these institutions were selected for the present study. Item responses were intercorrelated for each of the schools, producing five 18 by 18 matrices of tetrachoric coefficients of correlation.

Each of these five matrices was factor analyzed, and three factors accounting for the most variance were selected from each of the analyses. Each of these sets of three factors was rotated analytically, using the "varimax" criterion.

TABLE 73

SCHOOL 5

EIGHT ITEMS RANK ORDERED BY HIGHEST FACTOR
LOADINGS ON ROTATED FACTOR C

Item No.	Factor C	A	B	Item
47.	.848	.143	.023	A person who has bad manners, habits, and breeding can hardly expect to get along with decent people.
51.	.664	−.293	.341	The wild sex life of the old Greeks and Romans was tame compared to some of the goings on in this country, even in places where people might least suspect it.
45.	.606	.517	−.161	Every person should have complete faith in some supernatural power whose decisions he obeys without question.
49.	.600	.567	.251	There is hardly anything lower than a person who does not have great love, gratitude and respect for his parents.
52.	.514	.095	.049	No sane, normal, decent person could ever think of hurting a close friend or relative.
29.	.494	.228	.434	Obedience and a proper respect for authority should be the very first requirements for a good citizen.
46.	.411	.250	.183	When a person has a problem or worry, it is best for him not to think about it, but to keep busy with more cheerful things.
24.	.355	.772	.121	There is hardly anything lower than a person who does not feel great love, gratitude and respect for our flag.

To determine their stability the three factors thus obtained from each of the five schools were compared, in terms of items loading highest on them, with the three factors from Midwest University studied in the previous research. The three factors, A, B, and C generally shared similar items with Factors I′, II′, and III′, respectively, indicating that Factors I′, II′, and III′ are reasonably stable over several populations. Factor II′ was the most stable, or invariant, over the several populations.

Factor A, which in all schools was similar to Factor I′, was in several schools also similar to Factor III′. Factor C, in all schools

TABLE 74

School 5

Number of Items Common to Three Factors
(A, B, C) from School 5 and Three Factors
(I', II', III') from School 6

School 5 Factor	No. of Items Common	School 6 Factor
A	6	I'
B	1	I'
C	4	I'
A	3	II'
B	6	II'
C	3	II'
A	4	III'
B	4	III'
C	4	III'

similar to Factor III', was in several schools similar to Factor I' as well. Thus Factors I' and III' appear not to be as stable as Factor II'.

It was suggested that item content might be responsible for this lack of factorial invariance, since in constructing the F Scale (some of the items from which were included in the F' Scale used here), Adorno et al. (1950) attempted to develop items which would measure more than one facet of authoritarianism at a time.

279

XI TEACHER AUTHORITARIANISM VERSUS TEACHING EFFECTIVENESS AS PERCEIVED BY STUDENTS

W. H. Vermillion, Jr., W. H. Leftwich,[1] and H. H. Remmers.

Teaching effectiveness is a very complex activity and difficult to define since many variables could influence a teacher's performance. Among these are the traits which comprise his personality. In recent years, a personality syndrome which has received considerable attention is authoritarianism. The study herein reported is an investigation of the correlation between this personality variable, authoritarianism, and a measure of teaching performance, university student ratings. Specifically, the hypothesis being investigated is that the degree of authoritarianism possessed by an instructor will have a statistically significant non-zero correlation with the "goodness" of his teaching performance as evaluated by his students.

As will be clear from Chapters VIII and X, probably the best-known measure of authoritarianism is the original F Scale; the authors, as previously indicated, were guided by two primary purposes: (1) To provide a covert measure of prejudice without mentioning minority groups, or current political-economic groups; (2) to provide, in their words, "a valid estimate of anti-democratic tendencies at the personality level" (Adorno *et al.*, 1950, p. 222). The authors derived and defined a number of variables which would estimate these personality characteristics. These variables were considered to comprise a syndrome in the person that renders him receptive to anti-democratic propaganda. "One might say, therefore, that the F Scale attempts to measure the potentially anti-democratic personality" (Adorno *et al.*, 1950, p. 228).

Successive forms of the F Scale, revised on the basis of item analysis, resulted in a final 30-item form with a mean reliability coefficient (based on split-half correlation) of .90. To determine the inter-item relations of this form, an item-by-item correlation matrix was computed using results from a sample size of 517. The average coefficient was .13; the range was −.05 to .44. When each item was compared to the rest of the scale, the mean r was .33 and the range .15 to .52. The authors concluded that, "Despite the scale's relative lack of surface homogeneity, however, we are justified in speaking of an F pattern or syndrome, for the items do 'hang together' in the sense that each is significantly correlated with the scale as a whole" (Adorno *et al.* [1950], p. 261). Melvin (Eysenck, 1954) subjected this matrix to factor analysis and found a very strong general factor which substantiates the claim that the scale is essentially unidimensional. For the reader's convenience the F′ Scale is repeated here.

Struening (1957, p. 34) summarizes: "It appears that Adorno and his co-authors have constructed a highly reliable, essentially unidimensional (at least on college women) scale."

Struening (1957) developed empirically a modification of the F Scale, designated the F′ Scale (See Chapter IX) and designed for use with a university faculty population, which consists of 18 items (Table 75), 13 of which were selected from the various forms of the F Scale. The remaining five items are similar in content to original F Scale items. The following considerations were the bases for the selection of items: "(a) They must not antagonize the respondents; for this reason some of the extremely ambiguous items were omitted; (b) They must break the responding population into two reasonably equal groups in terms of agreedisagree responses; for this reason extremely over-simplified and superstitious items were excluded." (Struening, [1957], p. 35). The items were administered to 911 faculty members (Approximately 50 per cent) of a Midwestern university, the item responses intercorrelated and factor analyzed.

Three factors accounted for 74.9% of the variance. Factor I, labeled the "General Factor," accounted for 63.6% of the common variance while Factors II and III accounted for 6.4% and 4.9% respectively. The 18 items of the F′ Scale item responses were weighted in proportion to their loadings on Factor I (See Table

TABLE 75

THE F' SCALE

Item	Scoring Weight	
	Agree	Disagree
People without a deep and unquestionable faith in Almighty God should not be trusted in public office.	6	0
There is hardly anything lower than a person who does not feel a great love, gratitude, and respect for our flag.	8	0
Americans are getting soft; most people need stricter discipline and the will to defend their interests.	4	0
Most people don't realize how much our lives are controlled by plots hatched in secret by others.	2	0
Obedience and a proper respect for authority should be the very first requirements of a good citizen.	8	0
It's a mistake to trust any nation until we are completely sure of them.	2	0
An insult to our honor should always be punished.	6	0
If people would talk less and work more, everybody would be better off.	5	0
Every person should have complete faith in some supernatural power whose decisions he obeys without question.	5	0
When a person has a problem or worry, it is best for him not to think about it, but to keep busy with more cheerful things.	1	0
A person who has bad manners, habits, and breeding can hardly expect to get along with decent people.	2	0
What youth needs most is strict discipline, rugged determination, and the will to fight for family and nation.	9	0
There is hardly anything lower than a person who does not feel a great love, gratitude, and respect for his parents.	9	0
The wild sex life of the old Greeks and Romans was tame compared to some of the goings on in this country, even in places where people might least suspect it.	2	0
No sane, normal, decent person could ever think of hurting a close relative or friend.	4	0
Books and movies ought not to deal so much with the unpleasant and seamy side of life; they		

TABLE 75 (Continued)

Item	Agree	Disagree
ought to concentrate on themes that are entertaining or uplifting.	3	0
When you come right down to it, it's human nature never to do anything without an eye to one's profit.	1	0
Some leisure is necessary, but it is good hard work that makes life interesting and worthwhile.	3	0

75). Using these weights he computed an internal consistency of .79. With the present sample, an analysis of variance technique revealed a very similar internal consistency of .78. Since "what, precisely, is measured by the F Scale just isn't known" (Struening [1957], p. 70), the validity of the derived F' Scale must rest upon the scale authors' "ability to accurately infer what is measured by the items which define a factor." (p. 71)

Although a universally acceptable method of teacher evaluation is not available, student ratings of their instructors appears to be one of the most fruitful; hence, it was used as a criterion measure in this study. Considerable work has been expended toward devising reliable and valid instruments for evaluating teaching performance via this technique (Davenport, 1944; Bendig, 1952) Crannell, 1953; Ruja, 1953; Remmers, 1960). A recent survey of 584 colleges and universities disclosed that student ratings and opinions (informal) were cited most often by the colleges as aids to be used in the evaluation of teachers (Gustad, 1961). Leftwich ([1961], p. 11) concluded, after discussing the advantages and disadvantages of student ratings: "Although there is continued objection to the use of such ratings, the reasons being offered concerning their susceptibility to certain contaminating influences, the weight of the evidence supports their continued use."

The particular rating instruments employed in this study were the ten instructor personality traits of the *Purdue Rating Scale for Instruction* or PRSI (Brandenburg and Remmers, 1927). It is a 26-item graphic scale which enables students to rate their instructors and their courses on characteristics judged important in the educational process. Items one through ten (Table 76) deal with instructor qualities and thus were the items chosen to comprise the criterion. In the construction of the PRSI, these items were chosen from a variety of sources "as being among the most important contributors to the 'generalized attitude' towards an instructor and the most important traits where 'good' and 'poor' instructors are seen to differ" (Remmers [1960], p. 2). The manual of instructions reports reliabilities for each of the ten items to vary from .810 to .933 on one sample and .957 to .943 on another using the Horst (1949) reliability formula for unequal numbers

TABLE 76

THE CORRELATION BETWEEN STUDENTS' RATINGS OF 65 TEACHERS ON
THE TEN PERSONALITY TRAITS OF THE PURDUE RATING SCALE FOR
INSTRUCTION AND THE INSTRUCTOR'S F' SCORE

Item	r	t
1. Interest in Subject	$-.082$	$-.658$
2. Sympathetic Attitude toward Students	$-.022$	$-.176$
3. Fairness in Grading	.198	1.616
4. Liberal and Progressive Attitude	$-.095$	$-.764$
5. Presentation of Subject Matter	$-.085$	$-.683$
6. Sense of Proportion and Humor	$-.095$	$-.764$
7. Self-Reliance and Confidence	$-.224$	$-1.829*$
8. Personal Peculiarities	.032	.256
9. Personal Appearance	.113	.909
10. Stimulating Intellectual Curiosity	$-.151$	-1.221
Mean Rating	$-.082$	$-.658$

* Significant at .10 level; N = 65

$$t63(.90) = 1.665$$
$$t63(.95) = 1.993$$

of raters. In addition, it reports internal consistency coefficients (Horst Formula) for the items used in this study, based on a sample of 59 teachers and 1,908 students, to range from .67 to .91 with only one coefficient below .87. The validity of the PRSI is inferred from its reliability. According to Remmers ([1960], p. 7), the scale "purports to measure the student's judgments of the instructor . . . to the extent that the students agree among themselves, and to the extent that each student is self-consistent in his judgments, we are able to say that the scale is valid." This is in accord with the observation of Tiffin and McCormick ([1958], p. 244) that "the validity of merit ratings may have to be inferred from their reliability."

PROCEDURE

A total of 2,833 student ratings on instructors in 101 classes were obtained using the PRSI as a rating instrument. The number of students rating each of the 65 instructors (some instructors taught several classes) ranged from six to 276 with a median of 34. Concurrently, each instructor completed a questionnaire entitled "A Survey of Social Issues." Hidden within this questionnaire were the items which comprised the F′ Scale.

The sample of instructors was composed of both full-time and part-time teaching staff volunteers of a Midwestern university. The sample represented a wide variety of courses in a large number of departments. Thirty of the instructors possessed the doctorate degree and 32 others the master's degree. Classified by academic rank, there were two full professors, 11 associate professors, 29 assistant professors, and 23 instructors. A wide range of age and experience was represented.

For each instructor, the mean rating on each of the ten items of the PRSI, as well as the mean of all ten items was computed. In addition, each instructors F′ Score was determined. The F′ Scores were then graphically compared with each of the 11 rating scores. Since none of the plots indicated a non-linear relationship, Pearson r's were computed.

DISCUSSION

The original hypothesis of a non-zero correlation between an instructor's measured degree of authoritarianism and his rating by his students is rejected. As shown in Table 76, none of the correlations were significantly different from zero at the .05 level. One item, Self-Reliance and Confidence, was significantly different at the .10 level. With 11 correlations however, one will be expected to be statistically significant at this level as a result of sampling errors alone.

It appears reasonable to conclude, therefore, that, to the extent that this sample is representative of college instructors and to the extent that the F' Scale is an accurate measure of authoritarianism, there is no consistent relationship between an instructor's degree of authoritarianism and his ratings by his students. Due to the similarity of the F' Scale and the F Scale, this would also appear to make suspect the original F Scale as an instrument to aid in identifying and selecting instructors judged capable by their students.

SUMMARY

The hypothesis that there is a significant, non-zero correlation between an instructor's measured degree of authoritarianism and his rating by his students was tested on 65 instructors at a Midwestern university, each rated by one or more of their classes with the first ten items of the Purdue Rating Scale for Instruction. Each instructor completed a questionnaire which included items comprising an authoritarianism scale. The correlations between the items of the PRSI and the authoritarianism scale were computed. None were statistically significant at the .05 level of significance. It was concluded that there is no consistent relationship between student ratings of instructors and the instructor's degree of authoritarianism as measured by this scale.

NOTE

1. Now at the University of Richmond.

Appendix A

Question Sheet

THE PURDUE OPINION PANEL

Poll Number 30, October 1951

Please answer all questions frankly. Do not sign your name on this sheet or on the ballot. No one will ever know how you have marked your ballot. It is important that you answer *all* questions. Please follow these directions:

Read the question and decide upon your answer.
Notice the number and letter of that answer.
Draw a line through that number and letter on these pages.
Find the bracket on the card with the number and letter inside it.
Make a SOLID BLACK LINE through the number and letter from
one end of the bracket to the other.

INFORMATION ABOUT MYSELF, MY HOME,
AND MY PARENTS

1. I am a
   (1A) Boy
   (1B) Girl
2. I am in
   (1D) Grade 10
   (1C) Grade 9
   (1E) Grade 11
   (1F) Grade 12 or graduated
3. I live in an area which is chiefly (the person giving you these sheets will tell you which to mark.)
   (1G) Rural
   (1H) Urban
4. The political party I prefer is
   (1I) Democratic party
   (1J) Republican party
   (1K) Some other party
   (1L) No party
5. My religion is
   (2A) Protestant

287

(2B) Catholic
(2C) Jewish
(2D) Some other
(2E) None

6. SCHOOLING OF MY MOTHER. My mother
   (2F) Did not finish the eighth grade
   (2G) Finished eighth grade
   (2H) Had some high school but did not finish
   (2I) Finished high school
   (2J) Had some college but did not graduate
   (2K) Graduated from college

7. HOUSE AND HOME. We have the following at our home:
   (Mark with an X *on this paper* each item you have in your home.
   ____ A vacuum cleaner
   ____ An electric or gas refrigerator
   ____ A bathtub or shower with running water
   ____ A telephone
   ____ Two automobiles (don't count trucks)
   ____ I have had paid lessons in dancing, drama, expression, art, or
   music outside of school

   Now count the number of X's that you have marked above. Locate
   that number in the list below. On the ballot card find the number
   and letter which stand for your answer. Blacken the space that
   has that number and letter inside of it.

   (3A) None
   (3B) One
   (3C) Two
   (3D) Three
   (3E) Four
   (3F) Five
   (3G) Six

8. Regarding my religious beliefs and practices, I would say that
   (4A) I feel very strongly about them
   (4B) I feel somewhat strongly about them
   (4C) I feel very mildly about them
   (4D) I feel indifferent about them

9. Newspapers and magazines should be allowed to print anything
   they want except military secrets.
   (4E) Agree

288

(4F) Disagree

(4G) Uncertain

10. The greatest threat to democracy in the U. S. comes from foreign ideas and foreign groups.

(4H) Agree

(4I) Disagree

(4J) Uncertain

11. Obedience and respect for authority are the most important virtues that children should learn.

(5A) Agree

(5B) Disagree

(5C) Uncertain

12. The government should have control of the railroads and airlines.

(5D) Agree

(5E) Disagree

(5F) Uncertain

13. Religious belief and worship should not be restricted by laws.

(5G) Agree

(5H) Disagree

(5I) Uncertain

14. In these times, patriotism and loyalty to established American ways are the *most* important requirements of a good citizen.

(5J) Agree

(5K) Disagree

(5L) Uncertain

15. Whatever serves the interests of government best is generally right.

(6A) Agree

(6B) Disagree

(6C) Uncertain

16. The government should abolish all rights of inheritance to insure equality of opportunity.

(6D) Agree

(6E) Disagree

(6F) Uncertain

17. The government should prohibit some people from making public speeches.

(6G) Agree

(6H) Disagree

(6I) Uncertain

18. Immigration of foreigners into this country should be greatly restricted, since it may mean lowering national standards.
   (6J) Agree
   (6K) Disagree
   (6L) Uncertain

19. In some cases, the police should be allowed to search a person or his home even though they do not have a warrant.
   (7A) Agree
   (7B) Disagree
   (7C) Uncertain

20. Most basic industries, like mining and manufacturing, should be owned by the government.
   (7D) Agree
   (7E) Disagree
   (7F) Uncertain

21. Most children these days need more discipline.
   (7G) Agree
   (7H) Disagree
   (7I) Uncertain

22. Some criminals are so bad that they shouldn't be allowed to have a lawyer.
   (7J) Agree
   (7K) Disagree
   (7L) Uncertain

23. Foreign countries have very little to contribute to American progress.
   (8A) Agree
   (8B) Disagree
   (8C) Uncertain

24. Our modern society is moved chiefly by the desire for profit.
   (8D) Agree
   (8E) Disagree
   (8F) Uncertain

25. Some religious groups should not be allowed the same freedom as others.
   (8G) Agree
   (8H) Disagree
   (8I) Uncertain

26. Most criminals and moral misfits should be prevented from having children.
   (8J) Agree

(8K) Disagree

(8L) Uncertain

27. If a person is accused of a crime he should always have the right to know who is accusing him.

(9A) Agree

(9B) Disagree

(9C) Uncertain

28. We should firmly resist any attempts to change the American way of life.

(9D) Agree

(9E) Disagree

(9F) Uncertain

29. Certain groups should not be allowed to hold public meetings, even though they gather peaceably and only make speeches.

(9G) Agree

(9H) Disagree

(9I) Uncertain

30. Most history is the story of the fight for power between different classes: master and slave, landowner and peasant, management and labor.

(9J) Agree

(9K) Disagree

(9L) Uncertain

31. What this country needs most is a few strong, courageous, tireless leaders in whom the people can put their faith.

(10A) Agree

(10B) Disagree

(10C) Uncertain

32. Foreigners in this country should always be allowed the same basic freedoms that citizens have.

(10D) Agree

(10E) Disagree

(10F) Uncertain

33. A large mass of the people are not capable of determining what is and what is not good for them.

(10G) Agree

(10H) Disagree

(10I) Uncertain

34. Local police may sometimes be right in holding persons in jail without telling them of any formal charge against them.

(10J) Agree

(10K) Disagree

(10L) Uncertain

35. There will always be strong groups and weak groups, and it is best that the strong continue to dominate the weak.

(11A) Agree

(11B) Disagree

(11C) Uncertain

36. In some criminal cases, a trial by jury is an unnecessary expense and shouldn't be given.

(11D) Agree

(11E) Disagree

(11F) Uncertain

37. The price of goods we buy should depend only upon the cost of making them.

(11G) Agree

(11H) Disagree

(11I) Uncertain

38. The American way of life is superior in nearly all respects to any other.

(11J) Agree

(11K) Disagree

(11L) Uncertain

39. In some cases, the government should have the right to take over a person's land or property without bothering to go to court.

(12A) Agree

(12B) Disagree

(12C) Uncertain

40. The right of some working groups to call a strike should be abolished, as it is a threat to democracy and not in the general interest of society.

(12D) Agree

(12E) Disagree

(12F) Uncertain

41. The police or F.B.I. may sometimes be right in giving a man the "third degree" to make him talk.

(12G) Agree

(12H) Disagree

(12I) Uncertain

42. All banks and all credit should be run by the government.

(12J) Agree

(12K) Disagree

(12L) Uncertain

43. Some important organizations in the U. S. have objected to flying the United Nations flag above the U. S. flag. Do you agree or disagree with them?

(13A) Agree

(13B) Disagree

(13C) Uncertain

44. Persons who refuse to testify against themselves (that is, give evidence that would show that they are guilty of criminal acts) should either be made to talk or severely punished.

(13D) Agree

(13E) Disagree

(13F) Uncertain

45. The average citizen does not show enough respect for the U. S. flag.

(13G) Agree

(13H) Disagree

(13I) Uncertain

46. Large estates, on which the land lies idle and unused, should be divided up among the poor for farming.

(13J) Agree

(13K) Disagree

(13L) Uncertain

47. Some of the petitions which have been circulated should not be allowed by the government.

(14A) Agree

(14B) Disagree

(14C) Uncertain

48. Have you heard about Senator McCarthy's efforts to discover and remove communist influence in our government?

(14D) Yes

(14E) No

(14F) Uncertain

49. If you answered "yes" to Q. 48, would you say that you approve or do not approve of his methods? (If you did not answer "yes" to Q. 48, do not answer this question).

(14G) Approve

(14H) Do not approve

(14I) Uncertain

50. Do you think that loyalty oaths should be required of all government employees, or only of those in positions involving security or secrecy?
    (15A) Req'd of all
    (15B) Req'd only of security employees
    (15C) Not req'd of any
    (15D) Uncertain

51. Should or should not teachers in our schools and colleges be required to sign a special non-communist oath?
    (15E) Should
    (15F) Should not
    (15G) Uncertain

52. Police and other groups have sometimes banned or censored certain books and movies in their cities. Should they or should they not have power to do this?
    (15H) Should
    (15I) Should not
    (15J) Uncertain

53. It has been suggested that persons who refuse to serve in the Army or "fight for their country" should be deprived of their right to vote. Do you agree or disagree with this idea?
    (16A) Agree
    (16B) Disagree
    (16C) Uncertain

54. Should or should not a foreigner visiting this country be permitted to criticize our government?
    (16D) Should
    (16E) Should not
    (16F) Uncertain

55. Some cities have passed laws against printing or selling any communist literature. Do you think such laws should or should not be passed?
    (16G) Should
    (16H) Should not
    (16I) Uncertain

56. In peacetime, do you think that members of the Communist party in this country should be allowed to speak on the radio?
    (16J) Should
    (16K) Should not
    (16L) Uncertain

57. Do you think that a person suspected of being a communist should be fired from his job even if there is no proof that he is actually a communist?
    (17A) Should
    (17B) Should not
    (17C) Uncertain
58. Do you or do you not think that our schools should compare and contrast democracy as it works in the U. S. with communism as it works in Russia?
    (17D) Should
    (17E) Should not
    (17F) Uncertain
59. Do you think that most of the recent disloyalty charges that have been brought against persons in government positions have done more to *protect* our freedoms or more to *threaten* them?
    (17G) To protect
    (17H) To threaten
    (17I) Neither or undecided
60. If ordinary citizens make accusing statements about others, without evidence or proof, they can be sued for slander or libel. Do you think that members of Congress trying to uncover dangerous influences in the government should have to obey the same laws or not?
    (17J) Should
    (17K) Should not
    (17L) Uncertain

WHAT I BELIEVE TO BE TRUE

(If you don't know the answer, guess.) Do not omit any questions.
61. Bernard Baruch is
    (18A) A member of the U. S. cabinet
    (18B) A member of Congress
    (18C) A Supreme Court judge
    (18D) None of these
62. The present Secretary of Defense is:
    (18E) George Marshall
    (18F) General Eisenhower

(18G) Robert Lovett

(18H) Dean Acheson

63. The U. S. has signed a peace treaty with Germany.

(18I) True

(18J) False

64. The federal government has made it illegal to be a communist in the U. S.

(18K) True

(18L) False

65. The Constitution of the U. S. provided for the President's cabinet

(19A) True

(19B) False

66. Women gained the right to vote about the year

(19C) 1791

(19D) 1880

(19E) 1902

(19F) 1920

67. All thirteen of the original states had ratified the Constitution by the year 1787.

(19H) True

(19I) False

68. Congress has recently passed a universal military training law.

(19J) True

(19K) False

69. Communism was relatively unheard of before the year 1930 or so.

(20A) True

(20B) False

70. The Constitution of the U. S. drew many ideas about the rights of man from early English writers.

(20C) True

(20D) False

71. Have you had, or are you now taking a course in Civics or U. S. Government?

(20E) Have taken

(20F) Now taking

(20G) Have not taken any

Question Sheet

THE PURDUE OPINION PANEL
Poll Number 35, October 1952

To answer the questions on this poll, you will need one of the special pencils that your teacher will give you and the envelope containing the ballot cards. Look through this question sheet now to see that there are no blank pages. If you do not have three sheets, each printed on both sides, get a new one from your teacher. Also, look at the envelope containing the ballot cards. Make sure it is the same one that you used for the first poll, and has your name on it. Take the *WHITE* card from the envelope, and use it for answering this poll.

Please answer all questions honestly. Notice that you do *not* sign your name on this sheet nor on the ballot card. No one will ever know how you marked your ballot. It is important that you answer *all* questions. Please follow these directions:

Read the question and decide upon your answer.
Notice the number and letter of that answer.
Draw a line through that number and letter on these pages.
Find the bracket on the ballot card with that number and letter inside it.
Make a SOLID BLACK LINE through the number and letter from one end of the bracket to the other.

INFORMATION ABOUT MYSELF, MY HOME,
AND MY PARENTS

1. I am a
   (1A) Boy
   (1B) Girl
2. I am in
   (1C) Grade 9
   (1D) Grade 10
   (1E) Grade 11
   (1F) Grade 12 or graduated

297

3. I live in an area which is chiefly (the person giving you these sheets will tell you which to mark):
   (1G) Rural
   (1H) Urban

4. The political party which I prefer is
   (1I) Democratic party
   (1J) Republican party
   (1K) No party
   (1L) Some other party

5. If the ballot card you are using is *not* from the same envelope that you were given for the first two polls of the year, mark one of the following:
   (2A) This card is from a different envelope.
   (2B) I did not take one or both of the first two polls.

6. SCHOOLING OF MOTHER. My mother
   (2C) Did not graduate from high school
   (2D) Graduated from high school but did not graduate from college
   (2E) Graduated from college

7. On the average, I go to religious services
   (2F) Three or more times a week
   (2G) About twice a week
   (2H) About once a week
   (2I) About once or twice a month
   (2J) A few times a month
   (2K) Practically never or never

8. HOUSE AND HOME. We have the following at our home: (mark with an X *on this* page each item you have in your home, then follow the directions below).
   _____ A vacuum cleaner
   _____ An electric or gas refrigerator
   _____ A bathtub or shower with running water
   _____ An automatic dishwasher
   _____ Two automobiles (don't count trucks)
   _____ Part time or full time paid help for the *home*
   _____ I have had paid lessons in dancing, drama, expression, art or music outside of school

   Now count the number of X's that you have marked above. Locate that number in the list below. On the ballot card find the number and letter for that answer. Blacken the space that has that number and letter inside it.

298

(3A) None   (3E) Four
(3B) One   (3F) Five
(3C) Two   (3G) Six
(3D) Three   (3H) Seven

You may recognize some of the following questions as ones that were asked in last fall's election poll. However, we are interested in learning how you feel about the candidates and issues of that election now, four months after the event, so answer the questions on the basis of the way you feel about them *now*. Don't try to recall how you or other people answered them last fall. Remember, we are interested in *your present opinions*.

9. Suppose last November's elections were going to be held over again and you could take part in them. For which of the following would you vote?
   (4A) Eisenhower-Nixon
   (4B) Stevenson-Sparkman
   (4C) Some other candidates

10. Which one of the following was *most* important in determining your choice for president?
    (4D) The candidate's personality and background
    (4E) The candidate's stand on foreign policy and world peace
    (4F) The candidate's stand on national policies
    (4G) The candidate's political party

11. How do you feel about President Eisenhower's appointments of cabinet members and other officers.
    (4H) Definitely satisfied
    (4I) Undecided; probably satisfied
    (4J) Undecided; probably dissatisfied
    (4K) Definitely dissatisfied

12. How do you feel about President Eisenhower's statements of policy and other action since his inauguration?
    (5A) Definitely satisfied
    (5B) Undecided; probably satisfied
    (5C) Undecided; probably dissatisfied
    (5D) Definitely dissatisfied

13. How do you feel about lowering the age requirement for voting from 21 to 18 in all states?
    (5E) Should be lowered
    (5F) Should stay as it is
    (5G) Undecided

14. Pupils of all races and nationalities should attend school together everywhere in this country.
    (5H) Agree
    (5I) Undecided; probably agree
    (5J) Undecided; probably disagree
    (5K) Disagree

15. People of different races should not dance together.
    (6A) Agree
    (6B) Undecided; probably agree
    (6C) Undecided; probably disagree
    (6D) Disagree

16. Swimming pools should admit people of all races and nationalities to swim in the same pool.
    (6E) Agree
    (6F) Undecided; probably agree
    (6G) Undecided; probably disagree
    (6H) Disagree

17. There should be laws against marriage between persons of different races.
    (6I) Agree
    (6J) Undecided; probably agree
    (6K) Undecided; probably disagree
    (6L) Disagree

18. Hotels are right in refusing to admit people of certain races or nationalities.
    (7A) Agree
    (7B) Undecided; probably agree
    (7C) Undecided; probably disagree
    (7D) Disagree

19. Our armed forces should not have officers of some races and nationalities.
    (7E) Agree
    (7F) Undecided; probably agree
    (7G) Undecided; probably disagree
    (7H) Disagree

20. People of different races and nationalities should be allowed to live in the same neighborhoods.
    (7I) Agree
    (7J) Undecided; probably agree
    (7K) Undecided; probably disagree
    (7L) Disagree

21. Public eating places should serve people of all races and nationalities, even at the same table if the customers want it that way.
    (8A) Agree
    (8B) Undecided; probably agree
    (8C) Undecided; probably disagree
    (8D) Disagree

22. Property owners or their agents should prevent people of some races or nationalities from living in the better neighborhoods.
    (8E) Agree
    (8F) Undecided; probably agree
    (8G) Undecided; probably disagree
    (8H) Disagree

23. All theaters should admit people of all races and nationalities, and allow them to sit anywhere they want.
    (8I) Agree
    (8J) Undecided; probably agree
    (8K) Undecided; probably disagree
    (8L) Disagree

24. There are people of some races and nationalities who are by nature less capable of advancement.
    (9A) Agree
    (9B) Undecided; probably agree
    (9C) Undecided; probably disagree
    (9D) Disagree

25. Any kind of people—no matter what race or national origin—can become 100% Americans.
    (9E) Agree
    (9F) Undecided; probably agree
    (9G) Undecided; probably disagree
    (9H) Disagree

26. One can't tell much about a person's character by his appearance.
    (9I) Agree
    (9J) Undecided; probably agree
    (9K) Undecided; probably disagree
    (9L) Disagree

27. Some politicians place too much emphasis upon the principle, "America for Americans."
    (10A) Agree
    (10B) Undecided; probably agree
    (10C) Undecided; probably disagree
    (10D) Disagree

28. The true American way of life is disappearing so fast that force may be necessary to preserve it.
    (10E) Agree
    (10F) Undecided; probably agree
    (10G) Undecided; probably disagree
    (10H) Disagree
29. People who complain about things in the U. S. should be sent out of this country if they don't like it.
    (10I) Agree
    (10J) Undecided; probably agree
    (10K) Undecided; probably disagree
    (10L) Disagree
30. People without a deep and unquestioning faith in Almighty God should not be trusted in public office.
    (11A) Agree
    (11B) Undecided; probably agree
    (11C) Undecided; probably disagree
    (11D) Disagree
31. There is hardly anything lower than a person who does not feel a great love, gratitude and respect for our flag.
    (11E) Agree
    (11F) Undecided; probably agree
    (11G) Undecided; probably disagree
    (11H) Disagree
32. Americans are getting soft; most people need stricter discipline and the will to defend their interests.
    (11I) Agree
    (11J) Undecided; probably agree
    (11K) Undecided; probably disagree
    (11L) Disagree
33. Even people who have wild ideas or don't use their heads should still have the right to vote.
    (12A) Agree
    (12B) Undecided; probably agree
    (12C) Undecided; probably disagree
    (12D) Disagree
34. Most people don't realize how much our lives are controlled by plots hatched in secret by others.
    (12E) Agree
    (12F) Undecided; probably agree

302

(12G) Undecided; probably disagree

(12H) Disagree

35. Criminals, especially those guilty of sex crimes, should have mental and medical help rather than severe punishment.

(12I) Agree

(12J) Undecided; probably agree

(12K) Undecided; probably disagree

(12L) Disagree

36. Obedience and a proper respect for authority should be the very first requirement of a good citizen.

(13A) Agree

(13B) Undecided; probably agree

(13C) Undecided; probably disagree

(13D) Disagree

37. Strict and forceful leaders who demand an unquestioning trust are *not* desirable in this country.

(13E) Agree

(13F) Undecided; probably agree

(13G) Undecided; probably disagree

(13H) Disagree

WHAT ABOUT OTHER COUNTRIES AND WORLD AFFAIRS?

38. We should have as little as possible to do with the foreign countries of the world.

(13I) Agree

(13J) Undecided; probably agree

(13K) Undecided; probably disagree

(13L) Disagree

39. The U. S. should be willing to give up some of its national power and independence to the United Nations in the interest of a better world.

(14A) Agree

(14B) Undecided; probably agree

(14C) Undecided; probably disagree

(14D) Disagree

40. In its relations with other countries the U. S. should depend more upon a discussion of problems than upon "get tough" actions.

(14E) Agree

(14F) Undecided; probably agree
(14G) Undecided; probably disagree
(14H) Disagree

41. Foreign countries have contributed a great deal to the *past* development of the American way of life.
(14I) Agree
(13J) Undecided; probably agree
(14K) Undecided; probably disagree
(14L) Disagree

42. It's a mistake to trust any nation until we are completely sure of them.
(15A) Agree
(15B) Undecided; probably agree
(15C) Undecided; probably disagree
(15D) Disagree

43. We should *not* limit and control immigration of foreigners into this country as much as we do now.
(15E) Agree
(15F) Undecided; probably agree
(15G) Undecided; probably disagree
(15H) Disagree

44. Despite what people say about human nature, all the people of the world will someday live peacefully together.
(15I) Agree
(15J) Undecided; probably agree
(15K) Undecided; probably disagree
(15L) Disagree

45. Foreign countries have very little to contribute to American progress *today*.
(16A) Agree
(16B) Undecided; probably agree
(16C) Undecided; probably disagree
(16D) Disagree

46. There is too much concern about danger to democracy from foreign ideas within this country.
(16E) Agree
(16F) Undecided; probably agree
(16G) Undecided; probably disagree
(16H) Disagree

47. An insult to our honor should always be punished.
(16I) Agree

(16J) Undecided; probably agree
(16K) Undecided; probably disagree
(16L) Disagree

48. We should encourage more new ideas rather than always keeping to the old, tried and established ways of doing things.
(17A) Agree
(17B) Undecided; probably agree
(17C) Undecided; probably disagree
(17D) Disagree

49. Most foreigners have annoying habits.
(17E) Agree
(17F) Undecided; probably agree
(17G) Undecided; probably disagree
(17H) Disagree

HOW DO YOU FEEL ABOUT TELEVISION?

You may not be able to answer some of the following questions if you do not have television in your area or if you do not have a television set in your home. Answer those questions for which you are able to give an opinion.

50. Can television programs be received in the area around your home?
(17I) Yes, reception is good
(17J) Yes, but reception is poor
(17K) No, there are no close stations

51. Is there a television set in your home?
(18A) No
(18B) Yes, we have had one for six months or less
(18C) Yes, we have had one between six months and a year
(18D) Yes, we have had one for a year or more

52. Do any of your relatives or friends have a television set that you may watch whenever you wish?
(18E) Yes
(18F) No

53. How long each day, on the average, did you watch television during the past week?
(18G) Less than one hour
(18H) One to two hours
(18I) Three to four hours

(18J) Five to six hours

(18K) More than six hours

54. How often during the past month did you go to the movies?

(19A) Once a month or less

(19B) Two or three times a month

(19C) Once a week

(19D) Two or three times a week

(19E) Four or more times a week

55. Do you think that watching television has interfered with your schoolwork?

(19F) Yes, very much

(19G) Yes, somewhat

(19H) No

56. Some people claim that too many television programs show things that young people shouldn't see, such as crime and improper behavior. How do you feel about this?

(19I) Such programs are very harmful to people my age.

(19J) Such programs are somewhat harmful to people my age.

(19K) Such programs are not harmful to people my age.

57. New, good movies and sports events such as championship fights, football games, etc. are sometimes not televised because it would reduce paid attendance. It has been suggested that such programs might be brought into the home on television, without commercials, if people would pay a special fee to the network. This fee would be a fixed price for the entire family no matter how many people watched the program. Would you and your family be willing to pay to see such programs in your own home if "pay as you see" television were available?

(20A) No, we would not pay

(20B) Yes, the most we would pay is 50¢ per program

(20C) Yes, the most we would pay is $1.00 per program

(20D) Yes, the most we would pay is $2.00 per program (or more).

58. Which of the following types of program do you enjoy on television? Check how often you would watch each type.

Plays, dramas .... (20E) Very often;
(20F) Now and then; (20G) Never

Sports events .... (20H) Very often;
(20I) Now and then; (20J) Never

Mystery or detective stories .... (21A) Very often;
(21B) Now and then; (21C) Never

Family comedy program .... (21D) Very often;
    (21E) Now and then; (21F) Never
Quiz shows, contest programs .... (21G) Very often;
    (21H) Now and then; (21I) Never
Variety shows (comedians, dancers) ...... (21J) Very often;
    (21K) Now and then; (21L) Never
Western movies .... (22A) Very often;
    (22B) Now and then; (22C) Never
Opera, symphonic concerts .... (22D) Very often;
    (22E) Now and then; (22F) Never

59. For each of the following groups or organizations, mark whether you are now or have been an active member (of any of the groups named or similar groups); whether you belonged but were not very active; or whether you have never been a member during your high school years.

    (a) Boy Scouts, Girl Scouts, Camp Fire Girls, etc.
        (22G) Very active; (22H) belonged, but not active; (22I) have not belonged.

    (b) YMCA, YWCA, Hi-Y, Y-Teens, YMHA
        (22J) Very active; (22K) belonged, but not active; (22L) have not belonged.

    (c) Church groups or religious organization, such as CYO, service groups, young people's clubs, etc.
        (23A) Very active; (23B) belonged, but not active; (23C) have not belonged.

    (d) Future Farmers of America, Future Homemakers of America, 4-H, etc.
        (23D) Very active; (23E) belonged, but not active; (23F) have not belonged.

    (e) American Junior Red Cross
        (23G) Very active; (23H) belonged, but not active; (23I) have not belonged.

    (f) High school fraternities, sororities or social clubs.
        (23J) Very active; (23K) belonged, but not active; (23L) have not belonged.

    (g) Other clubs or organizations (Describe briefly on back of ballot card)
        (24A) Very active; (24B) belonged, but not active; (24C) have not belonged.

Appendix C

The following brief explanation of scaling and unidimensionality was taken from Dr. Krech's study. Chapter IV.

Scaling and Unidimensionality

In our discussion of individuals and their attitudes, it is apparent that it is necessary to have units, or measures, or these attitudes. The purpose of an attitude scale is to assign individuals to a position somewhere between the opposite extremes of favoring or opposing something. Another important property of scales is that from a sample of attributes we can draw inferences about the universe of attributes. These scales have the effect of placing individuals along a continuum of an attitude (Krech and Crutchfield, 1948; Newcomb, 1950).

Louis Guttman developed the concept of unidimensionality. On a unidimensional scale persons who answer any given question favorably should, by definition, have higher ranks than persons who answer the same question unfavorably (Stouffer, 1950).

Guttman's (1950) definition of a scale is as follows:

For a given population of objects the multivariate frequency distribution of a universe of attributes will be called a scale if it is possible to derive from the distribution a quantitative variable with which to characterize the objects such that each attribute is a simple function of that quantitative variable. Such a quantitative variable is called a scale variable.

The preceding definition of a scale is the definition of a perfect scale, a perfection rarely found in actual practice. The deviation from perfection is measured by counting up the number of responses which would have been predicted wrongly for each person on the basis of his scale score, dividing these errors by the total number of responses, and subtracting the resulting fraction from one. The resulting number is called a "coefficient of reproducibility." In practice, a coefficient of .90 is considered the least acceptable value that a scale may have and still be considered a perfect scale (Guttman 1954; Remmers, 1954).

However, reproducibility is a necessary, but not sufficient, test of scalability. Four other criteria are to be met.

1. The reproducibility is affected by the range of marginal distributions to the extent that the reproducibility of an individual item can never be less than the largest percentage of respondents falling into

any one category, whether or not a scale exists. Thus for any sample of items one should try to have as wide a range of marginals as possible, and should have at least some marginals around 50–50.

2. The pattern of errors must be random. This is also a requirement for quasi-scales, which are cases of low reproducibility but otherwise acceptable scale requirements. These errors form a sort of gradient, which is the identifying mark of a quasi-scale.

3. The number of items that should be used on a pre-test can vary but should not be less than ten. If the marginals prove to be widely varied, fewer items may be used on the final scale.

4. The number of response categories is important in relationship to the number of items. The fewer the items, the larger the number of response categories that should be kept. Combining categories in such a case does not disturb rank order, except that two adjacent ranks are merged (Remmers, 1954; Stouffer, 1950).

In addition to the five mechanical criteria for a scale is the consideration of the universe of content. Before any scale construction is undertaken, the universe should be defined and its content judged to be homogeneous. Content, not scale analysis, defines the universe. This judgment is a qualitative, subjective and intuitive process, not a statistical one.

For determining whether or not a set of questions form a scale, four specific techniques have been used: the Scalogram Technique, the Cornell Trial Scoring and Graphic Technique, the Tabulation Technique, and the Least Squares Method. Since they are based on the same theory, all four techniques produce essentially the same results.

Although most social distance scales have used Thurstone's method of equal-appearing intervals, we shall not do so here. Rather we shall assign arbitrary weights to the response categories in much the same manner as Paisios did in his previously mentioned study. These weights will be only temporary and will not necessarily be the final weights given to the response categories. Rather, the final weights will be determined by scalogram analysis using the latest IBM methods.

The means were the scale values and the standard deviations were the measures of ambiguity. There were 39 statements rated by 60 judges on an 11-point scale. His statements were very similar to the 1933 Bogardus scale except for the extreme "would kill" statement (Dodd, 1935).

Paisios investigated the concept of Social Distance in Housing and used a five-point scale, with five items arbitrarily assigned weights of

0, 1, 2, 3, and 4. He says "there is no assumption that they (the items) represent equally spaced psychological distances." He found that the various ethnic groups of subjects, although they exhibited a uniform order of preference for the "selected out-groups, have been demonstrated to be functioning at three different levels of out-group tolerance." The population used in his study was the adult working force in two large steel companies (Paisios, 1954).

In attempting to construct our unidimensional social distance scales in rating behavior we shall use the concepts developed by Louis Guttman and others.

Appendix D

THE PURDUE OPINION PANEL
A Survey of Public Opinion

This survey is under the direction and authority of the Indiana Conference on Higher Education, which includes representatives from all colleges and universities in Indiana. We are interested in what college and university faculties and students feel about a number of social issues. We are sure that you have thought about and discussed many of these issues and have received information about them through newspapers, magazines, the radio, and various courses in the social sciences. The statements which make up this survey cover many points of view. You will probably find yourself agreeing with some statements, disagreeing with others, and being perhaps neutral about still others. We wish to emphasize that there are no "right" or "wrong" answers; the best answer is YOUR PERSONAL OPINION. You can be sure that, whatever your opinion may be on a certain issue, many people will agree with you, while others will disagree. This is what we want to find out: how is student and faculty opinion really divided on each of these socially important topics?

We also emphasize that your name is NOT required. Please read each statement carefully and mark it according to your first reaction. It is not necessary to take a lot of time for any one question.

Directions
1. Read the question and decide upon your answer.
2. Place a check mark opposite your answer.
3. Follow directions given separately with individual questions.
4. Please be sure to answer every item.

1. Write age in years:_____
2. Sex:
  _____ (1) Male
  _____ (2) Female
3. Marital Status
  _____ (1) Unmarried
  _____ (2) Married
4. Are you a member of a social fraternity or sorority?
  _____ (1) Yes
  _____ (2) No

311

5. Classification:
_____ (1) Freshman
_____ (2) Sophomore
_____ (3) Junior
_____ (4) Senior
_____ (5) Graduate Student
_____ (6) Special Student

6. Political Preference:
_____ (1) Democratic party
_____ (2) Republican party
_____ (3) Independent
_____ (4) Other
_____ (5) None

7. Mother's education: My mother
_____ (1) Did not finish the eighth grade
_____ (2) Finished the eighth grade but did not go to high school
_____ (3) Had some high school but did not graduate
_____ (4) Finished high school but did not go to college
_____ (5) Had some college but did not graduate
_____ (6) Graduated from college
_____ (7) Worked on advanced degree

8. I have: (write in number)
_____ (1) Older sister(s)
_____ (2) Older brother(s)
_____ (3) Younger sister(s)
_____ (4) Younger brother(s)

9. *House and Home.* The following is true of my family. (Mark an X in front of the appropriate items; then follow the directions below.) We have:
_____ (1) A vacuum cleaner
_____ (2) A bathtub or shower with running water
_____ (3) An electric or gas refrigerator
_____ (4) Two automobiles (don't count trucks)
_____ (5) An automatic dishwasher
_____ (6) A recreation room or game room
_____ (7) Part or full time help for the home
_____ (8) A summer cottage or cabin
Now count the number of X's that you have marked above. Locate that number in the list below, and circle the number.

1 2 3 4 5 6 7

312

10. Regarding my religious beliefs and practices, I would say that I feel:
_____ (1) Very strongly
_____ (2) Strongly
_____ (3) Moderately
_____ (4) Indifferently

11. Church attendance: I attend church
0 1 2 3 4 5–7 8–10 11 or more times per month. (Circle one)

12. Please write below the name of your major field of interest, such as chemistry, history, sociology, etc. If you have no major at present, write "none."

---

13. Religious Preference:
_____ (1) Protestant
_____ (2) Catholic
_____ (3) Jewish
_____ (4) Other
_____ (5) None
Please write in the following space the name of the denomination with which you are affiliated:

---

14. Before coming to your present college campus, were you a resident of the continental United States?
_____ (1) Yes
_____ (2) No

15. Before coming to your present college campus, were you a resident of the state of Indiana?
_____ (1) Yes
_____ (2) No

16. Are you:
_____ (1) White?
_____ (2) Negro?
_____ (3) Oriental?
_____ (4) American Indian?

17. The greater part of my life I lived
_____ (1) On a farm
_____ (2) In a town having a population less than 1000
_____ (3) In a town having a population of 1000–2500
_____ (4) In a town having a population of 2500–10,000

313

_____ (5) In a town having a population of 10,000–50,000

_____ (6) In a town having a population of over 50,000

18. My father's occupation is

_____

_____

(Describe in brief, giving name of occupation and type of specialized work, such as: salesman-insurance, foreman-machine shop, banker-cashier, teacher-high school, construction-carpenter, industry-lathe operator, etc. . . .)

19. (a) I am now attending

_____

(College or university in which you are enrolled)

(b) Do you plan to teach in high school or grade school?

_____ (1) Yes

_____ (2) No

_____ (3) Don't know at present

MY OPINIONS

20. One can't tell much about a person's character by his appearance.

_____ (1) Agree

_____ (2) Undecided; probably agree

_____ (3) Undecided; probably disagree

_____ (4) Disagree

21. The true American way of life is disappearing so fast that force may be necessary to preserve it.

_____ (1) Agree

_____ (2) Undecided; probably agree

_____ (3) Undecided; probably disagree

_____ (4) Disagree

22. People who complain about things in the U. S. should be sent out of this country if they don't like it.

_____ (1) Agree

_____ (2) Undecided; probably agree

_____ (3) Undecided; probably disagree

_____ (4) Disagree

23. People without a deep and unquestionable faith in Almighty God should not be trusted in public office.

_____ (1) Agree

_____ (2) Undecided; probably agree

314

_____ (3) Undecided; probably disagree

_____ (4) Disagree

24. There is hardly anything lower than a person who does not feel a great love, gratitude and respect for our flag.

_____ (1) Agree

_____ (2) Undecided; probably agree

_____ (3) Undecided; probably disagree

_____ (4) Disagree

25. Americans are getting soft; most people need stricter discipline and the will to defend their interests.

_____ (1) Agree

_____ (2) Undecided; probably agree

_____ (3) Undecided; probably disagree

_____ (4) Disagree

26. Even people who have wild ideas or don't use their heads should still have the right to vote.

_____ (1) Agree

_____ (2) Undecided; probably agree

_____ (3) Undecided; probably disagree

_____ (4) Disagree

27. Most people don't realize how much our lives are controlled by plots hatched in secret by others.

_____ (1) Agree

_____ (2) Undecided; probably agree

_____ (3) Undecided; probably disagree

_____ (4) Disagree

28. Criminals, especially those guilty of sex crimes, should have mental and medical help rather than severe punishment.

_____ (1) Agree

_____ (2) Undecided; probably agree

_____ (3) Undecided; probably disagree

_____ (4) Disagree

29. Obedience and a proper respect for authority should be the very first requirements of a good citizen.

_____ (1) Agree

_____ (2) Undecided; probably agree

_____ (3) Undecided; probably disagree

_____ (4) Disagree

30. Strict and forceful leaders who demand an unquestioning trust are not desirable in this country.

_____ (1) Agree

___ (2) Undecided; probably agree

___ (3) Undecided; probably disagree

___ (4) Disagree

31. We should have as little as possible to do with the foreign countries of the world.

___ (1) Agree

___ (2) Undecided; probably agree

___ (3) Undecided; probably disagree

___ (4) Disagree

32. The U.S. should be willing to give up some of its national power and independence to the United Nations in the interest of a better world.

___ (1) Agree

___ (2) Undecided; probably agree

___ (3) Undecided; probably disagree

___ (4) Disagree

33. In its relations with other countries the U. S. should depend more upon a discussion of problems than upon "get tough" actions.

___ (1) Agree

___ (2) Undecided; probably agree

___ (3) Undecided; probably disagree

___ (4) Disagree

34. Foreign countries have contributed a great deal to the past development of the American way of life.

___ (1) Agree

___ (2) Undecided; probably agree

___ (3) Undecided; probably disagree

___ (4) Disagree

35. It's a mistake to trust any nation until we are completely sure of them.

___ (1) Agree

___ (2) Undecided; probably agree

___ (3) Undecided; probably disagree

___ (4) Disagree

36. We should not limit and control immigration of foreigners into this country as much as we do now.

___ (1) Agree

___ (2) Undecided; probably agree

___ (3) Undecided; probably disagree

___ (4) Disagree

316

37. Despite what people say about human nature, all of the people of the world will someday live peacefully together.
_____ (1) Agree
_____ (2) Undecided; probably agree
_____ (3) Undecided; probably disagree
_____ (4) Disagree

38. Foreign countries have very little to contribute to American progress today.
_____ (1) Agree
_____ (2) Undecided; probably agree
_____ (3) Undecided; probably disagree
_____ (4) Disagree

39. There is too much concern about danger to democracy from foreign ideas within this country.
_____ (1) Agree
_____ (2) Undecided; probably agree
_____ (3) Undecided; probably disagree
_____ (4) Disagree

40. An insult to our honor should always be punished.
_____ (1) Agree
_____ (2) Undecided; probably agree
_____ (3) Undecided; probably disagree
_____ (4) Disagree

41. We should encourage more new ideas rather than always keeping to the old, tried and established ways of doing things.
_____ (1) Agree
_____ (2) Undecided; probably agree
_____ (3) Undecided; probably disagree
_____ (4) Disagree

42. Most foreigners have annoying habits.
_____ (1) Agree
_____ (2) Undecided; probably agree
_____ (3) Undecided; probably disagree
_____ (4) Disagree

43. Which one of the following do you think is most likely to happen in the future?
_____ (1) A destructive world war which destroys most of civilization
_____ (2) World domination by one of the major powers, without a destructive war

317

_____ (3) A peaceful change in world government

_____ (4) An absence of war, with independent nations but no world government

44. If people would talk less and work more, everybody would be better off.

_____ (1) Agree

_____ (2) Undecided; probably agree

_____ (3) Undecided; probably disagree

_____ (4) Disagree

45. Every person should have complete faith in some supernatural power whose decisions he obeys without question.

_____ (1) Agree

_____ (2) Undecided; probably agree

_____ (3) Undecided; probably disagree

_____ (4) Disagree

46. When a person has a problem or worry, it is best for him not to think about it, but to keep busy with more cheerful things.

_____ (1) Agree

_____ (2) Undecided; probably agree

_____ (3) Undecided; probably disagree

_____ (4) Disagree

47. A person who has bad manners, habits, and breeding can hardly expect to get along with decent people.

_____ (1) Agree

_____ (2) Undecided; probably agree

_____ (3) Undecided; probably disagree

_____ (4) Disagree

48. What youth needs most is strict discipline, rugged determination, and the will to fight for family and nation.

_____ (1) Agree

_____ (2) Undecided; probably agree

_____ (3) Undecided; probably disagree

_____ (4) Disagree

49. There is hardly anything lower than a person who does not feel a great love, gratitude and respect for his parents.

_____ (1) Agree

_____ (2) Undecided; probably agree

_____ (3) Undecided; probably disagree

_____ (4) Disagree

50. Wars and social troubles may someday be ended by an earthquake or flood that will destroy the whole world.

_____ (1) Agree

_____ (2) Undecided; probably agree

_____ (3) Undecided; probably disagree

_____ (4) Disagree

51. The wild sex life of the old Greeks and Romans was tame compared to some of the goings on in this country, even in places where people might least suspect it.

_____ (1) Agree

_____ (2) Undecided; probably agree

_____ (3) Undecided; probably disagree

_____ (4) Disagree

52. No sane, normal, decent person could ever think of hurting a close relative or friend.

_____ (1) Agree

_____ (2) Undecided; probably agree

_____ (3) Undecided; probably disagree

_____ (4) Disagree

53. Books and movies ought not to deal so much with the unpleasant and seamy side of life; they ought to concentrate on themes that are entertaining or uplifting.

_____ (1) Agree

_____ (2) Undecided; probably agree

_____ (3) Undecided; probably disagree

_____ (4) Disagree

54. When you come right down to it, it's human nature never to do anything without an eye to one's profit.

_____ (1) Agree

_____ (2) Undecided; probably agree

_____ (3) Undecided; probably disagree

_____ (4) Disagree

55. Some leisure is necessary, but it is good hard work that makes life interesting and worthwhile.

_____ (1) Agree

_____ (2) Undecided; probably agree

_____ (3) Undecided; probably disagree

_____ (4) Disagree

56. The institution which has been the most effective in fighting prejudice and discrimination is

_____ (1) The church

_____ (2) The school

_____ (3) Labor unions

319

_____ (4) The government

_____ (5) Chamber of Commerce

_____ (6) Fraternal Organizations, such as Kiwanis, Elks, Eagles, etc.

_____ (7) Other (Write in).

_____

_____

57. How do you feel about laws making it illegal for employers to refuse to hire qualified persons for jobs because of their color, nationality, or religion?

_____ (1) No government—federal, state, or local—has a right to tell employers how to hire people

_____ (2) Individual states should make such laws

_____ (3) Federal government should pass such a law

58. If you or any members of your family have ever been treated unfairly, was it because:

_____ (1) You are not of the "White race?"

_____ (2) People thought your nationality is not 100% American?

_____ (3) Of your religion?

_____ (4) Of none of these?

59. Pupils of all races and nationalities should attend school together everywhere in this country.

_____ (1) Agree

_____ (2) Undecided; probably agree

_____ (3) Undecided; probably disagree

_____ (4) Disagree

60. People of different races should not dance together.

_____ (1) Agree

_____ (2) Undecided; probably agree

_____ (3) Undecided; probably disagree

_____ (4) Disagree

61. Swimming pools should admit people of all races and nationalities, to swim in the same pool.

_____ (1) Agree

_____ (2) Undecided; probably agree

_____ (3) Undecided; probably disagree

_____ (4) Disagree

62. There should be laws against marriage between persons of different races.

_____ (1) Agree

_____ (2) Undecided; probably agree

____ (3) Undecided; probably disagree

____ (4) Disagree

63. Hotels are right in refusing to admit people of certain races or nationalities.

____ (1) Agree

____ (2) Undecided; probably agree

____ (3) Undecided; probably disagree

____ (4) Disagree

64. Our armed forces should not have officers of some races and nationalities.

____ (1) Agree

____ (2) Undecided; probably agree

____ (3) Undecided; probably disagree

____ (4) Disagree

65. People of different races and nationalities should be allowed to live in the same neighborhoods.

____ (1) Agree

____ (2) Undecided; probably agree

____ (3) Undecided; probably disagree

____ (4) Disagree

66. Public eating places should serve people of all races and nationalities, even at the same table if the customers want it that way.

____ (1) Agree

____ (2) Undecided; probably agree

____ (3) Undecided; probably disagree

____ (4) Disagree

67. Property owners or their agents should prevent people of some races or nationalities from living in the better neighborhoods.

____ (1) Agree

____ (2) Undecided; probably agree

____ (3) Undecided; probably disagree

____ (4) Disagree

68. All theaters should admit people of all races and nationalities, and allow them to sit anywhere they want.

____ (1) Agree

____ (2) Undecided; probably agree

____ (3) Undecided; probably disagree

____ (4) Disagree

Appendix E

PURDUE OPINION PANEL
SAMPLING SUGGESTIONS

One objective of opinion research is to generalize findings from a sample to the population from which the sample was obtained. The sample must be "representative" in order for this to be done with a calculable amount of error. One way to obtain a representative sample is to select a random one, that is, one in which all members of the population have an equal chance of being chosen. This may be done by drawing names out of a hat, where every name has an equal chance of being chosen, or by selecting every nth name from an alphabetical list of the names of the population. Where portions of the population are known to differ in important matters, this scheme may be generalized to sampling within these portions or segments, and having each represented in the sample in the proportion in which it exists in the population.

We hope to obtain a large enough unselected group of individuals of each of various kinds from each school so that our selection of every nth case, in proportion to be worked out beforehand, can approximate randomness. We shall suggest a number of possible procedures for fulfilling this aim. Among students, all major fields of study should be represented; each level of study, from freshman to graduate, should be present. Students included in the sample should be chosen to represent the variation of the state's college population on such variables as wealth, religion, race, course grades, marital status, veteran status, etc.

Participating institutions will differ in the ease with which they can supply usable samples. In schools with enrollments of five hundred or less, all students should complete the questionnaire at one time. All faculty members should answer the questionnaire. The questions should not, of course, be discussed before they are answered.

Schools of from 500 to perhaps 3,000 students may find it possible to fulfill the requirements of randomness by selecting classes or class sections of all levels in all departments taught by all instructors, so that half or less of each student body is sampled. Those selected should include students from all college levels and students subjected to all obvious educational influences. A minimum of 500 students is desired. If the enrollment is not more than about 700 or 800 it will be simplest to include them all.

Some institutions may wish to select a random sample from an alphabetical list of students and administer the questionnaires to those selected either at a given time and place or else in classes in which it may be convenient for selected students to take them separately. Social science departments may be interested in helping with such problems of administration. The questionnaire should be given at the same time to all participants in order to avoid the contaminating effects of discussion.

Campus mail facilities may be used to advantage, especially in sampling the faculty population. By this means all faculty members can be reached from one central point and distribution problems simplified. This procedure is being used at Purdue University.

Institutions having faculty members and graduate students in the field of attitude research may find them willing to assume responsibility for selecting a sample and administering the questionnaire. Where classes are conducted in polling research, graduate students in these classes may be allowed to do this as course work. This method is being used at Purdue University.

A matter apart from sampling problems is that of rapport and motivation. Students should be made to feel favorable toward the questionnaire; but the subject matter of the questionnaire should not be revealed in the attempt to gain a favorable attitude. The statement made to the Purdue sample is enclosed.

BIBLIOGRAPHY

Adelson, J. "A study of minority group authoritarianism," *J. abnorm. soc. Psychol.*, (1953), *48*, 477–485.

Adorno, T. W., *et al. The authoritarian personality.* New York: Harper & Brothers, 1950.

Albig, W. "Two decades of opinion study: 1936–1956," *Public Opin. Quart.*, (1957), *21*, 14–22.

Allen, D. A. "Antifeminity in men." *Am. soc. Rev.*, (1954), 19, 591–593.

Allport, G. W. "Attitudes," in C. Murchison's (ed.) *A handbook of social psychology.* Worcester, Mass.: Clark University Press, 1935.

————— "Prejudice, a problem in psychological and social causation," *J. of soc. Issues*, (1950), Supplement Series, No. 4.

————— *The nature of prejudice.* Boston: Beacon Press, 1954.

————— and Kramer, B. M. "Some roots of prejudice." *J. Psychol.*, 1946, *22*, 9–39.

————— and Vernon, P. E. *A study of values.* Boston: Houghton Mifflin Co., 1931.

Anikeeff, Alexis M. "Reciprocal Empathy: mutual understanding among conflict groups," Purdue University—*Studies in Higher Education*, 78, 1951.

Applezweig, D. G. "Some determinants of behavioral rigidity," *J. abnorm. soc. Psychol.*, (1954), *49*, 224–228.

Asch, S. E. "Studies in the principles of judgments and attitudes: II. Determination of judgments by group and by ego standards," *J. soc. Psychol.*, (1940), *12*, 433–465.

———— *Social psychology*. New York: Prentice-Hall, Inc., 1952.

Becker, Carl L. *Freedom and responsibility in the American way of life*. New York: Alfred A. Knopf, Inc., 1947.

Bendig, A. W. "A statistical report on a revision of the Miami Instructor Rating Sheet," *J. educ. Psychol.*, (1952), *43*, 423–429, (a).

Bendix, R. and Lipset, S. M. *Class, status and power*. Chicago: Free Press of Glencoe, 1953.

Benedict, R. *Patterns of culture*. Boston: Houghton Mifflin Co., 1934.

Bettelheim, B., and Janowitz, M. "Ethnic tolerance: A function of social and personal control," *Amer. J. Sociol.*, (1949), *55*, 137–145.

———— *Dynamics of prejudice*. New York: Harper & Brothers, 1950.

Bidney, D. *Theoretical anthropology*. New York: Columbia University Press, 1953.

Bird, C. and Monachesi, E. D. "Prejudice and discontent," *J. abnorm. soc. Psychol.*, (1954), *49*, 29–35.

Blake, R. R. and Ramsey, G. V. *Perception, an approach to personality*. New York: Ronald Press Co., 1951.

Block, J. and Block, J. "An investigation of the relationship between intolerance of ambiguity and ethnocentrism," *J. Pers.*, (1951), *19*, 303–311.

Bogardus, E. S. "Measuring social distance," *Journal of Applied Sociology*, (1925), *9*, 299–308.

———— "A Social distance scale," *Sociol. soc. Res.*, (1933), *17*, 265–271.

———— "Social distance and its practical applications," *ibid.*, (1938), *22*, 462–476.

———— "Measurement of personal-group relations," *Sociometry*, (1947), *10*, 306–311.

———— "Social distance in daily vocabulary," *Sociol. soc. Res.*, (1948a), *32*, 723–727.

———— "The intercultural workshop and racial distance," *ibid.*, (1948b) *32*, 798–802.

———— "The social distance differential," *ibid.*, (1948c), *32*, 822–887.

———— "Reducing racial tensions," *ibid.*, (1950), *35*, 50–57.

Borgatta, E. F. and Hays, D. G. "Some limitations on the arbitrary classification of non-scale response patterns in a Guttman scale," *Publ. Opin. Quart.*, (1952), *16*, 410–416.

Boring, E. G., Bridgman, P. W., Feigl, H., Israel, H., Pratt, C., and Skinner, B. F. "Symposium on operationism," *Psychol. Rev.* (1945), *52*, 241–294.

Box, G. E. P. "Some theorems on quadratic forms applied in the study of analysis of variance problems, I. Effect of inequality of variance in the one-way classification," *Ann. math. Statist.*, (1954), *25*, 294–302.

Brandenburg, G. C., and Remmers, H. H. "The Purdue Rating Scale for Instructors," *Educ. Administration and Supervis.*, (1927), *13*, 399–406.

Brown, R. W. "A determinant of the relationship between rigidity and authoritarianism," *J. abnorm. soc. Psychol.*, (1953), *48*, 469–476.

Bruner, J. and Postman, L. "Perception, cognition and behavior," *J. Pers.*, (1949), *18*, 14–31.

Campbell, D. T., and McCandless, B. R. "Ethnocentrism, xenophobia, and personality," *Human Relat.*, (1951), *4*, 185–192.

Cattell, R. B. *Factor analysis.* New York: Harper & Brothers, 1952.

Centers, R. "Attitudes and belief in relation to occupational stratification," *J. soc. Psychol.*, (1948a), *27*, 159–185.

—— "Motivational aspects of occupational stratification," *J. soc. Psychol.*, (1948b), *28*, 187–217.

—— *The psychology of social classes.* Princeton, N. J.: Princeton University Press, 1949.

Chapman, L. J., and Campbell, D. T. "Response set in the F Scale," *J. abnorm. soc. Psychol.*, (1957), *54*, 129–132.

Chein, Isadore. "Some considerations in combatting intergroup prejudice," *J. educ. Sociol.*, (1946), *19*, 412–419.

—— "The problems of inconsistency: a re-statement," *J. Soc. Issues*, (1949), *5*, No. 3, 52–61.

——, Deutsch, M., Hyman, H. and Jahoda, Marie. "Consistency and inconsistency in intergroup relations," (1949), *5*, No. 3.

Chesire, L., Saffin, M. and Thurstone, L. L. *Computing diagrams for the tetrachoric correlation coefficient.* Chicago: Univ. of Chicago Bookstore, 1933.

Christie, R. "Changes in authoritarianism as related to situational factors," *Amer. Psychologist*, (1952), *7*, 307–308. (Abstract)

—— and Cook, P. "A guide to published literature relating to the authoritarian personality through 1956," *J. Psychol.*, (1958), *45*, 171–200.

—— and Garcia, J. "Subcultural variation in authoritarian personality," *J. abnorm. soc. Psychol.*, (1951), *46*, 457–469.

——, Havel, Joan, and Seidenberg, B. "Is the F Scale irreversible?" *ibid.*, (1958), *56*, 143–159.

—— and Jahoda, Marie. *Studies in the scope and method of "the authoritarian personality."* Chicago: Free Press of Glencoe, 1954.

Cohn, T. S. "Is the F Scale indirect?" *J. abnorm. soc. Psychol.*, (1952), *47*, 732.

—— and Carsch, H. "Administration of the F Scale to a sample of Germans," (1954), *49*, 471.

Cooper, E. and Jahoda, Marie. "The evasion of propaganda: how prejudiced people respond to anti-prejudice propaganda," *J. Psychol.*, (1947), *23*, 15–25.

Corder, R. F. "A factorial approach to anti-democratic attitudes," Unpublished doctor's dissertation, purdue University, 1953.

—— "A factorial approach to anti-democratic attitudes," Purdue Univ., Division of Educational Reference: Studies in higher education, *82*, 1954.

Crannell, C. W. "A preliminary attempt to identify the factors in student instructor evaluation," *J. Psychol.*, (1953), *36*, 417–422.

Cronbach, L. J. "Response sets and test validity," *Educ. Psychol. Measmt.*, (1946), *6*, 475–494.

—— "Further evidence on response sets and test design," *ibid.* (1950), *10*, 3–31.

Culver, D. W. *Negro segregation in the methodist church.* New Haven Conn.: Yale University Press, 1953.

Cureton, E. E. "Validity." In Lindquist, E. F. (ed.). *Educational Measurement.* Washington: American Council on Education, 1951.

Darley, J. and Hagenah, T. *Vocational interest measurement: theory and practice.* Minneapolis: University of Minn. Press, 1955.

Davenport, K. S. "An investigation into pupil rating of certain teaching practices," *Purdue University—Studies in Higher Education,* 1944, No. 49.

Davidoff, Melvin D., Ph.D. "A study of empathy and correlates of prejudice toward a minority group," *Purdue University—Studies in Higher Education, 67,* 1949.

Davis, A. "American status system and the socialization of the child." In H. Murray, C. Kluckhohn, and D. Schneider's (eds.) *Personality in nature, society, and culture.* New York: Alfred A. Knopf, Inc., 1953.

—— and Havighurst, R. J. "Social class and color differences in child rearing." In H. Murray, C. Kluckhohn, and D. Schneider's (eds.) *Personality in nature, society, and culture.* New York: Alfred A. Knopf, Inc., 1953.

Dicks, H. V. "Personality traits and national socialist ideology," *Human Relat.*, (1950), *3*, 111–154.

327

Dimond, S. E., and Pflieger, E. F. *Dimond-Pflieger problems of Democracy test.* Yonkers, N. Y.: World Book Company, 1953.

Dodd, S. C. "A social distance test in the near east," *Amer. J. Sociol.*, 1935, *41*, 194–204.

Dodd, S. D. and Nehnevajsa, J. "Physical dimensions of social distance," *Sociol. soc. Res.*, (1954), *38*, 287–292.

Dollard, J. "Under what conditions do opinions predict behavior," *Publ. Opin. Quartl.*, (1948), *12*, 623–32.

—— and Miller, N. E. *Learning theory and psychotherapy.* New York: McGraw-Hill Book Co., 1950.

Drucker, Arthur J. "Relationships between citizenship attitudes, parental education, and other variables," Purdue University—*Studies in Higher Education, 71,* 1950.

Duffy, E. "A critical review of investigations employing the *Allport-Vernon Study of Values* and other tests of evaluative attitudes," *Psychol. Bull.,* (1940), *37*, 597–612.

—— and Crissy, W. J. "Evaluative attitudes as related to vocational interests and academic achievement," *J. soc. Psychol.,* (1940), *35*, 226–245.

Eager, J., and Smith, M. B. "A note on the validity of Sanford's authoritarian-equalitarian scale," *J. abnorm. soc. Psychol.* (1952), *47*:265–267.

Edwards, A. L. "Unlabeled fascist attitudes," *J. abnorm. soc. Psychol.,* (1941), *36*, 575–582.

—— "The signs of incipient fascism." *J. abnorm. soc. Psychol.,* (1944), *39*, 301–316.

—— and Kilpatrick, F. P. "A technique for the construction of attitude scales." *J. appl. Psychol.,* (1948), *32*, 374–384.

Elias, Gabriel. "The concept and an objective measure of homelessness," Purdue University—*Studies in Higher Education, 77,* (1951).

Evans, R. I. "Personal values as factors in anti-Semitism," *J. abnorm. soc. Psychol.,* (1952), *47*, 749–756.

Eysenck, H. J. "General social attitudes," *J. soc. Psychol.,* (1944), *49*, 207–227.

—— "Primary social attitudes: the organization and measurement of social attitudes," *Int. J. Opin. Attit. Res.,* (1947), *1*, 49–84.

—— "Primary social attitudes as related to social class and political party," *Brit. j. social.* (1951), *2*:198–209.

—— "Primary social attitudes: a comparison of attitude patterns in England, Germany, and Sweden," *J. abnorm. soc. Psychol.,* (1953), *47*, 563–568.

——— "The logical basis of factor analysis," *Amer. Psychologist,* (1953), *8,* 105–114.

——— *The psychology of politics.* London: Routledge & Kegan Paul Ltd., 1954.

——— and Crown, S. "An experimental study in opinion-attitude methodology," *Int. J. Opin. Attit. Res.,* (1949), *3,* 47–86.

Ferguson, L. W. "Primary social attitudes," *J. Psychol.,* (1939), *8,* 217–223.

——— "The stability of the primary social attitudes 1. religionism and humanitarianism," *ibid.,* (1941), *12,* 283–288.

——— "The isolation and measurement of nationalism," *J. soc. Psychol.,* (1942), *16,* 215–228.

Fisher, J. "The memory process and certain psycho-social attitudes with special reference to the law of Pragnanz," *J. Pers.,* (1951), *19,* 406–420.

Flowerman, S. H. "The uses of propaganda to reduce prejudices: a refutation," *Int. J. Opin. Attitude Res.,* (1949), *3,* 99–108.

——— "Portrait of the authoritarian man," *The New York Times Magazine,* Apr. 23, 1950.

Forster, A. and Epstein, B. *The trouble makers.* New York: Doubleday and Company, Inc., 1952.

Forster, N. C., Vinacke, W. E., and Digman, John M. "Flexibility and rigidity in a variety of problem situations," *J. abnorm. soc. Psychol.,* (1955), *50,* 211–216.

Frenkel-Brunswik, E. "Some personality factors in anti-Semitism," *J. Psychol.,* (1945), *20,* 271–291.

——— "A study of prejudice in children," *Human Relations* (1948), *1,* 295–306.

——— "Intolerance of ambiguity as an emotional and perceptual variable," *J. Pers.,* (1949), *18,* 108–143.

——— "Patterns of social and cognitive outlook in children and parents," *Amer. J. Orthopsychiat.,* (1951), *21,* 543–558.

——— "Social research and the problem of values: a reply," *J. abnorm. soc. Psychol.,* (1954), *49,* 466–471.

Fromm, E. *Escape from freedom.* New York: Rinehart & Co., 1941.

——— *Man for himself.* New York: Rinehart & Co., 1947.

——— *Psychoanalysis and religion.* New Haven, Conn.: Yale University Press, 1950.

——— *Autorität und Familie,* Studien aus dem Institut für Sozialforschung, Librairie Felix Alcan, Paris, 1936. Cited in R. Christie and Marie Jahoda, *Studies in the scope and method of "the authoritarian personality."* Chicago: Free Press of Glencoe, 1954.

Fromm, E. *The sane society.* New York: Rinehart & Co., 1955.

Fruchter, B. *Introduction to factor analysis.* New York: D. Van Nostrand Co., 1954.

———, Rokeach, M., and Novak, E. G. "A factorial study of dogmatism, opinionation, and related scales," *Psychol. Repts.,* (1958), *4,* 19–22.

Gage, N. L. "Scaling and factorial design in opinion poll analysis," Purdue University—*Studies in Higher Education, 61,* 1947.

——— and Remmers, H. H. "Opinion polling with mark-sensed punch cards," *J. applied psychol.* (1948), *32,* 1:88–91.

Gates, Dorothy J. "A factor analytic study of the dimensions of anti-democratic attitudes," Unpublished master's thesis. Purdue Univ., 1956.

Goodenough, W. H. "A technique for scale analysis," *Educ. psychol. Measmt.,* (1944), *4,* 179–190.

Goodstein, L. D. "Intellectual rigidity and social attitudes," *J. abnorm. soc. Psychol.,* (1953), *48,* 345–353.

Gordon, T. and Cartwright, D. "The effects of psychotherapy upon certain attitudes toward others," In C. Rogers and R. Dymond's *Psychotherapy and personality change.* Chicago: The University of Chicago Press, 1954.

Gough, H. G. "Studies of social intolerance: I. Some psychological and sociological correlates of anti-Semitism," *J. soc. Psychol.,* (1951), *33,* 237–246.

——— "Studies of social intolerance: II. A personality scale for anti-Semitism," *ibid.,* (1951), *33,* 247–255.

——— "Studies of social intolerance: III. Relationship of the *Pr* scale to other variables," (1951), *33,* 257–262.

——— "Studies in social intolerance: IV. Related social attitudes," *ibid.,* (1951), *33,* 263–269.

———, Harris, D. B., and Martin, W. E. "Children's ethnic attitudes II. Relationship to parental beliefs concerning child training," *Child Development,* (1950), *21,* 169–181.

Grace, H. A. "A note on the relationship of hostility and social distance," *J. educ. Psychol.,* (1952), *43,* 306–308.

Grace, H. S. "The geo-ethnic preference inventory: world cultures and artistic thinking," *J. educ. Psychol.,* (1951), *42,* 206–214.

Green, B. T. "Attitude measurement," In G. Lindzey's (ed.) *Hand-*

book of social psychology I. Cambridge, Mass.: Addison-Wesley Publishing Co., 1954. Pp. 335–369.

Greenberg, H., Chase, A. L., and Cannon, T. M. Jr. "Attitudes of white and Negro high school students in a west Texas town toward school integration," *J. appl. Psychol.*, (1957), *41*, 27–31.

Guilford, J. P. *Fundamental statistics in psychology and education.* New York: McGraw-Hill Book Company, Inc., 1950 (2nd Edition).

────── "When not to factor analyze," *Psychol. Bull.*, (1952), *49*, 26–37.

────── *Psychometric methods.* New York: McGraw-Hill Book Company, Inc., 1954 (2nd Edition).

────── "Factor analysis in a test development program," *Psychol. Rev.*, (1955), *5*, 79–94.

Gulliksen, H. *Theory of mental tests.* New York: John Wiley & Sons, Inc., 1950.

Gump, P. V. "Anti-democratic trends and student reaction to President Truman's dismissal of General MacArthur," *J. Soc. Psychol.*, (1953), *38*, 131–135.

Gurnee, H., and Baker, Elizabeth. "The social distance of some common social relationships." *J. abnorm. soc. Psychol.*, (1938), *33*, 265–269.

Gustad, J. "Policies and practices in faculty evaluation," *The Educ. Rec.*, (1961), *42*, 194–211.

Guttman, L. "A basis for scaling qualitative data," *Amer. soc. Rev.*, (1944), *9*, 139–150.

────── "The Cornell technique for scale and intensity analysis," *Educ. and psychol. meas.* (1947), *7*, 247–279.

────── "The basis for scalogram analysis. In *Measurement and prediction.* Princeton, N. J. Princeton Univ. Press, 1950. Pp. 60–90.

────── "The principle components of scalable attitudes." In P. F. Lazarsfeld's, *Mathematical thinking in the social sciences.* Chicago: Free Press of Glencoe, 1954. Pp. 216–257.

Haimowitz, M. L. and Haimowitz, N. R. "Reducing ethnic hostility through psychotherapy," *J. soc. Psychol.*, (1950), *31*, 231–241.

Hall, Wilbur. "The effect of defined social stimulus material upon the stability of attitude toward labor unions, capital punishment, social insurance, and Negroes," In *Further Studies in Attitudes, Series III, Studies in Higher Education* (Purdue University), 1938. Pp. 34, 7–19.

Hansen, M. H., Horwitz, W. N., and Madow, W. G. *Sample survey methods and theory,* Vol. I. New York: John Wiley & Sons, Inc., 1953.

Harding, J., Kotner, B., Proshansky, H., and Chein, I. In G. Lindzey's (Ed.), *Handbook of social psychology*. Cambridge, Mass.: Addison-Wesley Pub. Co., 1954. Pp. 1021–1061.

Harper, M. H. "Social beliefs and attitudes of American educators," In G. Murphy, Lois B. Murphy, & T. M. Newcomb's (Eds.) *Experimental social psychology*. New York: Harper & Brothers, 1937.

Harris, A. J., Remmers, H. H., and Ellison, C. G. "The relation between liberal and conservative attitudes in college students and other factors," *J. soc. Psychol.*, (1932), *3*, 320–335.

Heath, R. W., Maier, M. H., Remmers, H. H., and Silance, D. L. "Knowledge of democracy, current events, and segregation," *Purdue Opinion Panel*, Number 7, November, 1956.

Hill, M. "Some problems of social distance in intergroup relations," In Sherif and Wilson's (Eds.), *Group relations at the crossroads*. New York: Harper and Brothers, 1953. Pp. 285–307.

Hoffer, E. *The true believer*. New York: Harper & Brothers, 1951.

Hoffman, M. "Some psychodynamic factors in compulsive conformity," *J. abnorm. soc. Psychol.*, (1953), *48*, 383–393.

Hofstaelter, P. R. "A factorial study of prejudice," *J. Pers.*, (1952), *21*, 229–239.

Hollingshead, A. *Elmtown's youth*. New York: John Wiley & Sons, 1949.

Horkheimer, M. "Authoritarianism and the family today." In Anshen, R. M., (ed.). *The family: its function and destiny*, New York: Harper & Bros., 1949.

Horney, K. *New ways in psychoanalysis*. New York: W. W. Norton & Co., 1939.

———— *Our inner conflicts*. New York: W. W. Norton & Co., 1945.

———— *The neurotic personality of our time*. New York: W. W. Norton & Co., 1937.

Horst, P. "A generalized expression for the reliability of measures," *Psychometrika*, (1949), *14*, 21–31.

————, et al. *The prediction of personal adjustment*. New York: Social Science Research Council, 1941.

Horton, Roy E. "American freedom and the value of youth." Unpublished doctorate thesis, Purdue University, 1955.

————, Mainer, R. E., and Remmers, H. H. *Youth and the 1952 election*. Lafayette, Ind.: Div. Educ. Ref., Purdue University, 1952.

Hotelling, H. "Analysis of a complex of statistical variables into principal components," *J. educ. Psychol.*, (1933).

Hoult, T. F. "Native New Mexicans and interethnic accommodation," *Sociol. soc. Res.,* (1954), *28,* 233–238.

Hovland, C. I., Lumsdaine, A. A., and Sheffield, F. D. *Experiments in mass communications.* Princeton, N. J.: Princeton University Press, 1949.

———, Janis, I. L., and Kelley, H. H. *Communication and persuasion.* New Haven, Conn.: Yale University Press, 1953.

Howells, T. H. "A comparative study of those who accept as against those who reject religious authority," Univ. of Iowa: *Studies in character,* 2, 1928.

——— "An experimental study of persistence," *J. abnorm. soc. Psychol.,* (1933), *28,* 14–29.

Hoyt, C. J. "Test reliability obtained by analysis of variance," *Psychometrika,* (1941), *6,* 153–160.

Huffman, P. E., and Levinson, D. J. "Authoritarian personality and family ideology: A scale for the measurement of traditional family ideology," *Amer. Psychologist,* (1950), *5,* 307.

Hyman, Herbert. "Inconsistencies as a problem in attitude measurement," *J. social issues* (1949), *5,* 38–42.

Jahoda, Marie. "Consistency and inconsistency in intergroup relations," Part I. *J. social issues* (1949), *5,* 4–11.

James, W. *Varieties of religious experience.* New York: Random House, Inc., 1903.

Jenkins, W. L. "An improved method for tetrachoric r," *Psychometrika,* (1955), *20,* 253–258.

Jones, M. B. "Authoritarianism and intolerance of fluctuation," *J. abnorm, soc. Psychol.,* (1955), *50,* 125–126.

Kagan, Henry E. *Changing the attitude of Christian toward Jew: a psychological approach through religion.* New York: Columbia University Press, 1952.

Kaiser, H. F. "The varimax criterion for analytic rotation in factor analysis," *Psychometrika,* (1958), *23,* 187–199.

Kardiner, A. and Linton, R. *The psychological frontiers of society.* New York: Columbia University Press, 1945.

——— and Ovesey, L. *The mark of oppression.* New York: W. W. Norton & Co., 1951.

Kates, S. L. and Lutfy, N. B. "Authoritarian ideology and attitudes on parent-child relationships," *J. abnorm. soc. Psychol.,* (1955), *51,* 13–16.

Katz, D., Cartwright, D., Eldersveld, S., and Lee, A. McC. *Public opinion and propaganda.* New York: The Dryden Press, 1954.

Kaufman, W. C. "Status, authoritarianism, and anti-Semitism," *The Am. J. of Soc.*, (1957), LXII, *4*, 379–382.

Kenny, D. T., and Ginsberg, Rose. "The specificity of intolerance of ambiguity measures," *J. abnorm. soc. Psychol.*, (1958), *56*, 300–304.

Kirkpatrick, C. "Religion and humanitarianism," *Psychol. Monogr.*, (1949), No. 63.

Kluckhohn, C., Murray, H. A., and Schneider, D. M. *Personality in nature, society and culture.* New York: Alfred A. Knopf, Inc., 1953.

Kogan, Nathan, and Downey, J. F. "Scaling norm conflicts in the area of prejudice and discrimination," *J. abnorm. & soc. Psychol.*, (1956). *53*, 292–295.

Krech, D., and Crutchfield, R. S. *Theory and problems of social psychology.* New York: McGraw-Hill Book Co., Inc., 1948.

Kriedt, P. H., and Clark, K. E. "Item analysis versus scale analysis," *J. applied psychol.* (1949), *33*, 114–121.

Kutner, B., Wilkins, Carol, and Yarrow, Penny R. "Verbal attitudes and overt behavior involving racial prejudice," *J. abnorm. soc. Psychol.*, (1952), *47*, 649–652.

Landis, P. H. and Hatt, P. K. *Population problems.* New York: American Book Company, 1954.

LaPiere, R. T. Attitudes vs. actions, *Soc. Forces*, (1934), *13*, 230–237.

Lasswell, H. D. *Psychopathology and politics.* Chicago: Univ. of Chicago Press, 1930.

Lawshe, C. H., Jr., "A nomograph for estimating the validity of test items," *J. appl. Psychol.*, (1942), *26*, 846–849.

—— and Baker, P. C. "A nomograph for estimating the validity of test items," Lafayette, Indiana: Purdue University, 1951.

Lazarsfeld, P. F., Berelson, B., and Gandet, H. *The people's choice.* New York: Duell, Sloan & Pearce, 1944.

Leftwich, W. H. "A comparison of graphic and forced-choice ratings of teaching performance at the college and university level," Ph.D Dissertation, Purdue University, 1961.

Levanway, R. W. "The effect of stress on expressed attitudes toward self and others," *J. abnorm. soc. Psychol.*, (1955), *50*, 225–226.

Lewin, K., Lippitt, R., and White, R. K. "Patterns of aggressive behavior in experimentally created social climates," *J. social psychol.* (1939), X, 271–299.

Lindquist, E. F. *Design and Analysis of Experiments in Psychology and Education.* Boston: Houghton Mifflin Co., 1953.

Lindzey, G. "Differences between highs and lows in prejudice and their implication for a theory of prejudice," *J. Pers.*, (1950), *19*, 16–40.

——— *Handbook of social psychology:* Vol. I., Cambridge, Mass.: Addison-Wesley Publishing Co., Inc., 1954a.

——— *Handbook of social psychology:* Vol. II., Cambridge, Mass.: Addison-Wesley publishing Co., 1954b.

Linton, R. *The cultural background of personality.* New York: Appleton-Century-Crofts, Inc., 1945.

Loescher, F. S. *The protestant church and the Negro.* New York: Association Press, 1948.

Look, "Are U. S. teenagers rejecting freedom?" February 26, 1952.

Lord, F. M. "Scaling," *Rev. educ. Res.*, (1954), *24*, 375–392.

——— "Nomograph for computing multiple correlation coefficients," *J. Amer. statist. Assoc.*, (1955), *50*, 1073–1077.

Luchins, A. S. "Rigidity and ethnocentrism: a critique," *J. Pers.*, (1949), *17*, 449–466.

——— "Personality and prejudice: a critique," *J. soc. Psychol.*, (1950), *32*, 79–94.

Lynd, R. S. and Lynd, H. M. *Middletown.* New York: Harcourt, Brace & Co., 1929.

——— *Middletown in transition.* New York: Harcourt, Brace & Co., 1937.

MacKenzie, B. K. "The importance of contact in determining attitudes toward Negroes," *J. abnorm. soc. Psychol.*, (1948), *43*, 417–441.

MacKinnon, W. S., and Centers, R. "Authoritarianism and urban stratification," *Amer. J. Sociol.*, (1956), *61*, 610–620.

McNemar, Quinn. "General review and summary: opinion-attitude methodology," *Psychol. Bull.*, (1946), *43*, 289–374.

Maier, M. H. "Dogmatism related to attitudes toward adolescence as an institution," Unpublished doctoral dissertation, Purdue Univ., 1959.

Mainer, R. E. "Attitude change in intergroup education programs," Purdue University—*Studies in Higher Education, 83*, August, 1954.

Malinowski, B. *Magic, science and religion.* Chicago: Free Press of Glencoe, 1948.

Masling, J. M. "How neurotic is the authoritarian," *J. abnorm. soc. Psychol.*, (1954), *49*, 316–318.

Maslow, A. H. "The authoritarian character structure," *J. soc. Psychol.*, (1943), *18*, 401–411.

Marx, Karl. *Capital, the Communist Manifesto, and other writings.* New York: Modern Library, 1932.

May, R. *Man's search for himself*. New York: W. W. Norton & Co., 1953.

———— *The meaning of anxiety*. New York: The Ronald Press, 1950.

Mead, M. *Male and female*. New York: William Morrow & Co., 1949.

Meer, S. J. "Authoritarian attitudes and dreams," *J. abnorm. soc. Psychol.*, (1955), *51*, 74–78.

Merton, R. K. *Social theory and social structure*. Chicago: Free Press of Glencoe, 1949.

Meyer, J. K. "Sociopsychological correlates of authoritarianism and response set in authoritarianism," Unpublished doctoral dissertation, Purdue Univ., 1957.

Miller, Arthur. *Death of a salesman*. New York: Viking Press, Inc., 1949.

Miller, N. E., and Bugelski, R. "Minor studies of aggression II. The influence of frustration imposed by the in-group on attitudes toward Negroes," *J. Psychol.*, (1948), *25*, 437–442.

Milton, O. "Presidential choice and performance on a scale of authoritarianism," *Am. Psychol.*, (1952), *7*, 597–598.

Moreno, J. L. (ed.) *Sociometry and the science of man*. New York: Beacon House, 1956.

Mowrer, O. H. "Learning theory," *J. educ. Research*, (1952), 46, 475–495.

———— *Learning theory and personality dynamics*. New York: The Ronald Press, 1950.

Murphy, G., Murphy, Lois B. & Newcomb, T. M. *Experimental social psychology*. New York: Harper & Brothers, 1937.

———— and Likert, R. *Public opinion and the individual*. New York: Harper & Brothers, 1938.

Murphy, L. B. and Murphy, G. *Experimental social psychology*. New York: Harper & Brothers, 1931.

Mussen, Paul H. "Some personality and social factors related to changes in children's attitudes toward Negroes," *J. abnorm. soc. Psychol.*, (1950), *45*, 423–441.

Myers, M. S. "The latent role of religious orientation," *Studies in Higher Education LXXVIII*. Lafayette, Indiana: Purdue University, 1951.

Myrdal, Gunnar. *An American Dilemma*. New York: Harper & Brothers, 1944.

Nelson, E. "Attitudes: I. Their nature and development," *J. gen. Psychol.*, (1939), *21*, 367–399.

Newcomb, T. M. *Personality and social change*. New York: The Dryden Press, 1943.

―――― *Social psychology*. New York: The Dryden Press, 1950.

Norton, J. A. *Tests of equality of means when the estimators possess unequal variances*. Lafayette, Ind.: Purdue University, 1955.

O'Connor, P. "Ethnocentrism, intolerance of ambiguity, and abstract reasoning ability," *J. abnorm. soc. Psychol.* (1952), *47*, 526–530.

O'Neil, W. M., and Levinson, D. J. "A factorial exploration of authoritarianism and some of its ideological concomitants," *J. Pers.*, (1954), *22*, 449–463.

Ostle, B. *Statistics in research*. Ames, Iowa: Iowa State College Press, 1954.

Paisios, J. *Social distance and housing*. Unpublished doctor's dissertation, Purdue University, August 1954.

Papuchis, Ann T. *Social distance patterns between and among Negro and white residents of an urban transition area*. Unpublished M.A. dissertation, Vanderbilt University, 1948.

Park, R. E. "The concept of social distance," *J. appl. Sociol.*, (1924), *8*, 339–344.

Parten, Mildred. *Surveys, Polls, and Samples*. New York: Harper & Brothers, 1950.

Pearl, D. "Ethnocentrism and the self concept," *J. soc. Psychol.*, (1954), *36*, 137–147.

―――― "Psychotherapy and ethnocentrism," *J. abnorm. soc. Psychol.*, (1955), *50*, 227–230.

Perlmutter, H. J. "Some characteristics of the xenophilic personality," *J. psychol.*, (1954), *38*, 291–300.

Postman, L., Bruner, J. S., and McGinnes, B. "Personal values as selective factors in perception," *J. abnorm. soc. Psychol.*, (1948), *83*, 142–153.

Prothro, E. T. "Ethnocentrism and anti-Negro attitudes in the Deep South," *J. abnorm. soc. Psychol.*, (1952), *47*, 105–108.

―――― and Jensen, J. A. "Interrelations of religious and ethnic attitudes in a selected southern population," *J. soc. Psychol.*, (1950), *32*, 45–49.

―――― and Keehn, J. D. "The structure of social attitudes in Lebanon," *J. abnorm. soc. Psychol.*, (1956), *53*, 157–160.

―――― and Miles, O. K. "Social distance in the deep South as measured by a revised Bogardus scale," *J. soc. Psychol.*, (1953), *37*, 171–174.

―――― and Milikian, A. "The California public opinion scale in an authoritarian culture," *Publ. Opin. Quartl.*, (1953), *17*, 353–362.

Remmers, H. H. "Propaganda in the schools—Do the effects last?" *Public Opinion Quarterly,* (April 1938), *2,* 197–210.

—— "Measuring the public opinion of tomorrow," *The Indiana Teacher,* May, 1941.

—— "Further studies in attitudes," Series V. Purdue University—*Studies in Higher Education, 45,* June, 1942.

—— "The Purdue opinion poll for young people," *Scientific monthly,* (1945), *60,* 292–300.

—— "Changes in attitudes towards Germans, Japanese, Jews, and Nazis as affected by war," *Sch. and Soc.,* (1946), *63,* 118–119.

—— "Some determinants of discrimination in higher education," *School and Society* (1953), 77, p. 4.

—— *Introduction to opinion and attitude measurement.* New York: Harper and Brothers, 1954.

—— "Early socialization of attitudes," *American Voting Behavior* (Chapter 2) by Burdick and Brodbeck, 1959, pp. 55–67.

—— "The American adolescent today," *Collier's Annual Encyclopedia,* 1960a, p. 3 ff.

—— *Manual of instruction for the Purdue Rating Scale for Instructions.* West Lafayette, Indiana: University Book Store, 1960b.

——, Horton, R. E., and Mainer, R. E. "Does youth believe in the Bill of Rights?" *Purdue Opinion Panel,* 1951, Report 30.

—— "Youth and the 1952 election." *Purdue Opinion Panel,* 1952, Report 33.

—— "Youth looks at peers, problems and parents," *Purdue Opinion Panel,* 1953, Report 34.

—— "Candidates and issues of the 1952 election as seen six months later," *Purdue Opinion Panel,* 1953, Report 35.

—— and Kirk, R. B. "Scalability and validity of the socio-economic status items of the Purdue Opinion Panel," *J. applied psychol.* (1953), *37,* 384–386.

—— and Radler, D. H. *The American Teenager.* Indianapolis: Bobbs-Merrill, 1957.

—— "Teenage attitudes," *Scientific American* (1958), *6,* 25–30.

—— and Steinberg, M. "Relationships between 8 variables and F-test scores of teachers," *J. educ. Psychol.,* (1954), *45,* 427–431.

—— and Wood, W. F. "Changes in attitudes toward Germans, Japanese, Jews and Nazis, *Sch. and soc.,* (1947), *65,* 484–487.

Riley, M. W., Riley, J. W. (Jr.), and Toby, J. *Sociological studies in scale analysis.* New Brunswick, N. J.: Rutgers Univ. Press., 1954.

Roberts, A. H., and Jessor, R. "Authoritarianism, punitiveness, and perceived social status," *J. abnorm. soc. Psychol.*, (1958), *56*, 311–314.

────── and Rokeach, M. "Anomie, authoritarianism and prejudice: a replication," *Am. J. of Soc.*, (1956), *61*, 355–358.

Roe, A. "A psychological study of eminent biologists," *Psychol. Monogr.*, (1951a), No. 31, 1–68.

────── "A psychological study of eminent physical scientists," *Genet. psychol. Monogr.*, (1951), *43*, 121–239.

────── Analysis of group Rorschachs of psychologists and anthropologists and a comparison with biological and physical scientists. *Psychol. Monogr.*, (1953), *67*, No. 2.

────── *The psychology of occupations.* New York: John Wiley & Sons, Inc., 1956.

Rogers, C. R. & Dymond, R. F. *Psychotherapy and personality change.* Chicago: The University of Chicago Press, 1954.

Rokeach, M. "Generalized mental rigidity as a factor in ethnocentrism," *J. abnorm. soc. Psychol.*, (1948), *43*, 259–278.

────── " 'Narrow-mindedness' and ethnocentrism," *Amer. Psychologist*, (1950), *5*, 308.

────── "Prejudice, concreteness of thinking and reification of thinking," *J. abnorm. soc. Psychol.*, (1951), *46*, 83–91.

────── "Toward the scientific evaluation of social attitudes and ideologies," *J. Psychol.*, (1951), *31*, 97–104.

────── "Dogmatism and opinionation on the left and on the right," *Amer. Psychol.*, (1952), *7*, 310.

────── "The nature and meaning of dogmatism," *Psychol. Rev.*, (1954), *61*, 194–204.

──────, McGoverny, W. C., and Denny, R. M. "A distinction between dogmatic and rigid thinking," *J. abnorm. soc. Psychol.*, (1955), *51*, 87–93.

────── "Political and religious dogmatism: An alternative to the authoritarian personality," *Psychol. Monogr.*, (1956), *70*, (Whole No. 425).

Rose, Arnold. "The use of propaganda to reduce prejudice," *Int. J. Opin. Attitude Res.*, (1948), *2*, 220–229.

Rosen, Irwin C. "The effect of the motion picture, 'Gentleman's Agreement,' on attitudes toward Jews," *J. Psychol.*, (1948), *26*, 525–536.

Ruja, H. "A student-centered instructor-rating scale," *Educ. Administration Supervis.*, (1953), *39*, 209–217.

Runner, J. R. "Social distance in adolescent relationships," *Amer. J. Sociol.*, (1937), *2*, 428–439.

Sanai, M. "An experimental study of social attitudes," *J. soc. Psychol.*, (1951), *34*, 235–264.

Sanford, F. H. *Authoritarianism and leadership.* Philadelphia: Stephenson, 1950.

Sanford, R. N. and Levinson, D. J. "Ethnocentrism in relation to some religious attitudes and practices," *Amer. Psychologist*, (1948), *3*, 350–351.

Sarbin, T. R. "Role theory." In G. Lindzey's (ed.) *Handbook of social psychology, I.* Cambridge, Mass.: Addison-Wesley Publishing Co., 1954. Pp. 223–238.

—— and Berdie, R. "The relation of measured interests to the Allport Vernon Study of Values," *J. appl. Psychol.*, (1940), *24*, 287–296.

Sargent, S. S. and Smith, M. W. (eds.) *Culture and personality.* New York: The Viking Fund, Inc., 1949.

Sarnoff, I. and Katz, D. "The motivational bases of attitude change," *J. abnorm. and soc. Psychol.*, (1954), *49*, No. 1, 115–124.

Sartin, A. Q., and Bell, H. V. Jr. "An evaluation of the Bogardus *Scale of Social Distance* by the method of equal-appearing intervals," *J. soc. Psychol.*, 1949, *29*, 85–91.

Schmalzried, N. T. "Socio-psychological vectors in the behavior and attitudes of children: I. Social acceptance as related to N variables." Purdue University—*Studies in Higher Education*, 65, 1949.

Schneider, Louis. "Some psychiatric views on 'Freedom' and the theory of social systems," *Psychiatry* (1949), *12*, 3, 251–264.

—— and Dornbusch, S. M. "Inspirational religious literature: from latent to manifest functions of religion," *The Am. J. of Soc.*, (1957), *62*, 476–481.

Scodel, A. and Freedman, M. L. "Additional observations on the social perceptions of authoritarians and non-authoritarians," *J. abnorm. soc. Psychol.*, (1956), *52*, 92–95.

—— and Mussen, P. "Social perceptions of authoritarians and non-authoritarians," *J. abnorm. soc. Psychol.*, (1953), *48*, 181–184.

Shaw, F. J. "A stimulus-response analysis of repression and insight in psychotherapy," *Psychol. Rev.*, 1946.

Shelley, H. P. "Response set and the California attitude scales," *Educ. Psychol. Measmt.*, (1956), *16*, 63–67.

Sherif, M. *The psychology of social norms.* New York: Harper & Brothers, 1936.

340

—— and Cantril, H. "The psychology of 'attitudes.' *Psychol. Rev.*, (1945), *52*, 295–319.

—— "The psychology of 'attitudes' " Part II, (1946), *53*, 1–24.

—— and Wilson, M. O. *Group relations at the crossroads.* New York: Harper & Brothers, 1953.

Shimberg, Benjamin. "The development of a needs and problems inventory for high-school youth," *Studies in Higher Education LXXII.* Lafayette, Indiana: Purdue University, 1949.

—— "The relationship between information and attitudes of high-school students on certain international issue," Purdue University— *Studies in Higher Education, 68,* 1949.

Siegel, S. "Certain determinants and correlates of authoritarianism," *Genet. Psychol. Monogr.,* (1954), *49,* 187–229.

Smith, M. B., Bruner, J. S., and White, R. W. *Opinions and personality,* New York: John Wiley & Sons, Inc., 1956.

Smuckler, R. H. and Balknap, G. M. *Leadership and participation in urban political affairs.* East Lansing: Michigan State University, Government Research Bureau, 1956.

Snock, D. D. "The effect of psychological stress on the intolerance of ambiguity," *J. abnorm. soc. Psychol.,* (1955), *50,* 177–182.

Spoerl, D. T. "Some aspects of prejudice as affected by religion and education," *J. soc. Psychol.,* (1951), *33,* 69–76.

Srole, Leo. *Social dysfunction, personality and social distance attitudes.* Paper read at meeting of American Sociol. Society, September, 1951.

—— "Social integration and certain corollaries: an exploratory study," *Amer. sociol. Rev.,* (1956), *21,* No. 6, 709–716.

Stagner, R. "Fascist attitudes: an exploratory study," *J. soc. Psychol.,* (1936a), *7,* 309–319.

—— "Fascist attitudes: their determining conditions. *J. soc. Psychol.,* (1936b), *7,* 438–454.

—— and Katzhoff, E. T. "Fascist attitudes: factor analysis of item correlations, *J. soc. Psychol.,* (1942), *16,* 3–9.

—— "Attitude toward authority: an exploratory study," *J. soc. Psychol.,* (1954), *40,* 197–210.

Stone, C. P. and Taylor, D. W. *Annual review of psychology.* Stanford, California: Annual Reviews, Inc., 1952.

—— *Annual review of psychology.* Stanford, California: Annual Reviews, Inc., 1953.

Stone, C. P. & McNemar, Q. *Annual review of psychology.* Stanford, California: Annual Reviews, Inc., 1954.

—— *Annual review of psychology.* Stanford, California: Annual Reviews, Inc., 1956.

Stouffer, S. A. "An overview of the contributions to scaling and scale theory," In *Measurement and prediction.* Princeton, N. J.: Princeton University Press, (1950), 3–45.

——, et al. *Measurement and prediction.* Princeton, N.J.: Princeton University Press, 1950.

—— "A technique for improving cumulative scales." *Publ. Opin. Quart.,* (1952), *16,* 273–291.

—— *Communism, conformity, and civil liberties.* New York: Doubleday & Co., 1955.

Strong, E. K. *Vocational interests of men and women.* Stanford, Calif.: Stanford Univ. Press, 1943.

Struening, E. L. "A study of certain social and religious attitudes of university faculty members." (Unpublished M.A. thesis.) Purdue University, 1951.

—— Unpublished term paper in seminar in social psychology, Purdue University, 1953.

—— Unpublished term paper in seminar in attitudes, Purdue University, 1955.

—— "The dimensions, distribution, and correlates of authoritarianism in a midwestern university faculty population," Unpublished doctoral dissertation, Purdue Univ., 1957.

—— and Spilka, B. "A study of certain social and religious attitudes of university faculty members," *Psychol. Newsletter,* (1952), *43,* 1–17.

Sullivan, P. and Adelson, J. *Ethnocentrism and misanthropy. J. abnorm. & soc. Psychol.,* (1954), *49,* 246–250.

Sutherland, E. H. *White collar crime.* New York: The Dryden Press, 1949.

Swanson, G. E., Newcomb, T. M., and Hartley, E. L. *Readings in social psychology.* New York: Holt & Co., 1952.

Taba, H. *et al. Curriculum in intergroup relations.* Washington, D. C.: American Council on Education, 1949.

Tawney, R. H. *The acquisitive society.* New York: Harcourt, Brace & Co.

—— *Religion and the rise of capitalism.* New York: New American Library, 1948.

Thorndike, R. L. "Reliability." In Lindquist, E. L. (Ed.) *Educational measurement*. Washington, D. C.: The American Council on Education, (1951). Pp. 560–620.

Thurstone, L. L. *Multiple factor analysis*. Chicago: The University of Chicago Press, 1947.

Tiffin, J., and McCormick, E. J. *Industrial psychology*. Englewood cliffs, New Jersey: Prentice-Hall, 1958.

Todd, J. E. "Social norms and the behavior of college students," *Teachers college contributions to education*, (1941), No. 833.

Tolman, E. C. *Collected papers in psychology*. Berkeley: University of California Press, 1951.

Tougas, R. "Ethnocentrism as a limiting factor in verbal therapy." In C. Rogers and R. Dymond's *Psychotherapy and personality change*. Chicago: The University of Chicago Press, 1954.

Turberville, G. "Social distance in Duluth," *Sociol. soc. Res.*, (1950), *34*, 415–423.

U. S. Bureau of the Census. *Statistical Abstract of the United States: 1953*. (Seventy-fourth edition.) Washington, D. C., 1953.

U. S. Department of Health, Education, and Welfare. *Biennial Survey of Education in the United States, 1949–50*. Chapter 1: Statistical Summary of Education, 1949–50. Chapter 2: Statistics of State School System, 1949–50. Washington, D. C., 1952.

Walker, H., and Lev, J. *Statistical inference*. New York: Henry Holt & Company, 1953.

Weber, M. *The protestant ethic and the spirit of capitalism*. New York: Charles Scribner & Sons, 1930.

Wells, W. D., Chiaravallo, G., and Goldman, S. "Brothers under the skin: A validity test of the F Scale," *J. soc. Psychol.*, (1957), *45*, 35–40.

Weltman, Naomi, and Remmers, H. H. "Pupils', parents' and teachers' attitudes—similarities and differences," *Purdue University Studies in Higher Education*, (1946), 56.

Wert, J. E., Neidt, C. O. and Ahmann, J. S. *Statistical methods in educational and psychological research*. New York: Appleton-Century-Crofts, Inc., 1954.

Wexler, Samuel. "An exploratory investigation of adolescent adjustment as measured by a forced-choice sentence completion test." Unpublished doctor's dissertation, Purdue University, 1953.

Williams, Robin M. Jr. *The reduction of intergroup tensions*. New York: Social Science Research Council, 1947.

Williams, R. J. and Wright, C. "Opinion organization in a heterogeneous adult population," *J. abnorm. soc. Psychol.*, (1955), *51*, 559–564.

Wilner, D. M., Walkley, R. P. and Cook, S. W. *Human relations in interracial housing.* Minneapolis, Minn.: University of Minnesota Press, 1956.

Wolfe, D. "Factor analysis to 1940," *Psychometric Monogr.*, No. 3., Chicago: The University of Chicago Press, 1940.